New Frontiers

HBJ BOOKMARK READING PROGRAM, EAGLE EDITION

Margaret Early

G. Robert Canfield

Robert Karlin

Thomas A. Schottman

Sara Krentzman Srygley

Evelyn L. Wenzel

Level 10

New Frontiers

HARCOURT BRACE JOVANOVICH, PUBLISHERS

Orlando   New York   Chicago   San Diego   Atlanta   Dallas

ACKNOWLEDGMENTS: For permission to reprint copyrighted material, grateful acknowledgment is made to the following sources:

ADDISON-WESLEY PUBLISHING COMPANY, INC.: On pp. 352 and 353, "Something to Do" (text & art); on pp. 492 and 493, "Bulbs and Cells" (text & art); and on p. 353, "To Think About" from *STEM Elementary School Science* and *Addison-Wesley Science STEM* by Verne N. Rockcastle, Frank R. Salamon, Victor E. Schmidt, Betty J. McKnight. Copyright © 1977 and 1980 respectively. "April: Specimen A" adapted from *A Snake-Lover's Diary*, © 1970 by Barbara Brenner, a Young Scott Book. Abridged and simplified version of *The Princess and the Admiral*, text © 1974 by Charlotte Pomerantz, a Young Scott Book.

ATHENEUM PUBLISHERS: "Lost and Found" from *See My Lovely Poison Ivy* by Lilian Moore. Copyright © 1975 by Lilian Moore.

CHILDRENS PRESS, CHICAGO: "The Lady in the Harbor" adapted from *The Story of the Statue of Liberty* by Natalie Miller.

COWARD, MCCANN & GEOGHEGAN, INC.: "A Very Special Place" adapted from *Museum Adventures: An Introduction to Discovery* by Herbert and Marjorie Katz. Copyright © 1969 by Herbert & Marjorie Katz.

THOMAS Y. CROWELL, INC.: "Weather is full of the nicest sounds . . ." from *I Like Weather* by Aileen Fisher. Text copyright © 1963 by Aileen Fisher. Text of "By Myself" from *Honey, I Love and Other Love Poems* by Eloise Greenfield. Copyright © 1978 by Eloise Greenfield.

DODD, MEAD & COMPANY, INC.: "I Meant to Do My Work Today" from *The Lonely Dancer* by Richard Le Gallienne. Copyright 1913 by Dodd, Mead & Company. Copyright renewed 1941 by Richard Le Gallienne.

E. P. DUTTON AND THE CANADIAN PUBLISHERS, MCCLELLAND AND STEWART LIMITED, TORONTO: "The Engineer" from *Now We Are Six* by A. A. Milne. Copyright 1927 by E. P. Dutton & Co., Inc. Renewal © 1955 by A. A. Milne.

M. EVANS AND COMPANY, INC., NEW YORK, NY 10017: Excerpts and adaptations titled "The Long Way Home" from *The Hopi Way* by Mary Elting. Copyright © 1969 by Mary Elting. Excerpts and adaptations titled "A Homecoming" from *A Mongo Homecoming* by Mary Elting and Robin McKown. Copyright © 1969 by Mary Elting and Robin McKown.

AILEEN FISHER: "Butterfly Wings" from *In the Woods, in the Meadow, in the Sky* by Aileen Fisher. Charles Scribner's Sons, NY, 1965.

FOUR WINDS PRESS, A DIVISION OF SCHOLASTIC MAGAZINES, INC.: From *The Secrets of Alkazar* by Allan Zola Kronzek. Copyright © 1976 by Allan Zola Kronzek.

NATALIE FRIENDLY: Excerpt (titled "Special Friendships") condensed from *Wildlife Teams* by Natalie Friendly.

HARCOURT BRACE JOVANOVICH, INC.—On pp. 68 and 69, "Review Practice—Syllables and Accent Marks, Possessive Nouns"; on pp. 354 and 355, from "Making Puppets" (text & art); on p. 333, from "To Remember"; and on pp. 283 and 284, "How Our Language Grows" in *Language for Daily Use*, Level Orange by Mildred Dawson et al. Copyright © 1978 by Harcourt Brace Jovanovich, Inc. On pp. 204 and 205, "Finding Words in a Dictionary" (text & art) from *Language for Daily Use*, Orange, Teacher's Explorer Edition, by Mildred A. Dawson et al. Copyright © 1978 by Harcourt Brace Jovanovich, Inc. On pp. 44 and 181, "Bar Graphs" (text & art) from *Growth in Mathematics*, Orange, by David W. Wells et al. Copyright © 1978 by Harcourt Brace Jovanovich, Inc. Excerpts on pp. 468 and 469, from "Food for Young Salmon" (text & art), on pp. 307 and 308, from "The Great Journey Begins," and on pp. 424 and 425, from "The Water We Drink," in *Concepts in Science*, Newton Edition, Orange, by Paul F. Brandwein et al. Copyright © 1975 by Harcourt Brace Jovanovich, Inc. On p. 155, Glossary Section; excerpts on pp. 494 and 495 from "How Can You Avoid Burns?" (text & art); on pp. 228 and 229, "Preventing Falls" (text & art); and on p. 42, section in "Learning from Other People" from *You Learn and Change* by Daniel A. Collins et al., Copyright © 1977 by Harcourt Brace Jovanovich, Inc. Excerpts on pp. 139, 141, 142, 152, and 153 from *The HBJ School Dictionary*. Copyright © 1977 by Harcourt Brace Jovanovich, Inc. "Barry: Hero of the Alps" abridged from *Barry: The Story of a Brave St. Bernard* by Bettina Hürlimann and Paul Nussbaumer. © 1967 by Atlantis Verlag AG Zurich.

HARPER & ROW, PUBLISHERS: "Helping" and "Ickle Me, Pickle Me, Tickle Me Too" from *Where the Sidewalk Ends: The Poems and Drawings of Shel Silverstein*. Copyright © 1974 by Shel Silverstein. Text of pages 37–44 (retitled "Winter Days and Winter Nights") from *Little House in the Big Woods* by Laura Ingalls Wilder. Copyright, 1932, as to text, by Laura Ingalls Wilder. Renewed 1959 by Roger L. MacBride. Chapter 35, text only, (retitled "Keeping House") from *On the Banks of Plum Creek* by Laura Ingalls Wilder. Copyright, 1937, as to text, by Harper & Row, Publishers, Inc. Renewed, 1965, by Roger L. MacBride. "Little Gray Home in the West," text only, from *These Happy Golden Years* by Laura Ingalls Wilder. Copyright, 1943, as to text, by Laura Ingalls Wilder. Copyright renewed 1971 by Roger L. MacBride.

GEORGE C. HARRAP & COMPANY LTD.: Excerpt (titled "The Dream Comes True") from *Tiger of the Snows* by Tenzing Norgay written in collaboration with James Ramsey Ullman.

D. C. HEATH AND COMPANY: Excerpt (text only) on p. 309 from "Problem Solving" in *Heath Elementary Mathematics* by Dilley, Ricker, and Jackson. © 1975 by D. C. Heath and Company, Lexington, Massachusetts.

HIGHLIGHTS FOR CHILDREN, INC.: Excerpt (titled "Flying High") from "Flying High on Hot Air" by Hal Schell from *Highlights for Children*, 1/75. Copyright © 1975, Highlights for Children, Inc., Columbus, Ohio.

HOLT, RINEHART AND WINSTON, PUBLISHERS: "Stopping by Woods on a Snowy Evening" from *The Poetry of Robert Frost* edited by Edward Connery Lathem. Copyright 1923, © 1969 by Holt, Rinehart and Winston. Copyright 1951 by Robert Frost.

ART CREDITS: The artists in this book and the pages on which their work appears are as follows:

vi

Contents

APPRECIATING LITERATURE

Part **2** Tell Me a Story

READING TO LEARN

Part **3** Achieving

137

APPRECIATING LITERATURE

Part **4** Songs Without Music

READING TO LEARN

Part 5 Communicating

APPRECIATING LITERATURE

Part 6 Fresh Starts

READING TO LEARN

Part 7 Enjoying the World

To the Reader

A book is a new frontier, a new world waiting for you to explore as you read. You will discover *New Frontiers* as you read this book. You will encounter *New Frontiers* in fact and fiction. You will learn about people and animals and the ways they live and work together. You will see how people set goals and reach them. You will learn about different kinds of communication. You will learn about interesting careers and hobbies. You will discover folktales, poems, stories, and a play, along with information about an author's life. In discovering *New Frontiers,* you will learn and practice skills that help you understand what you have read.

Your book, *New Frontiers,* is divided into eight parts. In Parts 1, 3, 5, and 7, you will learn to improve your reading skills through Skills Lessons, Vocabulary Studies, and Textbook Studies. The reading selections are yours to enjoy as you discover new information. In Parts 2, 4, 6, and 8, you will discover ways to understand and appreciate literature. The selections and poems are yours to enjoy as you laugh and cry with the characters and writers.

When you explore frontiers, you learn about new worlds and new ideas. And you learn about yourself. That is one of the most exciting adventures you can have. Go ahead— discover *New Frontiers.*

Part 1
Living and Working Together

Using Context Clues

STOP! That word tells you something. It doesn't tell you very much all by itself. But what if you saw *Stop* on a street sign? You would know that it means "Stop driving." On a test page, it might mean "Stop working. Do not write any more answers." A word means more to you when you think of it in its **context,** or setting.

In your reading, the context is made up of the other words around a word. Clues to help you with the meaning of a word may be in the same sentence as the word is. They may also be in other sentences around it. Using other words in the sentence or sentences to help you understand a word is called **using context clues.**

Read the sentences at the top of the next page. Use context clues to help you with the meaning of the word *ancient.* It appears in dark print (boldface).

Pompeii is a very old city. It was built more than 2,000 years ago. You can visit this **ancient** city today.

What does *ancient* mean? The context clues "more than 2,000 years ago" and "very old" help you know.

Try This

Read the sentences below. Choose the correct meaning for each word in boldface from the words below the sentences.

1. I read about **imaginary** animals. They are make-believe and don't look like any you will ever see.

   a. real   b. unreal

2. The lion **crouched** low, ready to leap. Its legs were bent. Its body was close to the ground.

   a. bent down   b. sat down

3. Make up a sentence for each word in boldface in sentences 1 and 2 above.

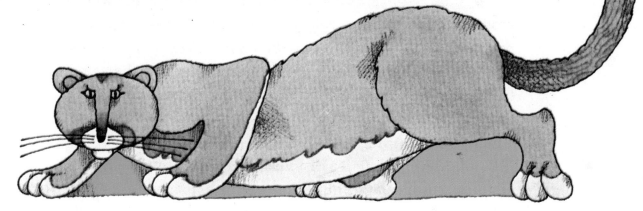

Definitions in Context

Sometimes the context may give more than just clues to the meaning of a word. A definition may be given. The definition may be in the same sentence as the word or in another. Read these sentences.

A **hamster** is a small animal that stores food in its cheeks.

My cousin is a **veterinarian.** That means she's a doctor that takes care of animals.

The definition of the word *hamster* is given in the same sentence as the word. Notice that the definition follows the word *is*. The meaning of *veterinarian* is given in a separate sentence. Its definition follows the word *means*.

Look for words such as *is, means, meant, are called,* and *or*. Such words may be clues that definitions may follow.

Try This

Read the following sentences. The words in boldface may be new to you. Use context clues to learn their meanings. Then use each word in a new sentence.

1. To **imitate** the call of a bird means to copy it.
2. Ellen watched the animal's **behavior.** This means she watched the way it acted.
3. A **symbol** is a mark or sign that is used to stand for something else.

Words with Many Meanings

A word may have more than one meaning. Then its meaning will depend on how the word is used. You can't tell which meaning such a word has until you read it in context. Therefore, context is very important when you read these words.

Here is a word: *pick.* Do you know what it means? Read the following sentences. See how the meaning of *pick* changes.

Pick a number from one to ten. (choose or select)
I don't like to **pick** fights. (stir up)
Pick an apple from the tree. (pull off)
Miners use a **pick** to split rocks. (pointed tool)

In each sentence, the word *pick* has a different meaning. The other words in the sentence help you tell what that meaning is.

5

Try This

Read each pair of sentences. The word in boldface has a different meaning in each sentence. Read the two meanings for the words given below the sentences. Tell which meaning belongs in place of the word in boldface in each sentence.

1. a. José will ride his horse in the **show** next week.
   b. Will you **show** me how to play this game?

   teach or explain   performance

2. a. We took a **picture** of our snow-covered house.
   b. **Picture** a giant table piled high with good food.

   imagine   photograph

6

VOCABULARY STUDY

Synonyms

I am Latoose Tralec, one of the greatest painters of all time! Allow me to show some of my <u>original</u> works. They are brand-new, the first of their kind.

Here is "The <u>Stout</u> Trout." It is a rather fat, thickset fish. Oh, such lovely colors!

And now, another great work— "The <u>Bumpy</u> Balloon." This balloon has parts that are rough and uneven. People say my paintings are silly. What do they know?

Oh dear, they're taking my paintings away. Maybe they do know something I don't....

Word Play

Synonyms are words that mean the same as other words. Give a synonym for each underlined word above.

When you meet a word you don't know, use the context to help you. In this selection you will find many new words that are defined in context.

Do you think you would like to belong to a family with over 1,000 people in it?

THREE-RING FAMILY

by Seymour Reit

Have you ever seen a circus? It's a wonder-world of clowns and acrobats, jugglers and dancers. You can see lion tamers and musicians, wire walkers and bareback riders. You can see people who fly from swings.

THE BIGGEST FAMILY ON EARTH

The Ringling Brothers and Barnum & Bailey Circus is called "The Greatest Show on Earth." It can also be called "The Biggest Family on Earth." There are over 1,000 people in it. The members of this "family" spend many months together each year. They live together and eat together. They also travel and work together.

Does your family have special names for people? The circus "family" does, too. People who take care of performing elephants are called *bull hands*. *Bull* is the name given to tame elephants in animal acts. A bull can be a male or a female elephant. *Hands* are workers. You can see how *bull hands* got their name.

Workers who load and unload trucks are *razorbacks*. In the past, these workers loaded cages onto trains. It took more than one worker to lift a cage. The workers lifted the cage with their backs. To stay together, they waited for the call, "Raise your backs!" The word *razorbacks* sounds like "Raise your backs!"

9

Here are some other names the circus "family" uses. *Flyers* are men and women who do tricks on the high swings. *Roustabouts* are people who set up the acts. All the performers are called *kinkers.*

FAMILY ACTS

Inside the big circus "family" are smaller, real families. Some of these families have *family acts.* A family act may have many members.

Circus children begin training when they are very young. A four-year-old is already learning the family act. A few years later, the child is in the act. Circus parents feel you are never too young to learn!

Family acts come from many lands. The Wallendas are a famous family from Germany. They do a daring high-wire act far above the ring.

The Wallendas' act has seven people in it. All seven people work together on one wire! Some balance on the

wire. Others stand on their shoulders. This is very dangerous. There have been bad falls. But the Wallendas keep going. When one member gets old, a young Wallenda takes over.

The Zacchini [zə·kē′nē] family is also well known. They're from Italy. Hugo Zacchini was called "The Human Cannonball." Why? He was "shot" from a giant cannon! The cannon had a steel spring inside. When the cannon went off—BANG!—Hugo came flying out! He sailed across the circus tent and landed in a small net.

When Hugo grew old, his son and his nephew took over. Now two Zacchinis are shot from the cannon.

MAKING PEOPLE LAUGH

Is there someone in your house who likes to clown around? The circus "family" has clowns, too.

Clowns are a favorite in every circus. You can tell clowns apart by their make-up. Clowns may change the way they dress, but they never change their faces. Their faces are very important. No clown can copy another clown's make-up.

Clowns think up their own acts. Some clowns work alone; some work together.

One act that many people like is the "Clown Car." A small car stops in the center ring. Out crawls one clown. Then another climbs out. Then another. A whole crowd of clowns all come from one tiny car!

How do they do it? Only the clowns know. And they never give away their secrets.

Emmett Kelly was a famous clown. He dressed as a tramp. He had a very sad face. Kelly would walk around with an old broom. Sometimes he would try to sweep up the bright circle of light made by a spotlight. He would sweep and sweep. He looked very silly trying to sweep the light away.

Emmett Kelly is no longer with the circus. Now Kelly's son carries on his father's act.

13

CIRCUS FAMILY DOCTOR

Does your family have a doctor? The circus "family" has a doctor, too. The doctor takes care of all the animals.

Animals get some of the same sicknesses that people get. Tigers get colds. Lions get headaches. Elephants get chills. Bears get toothaches. "Doc" always has something to worry about.

Suppose a lion's head hurts. What does the doctor do? The doctor treats the lion the way your doctor might treat you — with aspirin!

In many ways, the Ringling Circus "family" is like other families. And in many ways, it certainly is different! In what other family can you find a clown who dances with a baby pig? In what other family can you find several people who balance on one thin wire?

A famous person once said, "The circus is pure delight. It gives the feeling of a truly happy dream."

And it does!

Understanding What You've Read

1. Why can the Ringling Brothers and Barnum & Bailey Circus be called "the biggest family on Earth"?
2. State the special names that describe five circus jobs.
3. If you were part of the circus "family," which kind of work would you most like to do? Why?

Applying the Skills Lesson

1. What definition for each word below is given in the selection?

    razorbacks (p. 9)   kinkers (p. 10)

    roustabouts (p. 10)

2. What special meaning does each word below have in the context of the selection?

    flyer (p. 10)   ring (p. 10)

Using Context Clues to Find Meanings

In textbooks, the *context* may give the meaning of a new word. When the meaning for a word is given in what you read, the word is *defined in context*. See which words are defined in context below. Use the sidenotes to help you.

The *Building Skills* section that follows each textbook study will ask you to answer some questions about what you've just read.

Using Context Clues to Find Meanings in Social Studies

Since early times, people have asked questions about the solar system. What are Earth's neighbors really like? Can there be life on them like that on Earth?

Words in boldface are often defined in context. What words in these sentences help you know what *satellites* are?

Some of the planets are circled by smaller bodies called moons, or **satellites.** Earth's moon is a natural satellite. Earth is also circled by satellites that people have made. These satellites have helped us learn much about Earth's neighbors. In fact, by the time you read this, we may have found out many new things about the planets. See what you can find to add to the information you read here.

Earth's moon has a rocky surface covered with dust. There are many deep cracks and pits called **craters.** Some of them are miles across. The moon also has mountains. They are sharp and jagged because there's no wind or water to wear them down.

What word in this sentence is a clue that a definition may be given? What word is defined?

Earth's air ocean is its **atmosphere.** This envelope of moisture and gases keeps Earth from getting deathly hot during days and deathly cold during nights. The moon has no atmosphere. This means that it can't trap the sun's heat. There is no air to protect the surface from the bright rays of the sun. During the day, the moon is a very hot place. At night, the heat escapes quickly, and the moon is very cold.

The word *atmosphere* is explained in the context of this sentence and the next one. What words in these sentences help you know what *atmosphere* is?

—*Planet Earth*
Houghton Mifflin

Building Skills

1. What are *satellites, craters,* and *atmosphere?* Look back at the information given in the selection to help you explain these words.

2. Suppose you don't know the meaning of the words *solar system* and *moisture.* Where can you look to find their meaning?

Using Context Clues to Find Meanings in Science

This context tells you two things about *matter*. What are the two things?

You know that all matter has weight and takes up space. Rocks, water, animals—everything you can see is matter. But what about air? You cannot see air. Is air matter?

You don't have to see air to know that it is around you. Just step outdoors and feel the wind. Wind is moving air. Strong wind can overturn cars and knock down buildings. Air can do these things because it has weight and takes up space. So air is matter.

This sentence is a definition. What is wind?

The earth is surrounded by a layer of air. This layer of air goes above the earth for thousands of meters. All this air has great weight. This weight acts as a force on everything on the earth. This force is called **air pressure.**

From the context, can you tell what surrounded means?

Words in boldface are often explained. Is air pressure defined?

—*Understanding Your Environment*
Silver Burdett

Building Skills

Use the context clues in the selection to match the words below to the definitions. Use each word or word group only once.

    a. air pressure   b. wind   c. matter   d. force

1. anything that has weight and takes up space
2. the force of air in a limited space
3. moving air
4. power, energy, or strength

Sounds and Letters

Do you know the answer to this riddle: *Why couldn't the spy talk clearly?* You would if you knew the code the boy in the picture is using. The answer is given in Morse code. It says, "He had a code in his nose."

Letters are also a code. They stand for sounds. When you read aloud, you are using the code. When you read silently, you may "think" of the sounds that the letters stand for. Some people say that you are **decoding** when you figure out how to say words in print. Sometimes when you figure out how to say a printed word, you realize that you know what the word means. You have heard that word before.

In English, letters can stand for sounds in different ways. Let's review some of those ways.

Consonants

1. Most consonant letters stand for only one sound. However, letters such as g, c, and s can stand for more than one sound. Say each pair of words below. Listen for the different sounds that the letters in boldface stand for.

   goat   **g**entle   **c**arry   **c**ent   bu**s**   wa**s**

2. Two different consonant letters can stand for the same sound. Say the words below. Listen for the same sound in each pair of words.

   jam   **g**ym   **k**ey   **c**age   **z**oo   ha**s**

3. Two consonant letters next to each other in a word can stand for two sounds. These sounds are blended together, but you can hear each one. Say each of the words below. Listen for the sounds that the letters in boldface stand for.

   fly   **br**ight   **sp**end   **cr**awl   **st**udy   **pr**omise
   jum**p**   fou**nd**   po**st**   pai**nt**   ma**rk**   si**nk**

21

4. Two consonant letters next to each other in a word can stand for one sound. This sound is different from the sound that either letter stands for alone. Say each word below. Listen for the sound that the letters in boldface stand for.

show   **ch**ildren   **th**ink   fi**sh**   ea**ch**   wi**th**

Try This

1. Read each sentence below. Listen for the sound that each letter in boldface stands for. Do the letters stand for the same sound in both words? Answer *same* or *different*.

     a. The mouse kept the **c**amel **c**ompany.
     b. **J**umping through a hoop is a **g**ood trick.
     c. It's wi**s**e to stay on third ba**s**e.

2. Read each sentence below. Say the word in boldface. It has two consonant letters next to each other that stand for *one* sound. The sound is not the sound that either letter stands for alone. What are the two consonant letters?

     a. Don't drop the **china** cup.
     b. Would you like to go to the park **with** us?
     c. I **wish** I were taller.

3. Read each sentence below. Say the boldfaced word. It has two consonant letters next to each other that stand for two sounds blended together. Name the two consonant letters. Make up a new sentence using each of the boldfaced words.

a. We'll be ready in a **moment.**
b. It's Rita's turn to **speak.**
c. I would sweep up if I could find a **broom.**

Vowels

1. Every vowel letter can stand for at least two sounds—a *long* sound and a *short* sound. A long vowel sound is the same as the letter name. Say the words below. Listen for the long vowel sounds.

h**a**te	P**e**te	b**i**te	h**o**pe	c**u**te

What did you notice about the last letter in each word above? The letter *e* at the end does not stand for any sound.

The last three letters in many words are a vowel, a consonant, and an *e*. In most of these words, the final *e* tells you that the vowel before the consonant stands for a long sound. (Can you think of some that do not follow this rule?)

2. Say the words below. They look like the words in the box on page 24, but they don't end in *e*.

h**a**t p**e**t b**i**t h**o**p c**u**t

Notice how different the words sound. The vowel letters in these words stand for short vowel sounds.

3. Two vowel letters next to each other in a word usually stand for one sound. Say the words below.

r**oa**d t**ea**ch p**ai**n s**ee**d

In each word, the vowel sound is the long sound of the first vowel letter. Two vowel letters next to each other often stand for the long sound of the first vowel.

4. Two vowel letters next to each other in a word can also stand for other sounds. Say the words below. Listen for the vowel sound in each word. The vowel sound you hear is *not* the long sound of the first vowel.

r**ou**nd h**ea**d h**oo**d h**au**l w**ei**ght

5. Sometimes two vowel letters next to each other in a word stand for two sounds. Say the words below. Listen for the two sounds.

l**io**n d**ie**t sc**ie**nce

Try This

1. Read each sentence below. Say the words in boldface. Is the vowel sound in each word long or short?

   a. That's the **best** meal I ever **ate.**
   b. Let's get an ice **cream cone.**
   c. It's time to **feed** the **cat.**

2. Read each sentence below. Say the word in boldface. Listen to the vowel sound. Is it the same as the long vowel sound that the first vowel letter stands for? Answer *same* or *different*.

   a. Steve bought the biggest **loaf** of bread.
   b. One way to **cook** a chicken is to fry it.
   c. Peggy likes to look for shells on the **beach.**

VOCABULARY STUDY

Multiple Meanings

PROFESSOR I. M. SMART

Dear Professor Smart,

I'm bored with my life. My friends said, "Look for a **sideline.**" I found one at a football game and stood by it. I was knocked down by a quarterback! What went wrong?

Sincerely,
Aches and Pains

Dear Professor Smart,

I often fall off a chair while sitting in it. My friends say that I may have a problem with my **balance.** That's silly. I have $1,000 in my bank account.

Sincerely,
Shaky

Dear Shaky,

The balance in your bank account sounds fine. The other one doesn't. Can't you sit without falling? Try sitting on the floor!

Sincerely,
I. M. Smart

Dear Aches and Pains,

Aha! Your problem is one word with two meanings! Your friends meant for you to look for a sideline, "an extra job that pays and is interesting." The other sideline, "the line at the side of a football field," doesn't pay—except in black and blue marks.

Sincerely,
I. M. Smart

Word Play

1. Give two meanings for the words *sideline* and *balance.*
2. Use each word, *palm* and *watch,* in two sentences. Make the meaning of the word different in each sentence.
3. Write your own letter to I. M. Smart about a problem with two meanings for the word *marks.*

When you meet a word you think you don't know, try to decode it. Remember that two vowel letters next to each other often stand for one sound.

Going from a big, modern city in Africa to a tiny fishing village can be a strange and beautiful adventure. Pauline found this out when she went with her brother, Robert, to visit a Mongo fishing village in Africa — the village of their grandparents.

A Homecoming

by Mary Elting *and* Robin McKown *with the help of* Pauline

The Great Water

At last school vacation began! Robert came home from college in Europe. Now I could go to the village where my grandparents lived.

Early in the morning we were off in a cab to the riverboat dock. A great crowd of people was already there. They sat near the gate, with bags and bundles around them.

It was a beautiful ship with three decks. We were shown to our cabins. Quickly I put away my suitcase. Then I ran out to watch.

More and more people came on the ship. Giant machines lifted boxes onto the ship. Hours went by, and I began to be afraid we would never really leave. But at last the whistle sounded. We were moving out onto the river.

Near my home in Kinshasa, the river is very wide and very smooth. It is almost like a lake. Long ago, certain African people called the river *Nzadi* [ən·zä′dē], which means "Great Water." Now we call it the Congo.

What Does the Equator Look Like?

The air felt warmer every day because we were nearing the equator. What would the world look like there? Now I wished the riverboat would hurry so that I could find out.

My brother seemed surprised at me. Hadn't I learned in school that the equator is only an imaginary line around the earth, halfway between the North and South Poles? Of course I knew that. But I couldn't help expecting that somehow I could tell when we crossed that line.

Everything along the shore now looked greener. In Mbandaka [əm·bän′dä·kä], the town where we left the riverboat, I saw the greenest, tallest palms I had ever seen. My brother said it was rain that made them grow. Here near the equator it rains almost every day.

Not much farther to go, my brother told me. Less than an hour by automobile. A friend of my father's who worked in the town would take us there.

We left the town and followed a road that ran between tall rain-forest trees. Now we were stopping.

EQUATOR—there at the roadside stood a sign! An arrow on one half of the sign pointed north. On the other half, the arrow pointed south. If you stood next to the sign, your feet would touch the imaginary line that runs all the way around the earth.

New Sisters and Brothers

We were there, in my grandparents' village! I had been told what the village was like. Still it surprised me! There was a broad street leading down to the river's edge. Like our street in Kinshasa, this one ran between two rows of houses. But these houses had green rain-forest trees at their backs, and they were made of brown mud-bricks instead of cement. The sloping roofs came far out over the walls, just as they did at home. But these were not roofs I was used to. They were made from many layers of large, thin leaves.

Dozens of girls and boys streamed from the houses to meet us. They were dressed just like the children I knew at home. My grandmother and the other women wore *ifutas* [ē·fōō′täz], or long skirts, and turbans. The men had on pants and sport shirts like my brother's.

The moment I left the car, girls came up to me. All of these girls were my sisters. This does not mean that we had the same mother and father. It means that we were close relatives. You could call us cousins. In Mongo families, people believe that close relatives should feel and behave like sisters and brothers. So that is what we are called.

Chicken for Dinner

It was time for dinner, our first meal in the village. Our grandmother decided we should have something special. We were to have chicken in palm-oil sauce, with large helpings of rice and hot spices.

Our grandmother was proud of her cooking, so she made the dinner herself. First she served the men and children. Then she sat down and ate her own dinner. This was the way it was done in the village.

Many things in the village, I soon discovered, were different from things in the city. Here the children asked more questions. It seemed to me they never stopped asking. The grown-ups usually tried to answer. But one thing was the same, here and at home. Girls and boys in the village always obeyed their parents right away, just as we did in Kinshasa. No one questioned an order that a parent gave.

Mongo Village

I grew used to the village, and I liked sharing in the things that went on. All of our tasks were divided between men and women. This is the way it had been for hundreds of years.

The men and boys did the fishing. Often my brother went to the river to help.

Boys in the village had other tasks to do besides fishing. They climbed the tall palm trees to cut palm nuts. The nuts grew in prickly groups. When they were ripe, they turned a fine red-orange color.

Girls helped women make the nuts into sauce for cooking. First, my grandmother boiled the nuts until they turned soft. After the pot cooled a little, my sisters and I squeezed the warm pulp between our fingers. It turned into a thick red oil. This oil was what made our chicken taste so good.

My sisters also let me help them weave baskets from reeds and palm leaves.

The women used some of the bigger baskets to carry things to and from the fields or the market. These baskets were called *head baskets* because the women carried them on their heads. I had never done this at home because my mother did not. But many of our neighbors always carry things in head baskets.

Surprise and Home

I loved each hour of the days we spent in the village. Now they were almost over. That made me feel sad.

On the morning we were supposed to leave, my brother told me a wonderful secret. He had exchanged the riverboat tickets for two tickets on an airplane.

On the last morning, we said good-by to each family. We promised to come back soon.

The airplane was late, but at last it was ready. We began moving down the black runway. Black turned into green—green trees below us. All I could see was green now, except for a silver thread. That was the broad river winding through the forest.

After a while, the sound of the engine changed. The plane was flying lower. We were home.

Sometimes I dream about the village and my sisters. Sometimes they send me letters.

"Come back," the letters say.

And I answer, "Someday I shall!"

Understanding What You've Read

1. Why was Pauline going to the Mongo fishing village?
2. In the village, what were two tasks done by the boys? What were two tasks done by the girls?
3. If you visited such an African village, what would you enjoy doing most?

Applying the Skills Lesson

1. Say each word below. Is the vowel sound long or short?

   a. feel   b. leave   c. much   d. home

2. Say each word below. Do the two vowel letters next to each other stand for one sound or more than one sound?

   a. giant   b. weave   c. rain   d. broad

When you come to a word you don't know, think about the sounds the letters can stand for. Remember that each vowel letter can stand for at least two sounds.

Do you have horses and guinea pigs in your family? It's possible if you are part of . . .

The 4-H Club Family

by Danny Weiland *with* Sarah Rose Skaates

Can you picture living in a family with ten children, six horses, five dogs, and two hundred guinea pigs? That's the kind of place I live in. You can bet it's never dull here!

I'm Danny Weiland from Lancaster, Ohio. My family is a 4-H family.

Do you know about 4-H? It's an organization of clubs for young people. 4-H Clubs give us a chance to work on some great projects. We can learn more about things that interest us, and we can have fun doing it.

Both my mother and father work with 4-H Clubs. All of my sisters and brothers are or have been members. I'm the youngest in the family. I was able to join 4-H when I turned nine. But even before that, I took part.

Mom has loved horses and worked with them since she was a child. So it is no surprise that she works with a 4-H Club whose interest is horses.

The children who work with my mother have already learned some things about horses. They know how to show them at fairs and horse shows. My mom judges a lot of horse shows. So she can help the children learn more about judging the best horses and riders.

I'm just starting out with a horse project. Annie Dexter—my pony—and I spend hours together in the horse lot behind our house. There we work out for the shows. I have to know all kinds of things about taking care of Annie. Mom shows me how to hold the lead rope, how to get her to stand just right, and how to ride so Annie and I both look good.

Dad's 4-H Club is interested in guinea pigs. My brothers Paul and Eddie and I are also interested in guinea pigs. We've learned to feed them rabbit food and greens. We also have to keep their cages clean. Dad uses ground corncobs in the bottom of each cage. He adds hay in the winter to keep the animals warm. Each club member has his or her own pigs. Dad lets us breed them with his. We try for prize-winning offspring.

To be a winner, a guinea pig should have a stout body. It should be like a brick with rounded corners. The nose should be rounded, not pointed.

Dad sells some of his *cavies* [kā′vēz] for pets. Cavies is another name for guinea pigs. He keeps some for breeding and for shows.

Some people earn their living by raising and selling guinea pigs. But Dad does it only as a sideline. His main work is with copying machines. His office is behind our house.

Mom is in business, too. She has a tack shop right next to Dad's office. In a tack shop people buy things like saddles and riding boots.

It just happens to be that our family is mostly interested in animals. But there are many different kinds of projects for 4-H members. The 4-H Club was begun for farm children. But other children can enjoy 4-H now, no matter where they live. There are several different projects in cooking, sewing, woodworking, gardening, and photography.

Maybe you wonder what the letters stand for in 4-H. The four

H's are for Head (thinking), Heart (feeling), Hands (working), and Health. The 4-H motto is "To Make the Best Better."

I said there is a lot of fun in 4-H — and there is! First, there's the fun of doing things with friends. Then there's the fun of showing one's work at fairs.

Mom and Dad say it's easy to find a 4-H Club. Maybe there's a lucky 4-H clover waiting for you — if you're interested in looking for it. Happy hunting!

Understanding What You've Read

1. What special skill did Danny's mother teach to her 4-H Club?
2. What did Danny and his brothers learn about the feeding and care of guinea pigs?
3. Danny mentioned many projects 4-H members work on. If you were a 4-H member, which project would you like to work on? Why?

Applying the Skills Lesson

1. All the words below have two consonant letters next to each other. Say each word. Do the two consonant letters stand for one sound or two sounds?

   a. green   b. father
   c. show   d. lucky

2. Say the pairs of words below. One word in each pair has a long vowel sound. Which word is it?

   a. learn   each
   b. clover   round
   c. clean   earn

Using Sounds and Letters to Decode Words

You may find many words you don't know in your textbooks. When you see a new word, remember to use what you know about sounds and letters to help you decode it. Once you've said the word, you may find you already know it.

Read the following selections. Use the sidenotes to help you with the hard words.

Decoding Words in Health

In the word *traits*, the two vowel letters stand for the long sound of the first vowel letter. Say this word.

If you are not sure how to say *inherited*, use the glossary. You will also find what it means.

The letters *ph* stand for the same sound as the *ph* in *phone*. The *y* stands for the sound of the *i* in *is*. When you say this word, you may know that it means "of the body."

You are a special person. You are different from everyone else. The traits you inherited make you you. And what you have learned makes you you.

Merrie is a special person, too. There is no one just like her. The traits she inherited make her different. Perhaps you can name two of Merrie's physical traits.

Merrie is different in other ways. Guess what one other way might be. How did she become different in that way? Who helped her? How did what she has learned change the way she grows?

— *You Learn and Change:* Orange
Harcourt Brace Jovanovich

Building Skills

1. Say the word pairs below. Do the vowel letters in boldface stand for the same sound in each word?

   a. m**a**ke tr**ai**t   b. d**i**fferent   ph**y**sical

2. Look in the glossary to find the meaning of the word *inherited.* Use the word in a sentence.

Decoding Words in Mathematics

This selection shows a *bar graph.* A bar graph is a special kind of chart that compares a number of things or events. The notes below the graph will help you read it.

Michael is studying the planets. He learned that his pony Skippy would weigh different amounts on the different planets. He made a bar graph to show this.

43

This title tells you what the bar graph is about.

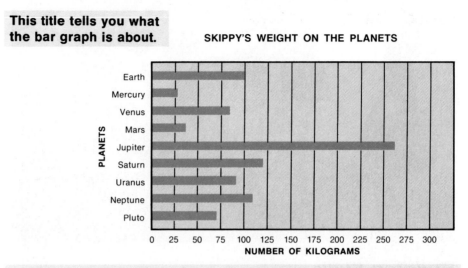

SKIPPY'S WEIGHT ON THE PLANETS

The words down the side of the graph tell what things are being compared. The numbers across the bottom are called a *scale*. By finding where each bar ends on the scale, you can tell how much Skippy weighs on each planet.

This word can be pronounced in two different ways. Look in the glossary for the two pronunciations.

The *u* in *Jupiter* and *Pluto* sounds like the *oo* in *pool*. Say these words.

Skippy weighs 100 kilograms on Earth. Skippy would weigh less on Mercury. Skippy would weigh more on Jupiter. Would Skippy weigh more or less on Pluto?

— *Growth in Mathematics:* Orange
Harcourt Brace Jovanovich

Building Skills

Say each word below. Listen for the vowel sounds. Tell whether the letter or letters in boldface stand for a long vowel sound or a short one.

planet   w**ei**gh   n**u**mber   p**o**ny

Word Parts

You're on your first airplane trip. The pilot has just announced that you're about to land. You look out the window. You see a strange picture. It's made up of long lines and little boxes. You think it's beautiful, but you don't know what it is. Then, as the plane goes lower, you see that the lines are roads and the boxes are houses and stores. You're looking at a town. Once you know what the parts are, you are able to make sense out of the whole picture.

When you come to words that seem strange, you can use the parts to help you understand them. When you look at each part, you often find you know how to say the word. You may also know what each part means. When you put the parts back together, you may know the meaning of the whole word.

Compounds

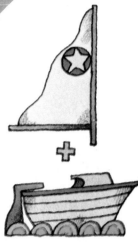

Some long words are made by joining two or more shorter words. In the word *sailboat,* you can see the two words *sail* and *boat.* Words like this are called **compound words.** In a compound word, the shorter words may tell you the meaning of the long word. You can tell the meaning of *sailboat* from the two shorter words. A *sailboat* is a boat that has sails.

Find the two compound words in this sentence: "I left my notebook in the classroom." What does each one mean? Right! A *notebook* is a book for notes. A *classroom* is a room for a class.

Sometimes a compound word may be made from two or more shorter words that do *not* help tell the meaning. Look at the word *understand.* It does not mean "stand under." You may not be able to use the shorter words in a compound word to help you know its meaning. But you can still use them to help you say the word. Once you say a word, you often find you already know the meaning.

Try This

Read the questions below. Notice the two shorter words in each compound word in boldface. Answer *yes* or *no* to each question. Make up a sentence using each compound word.

1. Can a **flashlight** help you in the dark?
2. Is a **firecracker** something warm to eat?
3. If you walked by the **roadside,** would you be walking by the side of the road?

46

Prefixes

Sometimes a part is added to the beginning of a word to make a different word. The word that the part is added to is called the **root word.** The part added to the beginning is called a **prefix.** Look at the word *unhappy.*

$$\text{unhappy} = \text{un} + \text{happy}$$

The prefix *un-* means "not." The root word is *happy*—a word you know. You can tell that *unhappy* means "not happy."

Some prefixes you may know are: *un-*, *dis-*, *re-*, *pre-*. The prefixes *un-* and *dis-* mean "not." The prefix *re-* means "again." The prefix *pre-* means "before."

Look at the words *preview* and *review*. Use the meaning of each prefix to help you understand these words.

             (before)   *(see or look at)*

So *preview* means "see or look at before."

review = re + view

             (again)   *(see or look at)*

So *review* means "see or look at again."

Try This

Read the sentences below. Look at the words in boldface. Notice the prefix and root word in each. What is the meaning of the whole word? Use each word in a new sentence.

1. Robin **reread** the book because she liked it so much.
2. People who don't think the same as you do are likely to **disagree** with your ideas.
3. The directions for the pie said to **preheat** the oven.
4. The **unusual** animal appeared very strange to me.

48

Suffixes

Sometimes a part is added to the end of a root word to make a different word. The part added at the end of a root word is called a **suffix.** Look at the word *peaceful.*

peaceful = peace + ful

The word *peace* can mean "a state of quiet or calm." The word part *-ful* means "full of." So the word *peaceful* can mean "full of quiet or calm."

Some suffixes you may know are: *-ful, -less, -ous, -able, -er.*

The suffix *-less* means "without." The suffix *-ous* means "having." The suffix *-able* means "able to." The suffix *-er* means "one who."

Sometimes the spelling of a root word is changed when a suffix is added. Look at the following list.

Word	=	Root Word	+	Suffix
plentiful	=	plenty	+	ful
penniless	=	penny	+	less
usable	=	use	+	able
winner	=	win	+	er

Notice what happens to *y* at the end of a root word before a suffix is added. Notice what letter is dropped from *use* before *-able* is added. Find the letter that is added to the word *win* before *-er* is added.

If you come to a long word that has a suffix, remember that the spelling of the root word may have changed. Once you have figured out what the root word is, you often will be able to say and understand the long word.

Try This

Read the sentences below. Look at the words in boldface. Notice the root word and suffix in each. What is the meaning of the whole word? Use each word in a new sentence.

1. The **farmer** worked all day plowing the field.
2. Nina looked at the **cloudless** sky.
3. His kind acts showed that he was a **merciful** king.

50

VOCABULARY STUDY

Compound Words

Hello. Bertha Snodgrass, director of the Compound Word Museum, speaking. You say you'd like to join our museum? Well, we only have compound words where the meanings of the shorter words help people to know the meaning of the compound word. Our newest words are **starfish, scoreboard,** and **seaplane.** We received starfish from Mortimer C. Urchin's *Words of the Sea* collection. A baseball team gave us scoreboard. And seaplane was given by the well-known flying company, *Ups and Downs.*

Well, what are you? A firecracker? I think you are calling the wrong place, Sir—or, Madam—or whatever you are. I know you're a compound word, but your two words don't tell what you mean. What? You say you'll just explode if you aren't allowed to join? Well, maybe we can start a new branch of the museum for your kind of compound word. . . .

Word Play

1. Give a definition for each word in boldface. Use the shorter words in each compound to explain its meaning.
2. With each short word below, make three compound words.

    some   room   day   grand   tooth

3. The two words of the compound do not always tell you what the compound means. For example, a *firecracker* is not "something warm to eat." Think of three compound words like *firecracker* and write a "daffy definition" for each one.

When you come to a long word you don't know, see if it contains a word you do know.

At the Olympics, people from all over the world learn about each other and from each other.

The OLYMPICS: A World Family

by Nicholas Pease

Many families enjoy playing games together. So do the "family of nations" that make up our world. Every four years, people from all over the world gather for the Olympic Games. Athletes from many lands come together. They take part in matches. The winners receive medals and honors.

History of the Olympic Games

The first Games were held many hundreds of years ago in Greece. Each city sent a team. Huge numbers of people went to watch the Games. Sports were very important to the people of Greece.

About one hundred years ago, Pierre de Coubertin studied the history of the Games. The Greek games gave him an idea. Greek cities could compete in peaceful ways. Why couldn't the countries of the world? Why not a *World Olympics?*

Coubertin acted on his idea. In 1896, the first modern Games were held. These Games were held in Greece, as the Games of old were. Only amateurs could enter. This meant people who played for the love of sport—not for money. Coubertin's idea worked well.

Modern-Day Heroes

Over the years the Olympics have brought out the best in athletes. In 1912, for example, Jim Thorpe won the two hardest events.

First he won the *pentathlon* [pen·tath′lən]. It is made up of five different contests. There are two each in running and throwing and one in jumping. The person who finished second had less than half the points Thorpe had.

Next Thorpe won the *decathlon* [di·kath′lən]. It has ten separate contests. Again he jumped, ran, and threw. Once more he won by many points.

Then a sad thing happened to Thorpe after the 1912 Games. Thorpe did not know it, but he had broken an Olympic rule. He had played baseball for money one summer. This meant he wasn't an amateur. His first-place gold medals were taken away. But the second-place winner refused them. He said Thorpe was still the greatest athlete of all time.

In 1982, the International Olympic Committee ruled that Thorpe had not really broken a rule. The gold medals were at last returned to Thorpe's family. This was almost thirty years after his death.

American track star Jesse Owens is still remembered for what he did in 1936. That year, he raced twelve times in the Games. In nine of those races he tied or broke Olympic records. He also tied or broke four world records. What he did may never be matched.

No one may ever equal what Mark Spitz did, either. In 1972 this swimmer from the United States won seven gold medals. He finished first in each race.

In 1976 Nadia Comaneci [kō′mə·nēch′] won three gold medals in gymnastics. This girl

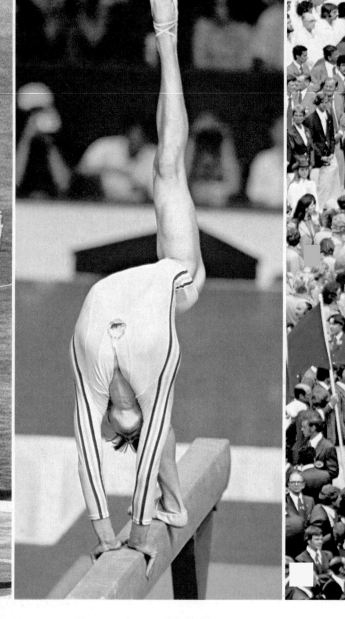

from Romania was only fourteen. She scored seven perfect marks of 10. No one had ever scored 10 before. In fact, the scoreboard could go only as high as 9.99!

Courage and Conquest

Skill is important. Sometimes courage is just as important.

In 1976 crowds cheered a gymnast from Japan. His act on the

54

Top, Mark Spitz, 1972 Gold Medalist in Munich, Germany.
Bottom left, Shun Fujimoto, 1976 Gold Medalist in Montreal, Canada.
Bottom right, Jesse Owens, 1936 Gold Medalist in Berlin, Germany.

rings was breathtaking. But his face showed pain. At the end of his act, he did a difficult triple turn. In landing, he stumbled just a little. Shun Fujimoto [shoŏn foo′jē·mō′tō] smiled bravely. But he had to be helped to the dressing room.

No one knew it then, but Fujimoto had just shown unbelievable courage. The day before, he had hurt himself. But he would not quit. That would have spoiled his team's chances of winning. So he hid his pain from the judges. He had done his whole graceful act with a broken leg.

Wilma Rudolph had polio as a child. For four years she lay in bed. When she finally got up, she could barely walk. But Wilma made up her mind to run. And run she did. In the 1960 Games, she won three gold medals. No American woman runner had ever done that before.

Bob Mathias was a thin and sickly child. In fact, he nearly died. Doctors warned him against pushing himself too hard. Still, he wanted to build up his body. Every day he trained. In time he became very strong.

By age seventeen, Mathias was able to join the 1948 Olympic team. He was the youngest man

ever to enter the decathlon. He surprised everyone by winning. And four years later he won it again. Bob Mathias is the only person so far to win it twice.

The Olympic Symbol

You may know the five-ring symbol of the Games. The colors of the rings were chosen with good reason. Every flag in the world can be joined together in the colors. These rings are connected. This shows how people of the world can be joined together in the friendly spirit of the Games.

The rings make a fitting sign of the dream held by Coubertin. He once wrote these words: "The important thing about the Olympic Games is not to win, but to take part. The important thing in life is not the triumph, but the struggle."

Understanding What You've Read

1. How often are the Olympic Games held?
2. How did the Japanese gymnast Shun Fujimoto show unbelievable courage?
3. What is the symbol of the Olympics? What reason is given for choosing the colors of the rings?

Applying the Skills Lesson

1. What is the root word in each of the following words?

   a. runner   b. graceful
   c. unbelievable   d. swimmer

2. What shorter words make up each of the compound words below?

   a. scoreboard   b. everything   c. himself

If a compound word gives you any trouble, see if there are words you know in it. The meanings of the shorter words may help you with the meaning of the compound word.

How would it feel to meet a part of your family you'd never met before?

THE LONG WAY HOME

by Mary Elting *with* Louis Mofsie

When Louis Mofsie was a boy, he lived with his family in New York City. Louis's mother belonged to a Winnebago Indian family. His father was a Hopi.

Louis's father came from a tiny Hopi village in Arizona. There, near the Painted Desert, his ancestors had built their homes long ago.

Louis himself had never seen the desert. Neither had his sister. Then one summer, their father and mother took them to visit the Hopi village. It was a summer full of wonderful surprises.

58

How We Came to Hopiland

What a long way it was! For three days and nights we traveled on the train—my father and mother, my sister, and I. Now we were in a bouncing pick-up truck. We were raising clouds of dust over great stretches of road.

The truck belonged to my uncle. As we rode along, he hummed to himself. At last I had to ask him why.

"I am making a new song about you," he said.

My uncle sang a bit of it then. I did not understand one word of it. He was singing in the Hopi language.

"The words tell a story," he said. "The story is about children who come from far away to stay with their people for a while. Hopi people love to have their sons and daughters come home."

My uncle drove on and on, across a rocky plain and into the Painted Desert. It is called "painted" because the earth itself is many-colored—purple, orange, yellow, green, gray.

Beyond the desert lies the land where the Hopi people live. If you are not an Indian, you might say it is the Hopi reservation. We have a different name for it. We call it "Land of the Peaceful People." The word *Hopi* means "People of Peace."

The road through Hopiland grew more rough —and lonely, too. We saw no houses—not even any animals. There was nothing but the wide, brown earth and tall clouds journeying across the bright sky.

Then I saw it—the village with its small houses made of brown stone. They were grouped together at the top of a steep, rocky cliff. You could hardly tell where the houses ended and the brown rock began.

Now I had two homes. They were so different and so far apart. Would I like this new one? I couldn't be sure. But I was very glad to get here. It was just sunset, and the sky and the whole earth turned red and gold.

Who Is Who

My sister woke me very early the next morning. All day we went visiting the members of our Hopi family. First we went to my grandmother's. She did not speak English. But I did not have to speak Hopi to know that I was welcome in my grandmother's home.

By the end of the day I discovered a surprising thing. I had not one father but three! My two new fathers were my father's brothers. But they were more than uncles, really. They thought of me as their son. The Hopi word for *father* and *uncle* is the same—*naa.*

It gave me a good new feeling. All three of my fathers loved me. All three would take care of me. That was the Hopi way, and it made me feel very comfortable and safe.

Finally, the visiting ended. Now everyone agreed that the time had come for me to receive a name of my own.

Of course, I had a first name and a family name already. In a Hopi village, my uncle explained, everyone knew everyone else, so nobody needed a family name. Because of this, Hopi children could be given several names that belonged only to them. Later they could pick the one they liked best. They could even choose a new name.

My father had chosen a name for himself when he first went to live in the city. The name he chose means "sharpshooter" in the Hopi language. But the Hopi word was a very long one. City people never could remember it. So he began using only the easiest part of it, which is Mofsie.

When I went to school, I was also called Mofsie. Like other city children, I was given a first name, too. Did I really need still another? I wondered. But I did not ask. I would wait and see.

My New Name

My grandmother chose my new name. It was a very old one, my uncle told me. Long ago it belonged to a man in our family who followed all the rules that Hopi people have for living happily together. He was patient, generous, and kind. He always showed that he felt peaceful toward the rest of the world.

My grandmother wanted me to be like this man, so she had made up her mind to give me his name. When I received it, there would be a very important ceremony.

On the morning of the ceremony, my mother and sister went with me to my grandmother's house. Around the room sat a row of women. Everyone sat very still, without a word.

The women nodded toward a spot where I was to sit. I took my place. Not a word had been spoken. Yet, I was sure that everyone had come here for a happy reason.

My grandmother rose and put a small tub of water and a towel on the floor. Next, she went to a storeroom. From it, she brought out an ear of corn, a bundle of leaves, and crushed roots from a plant, called *yucca*, which grew near the village. She put the roots into the small tub. Then she moved the long leaves through the water. A cloud of white bubbles foamed up! Yucca root makes bubbles in water, just as soap does.

Now my grandmother beckoned to the other women in the room. They formed a half-circle behind her. My mother and sister stood with them.

Last of all, I was motioned to kneel beside the tub of foam. Gently, my grandmother gathered up bubbles and rubbed them into my hair. Then she took the ear of corn and touched my head with it lightly—once. Then she touched it again and again.

My mother did just as my grandmother had done. Every woman in the room followed her. Each of them washed my hair. Then they very softly said a prayer while rubbing my head four times with the corn.

At last my grandmother wrapped a towel around my shoulders. She rubbed the water from my hair, powdered my face with corn meal, and spoke my new name: Lomahongva!

"Lo-May-Hong-Vah." I said it over slowly. It had a wonderful sound. In English it meant "Clouds-Standing-Straight-in-the-Sky." Those words had a fine sound, too.

Now the solemn part of the ceremony was almost over. Only one thing remained. I had to make my greeting to the sun.

If I had been born in the village, I would have been carried out into the sunshine for the first time when I was twenty days old. Since I was much too big to be carried, I could introduce myself.

I took the ear of corn that had been used in the ceremony, ran out, and raised it high in the sunshine. Then I ran back into the house.

64

What a change I found! The women were all talking in their soft, cheerful voices. They smiled at me and gave me presents. One gave me a blanket. Several gave me baskets. In our village, women make a kind of basket that is very beautiful. In a neighboring Hopi village, the women do not weave baskets, but they do make clay bowls. Someone gave me one of those fine, small bowls.

Like yucca bubbles, happiness rose up inside me. I felt as if I had been waiting all my life to celebrate a birthday here. I felt as if I had never had a real birthday before.

Understanding What You've Read

1. Why did Louis and his family go to Arizona?
2. What was the reason for Louis's special ceremony?
3. Why did Louis's grandmother choose Lomahongva as his Hopi name?

Applying the Skills Lesson

1. What is the root word in each word below?

   a. cheerful   b. happiness   c. beautiful

2. What two words make up each compound word below?

   a. Hopiland   b. sharpshooter
   c. storeroom   d. sunshine

Using Word Parts to Find Meanings

Use what you know about word parts as you read these selections. Some long words are made from two shorter words. Some are made by adding prefixes or suffixes to root words. Use the sidenotes to help you.

Using Word Parts to Find Meanings
   in Social Studies

This selection is part of a chapter on space. It tells how ideas about space travel have helped us in our daily lives.

> This word is made by adding the suffix *-less* to the root word *weight.* What does this suffix mean?

> Which part of this word means "teach" or "show"? Which part of this word means "again"?

Space technology is also used by institutions that work to keep us well. If you've ever broken a bone or been sick for a long time, you know how weak your muscles can get. The same thing happens to astronauts in space. Because their bodies are weightless, their muscles grow soft. They don't have to be used the way they are on Earth. The exercises that astronauts use can help people who have been sick to retrain their muscles.

Some of the moon trips used a moon rover. Wheels aren't much use on a surface as rough as the moon's.

The moon rover can go up and down slopes and across rough surfaces without getting stuck. How might a tool like this help people who are unable to walk?

The root word is _able._ What prefix was added?

Have you ever had trouble using a pen because you were writing uphill? Has anyone in your family ever cooked food and had it stick to the pan? Have you ever swallowed toothpaste foam and choked because it was full of detergent? The technology that has made space travel possible has solved these problems, too.

What two shorter words make this compound word?

Which word in this sentence is a compound word?

—*Planet Earth*
Houghton Mifflin

Building Skills

1. Look at the words below. The suffixes *-able* or *-less* have been added to words from the selection. Tell what each new word below means.

   a. trainable   b. useless   c. helpless

2. Match each word in Column 1 to its meaning in Column 2.

1	2
weightless	up a hill
retrain	not able
unable	paste for cleaning teeth
uphill	teach or show again
toothpaste	without weight

Using Word Parts to Find Meanings in Language Arts

You do not have to do the exercises in this selection. Use the sidenotes to help you use word parts to find meaning.

Which part of this word means "see"? Which part means "again"? What does *review* mean?

Review Practice

1. Decide how many syllables each word has. If the word has more than one syllable, decide where the accent belongs. Be ready to tell the class what you have decided.

handkerchief   lasso   about

through   cheerful

beginner   icy   potato

Would you hold a *kerchief* in your *hand*?

2. Write each sentence below. In place of each blank, write the possessive form of the noun in parentheses.

What does the suffix in *cheerful* mean?

How was *ice* changed to make this word?

First look for the root word in *possessive*. Then if you are not sure what this word means, look in the glossary.

1. Charles chewed all of his _____ gum. (sisters)

2. He used all of his _____ toothpicks. (mother)

3. He entered the _____ Art Show. (Children)

4. _____ toothpick and bubble gum sculpture won the "most original" prize. (Charles)

The root word *sculpt* can mean "to shape." *Sculpture* means "a work of art that is made by modeling figures or shapes."

—Language for Daily Use: Orange
Harcourt Brace Jovanovich

Building Skills

Look at each word below. Is the word a compound word? If it is, name the two shorter words in it. Is the word made of a root word and a suffix? If it is, name the root word and the suffix.

toothpick   sculpture   handkerchief   beginner

Syllables

Sometimes smaller parts are easier to handle. It may be easier to say a long word by attacking it in small parts. Then you can put the parts together. Sometimes when you say a word that seems hard, you may find you already know it.

One way to break apart the sounds in a word is to look for syllables. A **syllable** is a short word part with one vowel sound in it. When you say the word *bat,* you hear one vowel sound. *Bat* has one syllable. Say the word *begin.* Do you hear two vowel sounds? *Begin* has two syllables.

How the Dictionary Breaks Words into Syllables

Dictionaries show the syllables in words by using marks or spaces. Some dictionaries use a dot between the syllables. Others use a dash. Still others just use a blank space. Look at the different ways the word *transportation* is broken into syllables by different dictionaries.

trans·por·ta·tion   **trans-por-ta-tion**   **trans por ta tion**

Each dictionary breaks the word in the same places. Each shows that *transportation* has four syllables.

Word Parts and Syllables

Here are some dictionary entry words. Study them to find out some things about how words are broken into syllables. The notes following the words will give you some pointers.

dis·trust   rest·ful

A prefix is usually in a syllable by itself. So is a suffix. The prefix *dis-* in the word *distrust* is marked as a separate syllable by a dot. The suffix *-ful* in the word *restful* is also marked as a separate syllable by a dot.

break·a·ble

Sometimes a suffix has more than one syllable. How many vowel sounds are there in *-able*? Remember, a syllable has only one vowel sound.

air·line

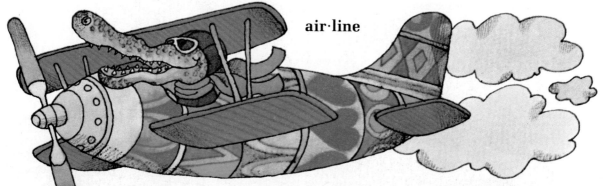

Airline is a compound word. What two shorter words do you see in it? How many syllables does *airline* have? Compound words always have at least two syllables—at least one for each short word. But compounds can have more than two syllables. How many syllables are in *airliner*?

Try This

1. Say the words below. How many syllables do you hear in each? Use each word in a sentence.

   a. restate   b. likable
   c. spotlight   d. carefully

2. Read the sentences below. Then say the words in boldface. How many syllables do you hear in each of the words in boldface?

   a. We are going to the **airport.**
   b. It was an **uneventful** meeting.
   c. Has **anybody** found my lunchbox?
   d. **Thanksgiving** is my favorite holiday.
   e. **Refreshments** will be served.

I love the 4th of July

I love Thanksgiving

Sounds and Syllables

If you know how to find the syllables in words, you may find it easier to decode them. You can try to say each part of a word and then put the parts together. Here are some more entry words. You will learn some more about syllables from them. Once again, there are notes to help you.

broad   ac·tu·al

Broad has only one syllable. The two vowel letters in *broad* stand for one sound. Remember that a syllable contains one vowel sound. Sometimes two vowel letters together stand for two sounds. When they do, each is in a separate syllable. Notice that *actual* has three syllables.

The two consonants together in *monkey* stand for two sounds. Most words like this are divided between the two consonants.

feath·er

Feather also has two consonants together in it. How many sounds does *th* stand for? When two consonants together stand for one sound, they are in the same syllable.

sup·per

The *pp* in *supper* also stands for one sound. But the dictionary breaks the word between the two p's. Often, in writing, a word with a double consonant in it is divided this way. But when you say the word, the double consonant has only one sound.

Try This

1. Say the words below. How many syllables do you hear in each? Use each word in a sentence.

   a. package   b. center   c. create

2. Read the sentences below. Say the words in boldface. How many syllables do you hear in each of these words?

   a. Our school is having a folk dance **festival.**
   b. I like to listen to music on the **radio.**
   c. Jenny helped **shear** the sheep.
   d. The **market** is always crowded on Saturdays.
   e. I saw a TV show about **lions.**
   f. **Dinner** is ready.
   g. I have a new **leather** jacket.

VOCABULARY STUDY

Antonyms

Interviewer:
We are visiting Heliotrope Cavendish, well-known author of adventure stories. His latest book is *When Worlds Collide, Do They Say Excuse Me?* How are you today, Mr. Cavendish?

Cavendish:
I feel **generous.** Yesterday I felt selfish, but not today. I also need a haircut.

Interviewer:
Tell me, where did you get your ideas for the people in your book? Is Queen Urpo like your sister, Novodka?

Cavendish:
The people in my book are all **imaginary.** They're not real, like Novodka or us.

Interviewer:
Does this story take place in the past? No one seems to be able to tell.

Cavendish:
I don't understand why. It's clear to me. My story takes place in the **future.** I never write about the past because it's over. The past makes me ill. I don't like to think about it. Do you want to hear about my new book—*What Do You Say After You Say Good-by?*

Interviewer:
Maybe in the future, Mr. Cavendish. But not now.

Word Play

1. Antonyms are words that mean the opposite of other words. Mr. Cavendish used antonyms for *generous, imaginary,* and *future.* Give an antonym for each word in boldface.

2. Give an antonym for each of the following words:

   fancy   muddy   deserted   major

3. Sometimes a prefix makes a word mean the opposite. The prefix *dis-* means "not," as in *disagree.* Add *dis-* to four other words to make their antonyms.

When you come to a long word you don't know, try saying it one syllable at a time.

Lynne Sommer and her family always wanted to live on an island. Now they sometimes see whales swimming by their house.

As Free as the Wind

by Lynne Sommer *as told to* Susanne Sommer

Have you ever dreamed about living on an island as Robinson Crusoe did? I'll bet you've thought about it. My family and I thought about it, too. Then we did it! We really moved to an island. It's not as deserted as Robinson Crusoe's island—there are 500 people living here. Yet, it's still an honest-to-goodness island.

It was quite a move for my family and me. None of us had ever lived on a farm before—and certainly not on a farm on an island! Mom and Dad felt that living on an island farm would give us more time together as a family. So, three years ago, Mom, Dad, my sister Karen, my brother Marc, and I packed our things and moved to Malcolm Island.

Malcolm Island is off the northern coast of British Columbia, Canada. When you come here, it seems like you're going to the end of the world. You have to take three ferry boats from Vancouver, Canada. The boat trips take many hours. The only other way to get here is by seaplane.

Living on an island farm is quite different from living in a big city in the United States. We've had to get used to a lot of things. In the States, my sister, brother, and I went to a large school. The school had two or three classrooms for each grade. But here the whole school has three classrooms—and just eighty-one children! There are only three teachers in the school.

Marc goes to high school, which is on another island. He takes the ferry to get there. He's gone from about 7:30 A.M. to 5:00 P.M.

Some of our holidays—such as Thanksgiving—are at different times than they are in the States. Our major holiday is Dominion Day. It falls on July 1. Every August, the small town of Sointula [swän·tōō′lə] on our island has a Salmon Festival. That's the biggest event of the year for everyone.

To go to a movie, we have to take a boat to another island, so we don't go very often. There are no circuses here. We don't have TV. But we see and do lots of things that you can't see and do in a city.

The ocean is right in front of our house. We sometimes see whales swimming by. Steamships that are going to Prince Rupert and Alaska pass right in front of our house, too.

Karen and I like to go exploring when we get the chance. We look for starfish. They are often very large and come in different colors, such as red, purple, and orange. We also like to watch the tiny fish swimming in little pools. We try to chase the crabs as they hurry across the sand, too.

Another thing Karen, Marc, and I like to do is to go to Mitchell Bay to visit friends. Mitchell Bay is ten miles from our house. We have to ride over an old, bumpy road to get there. There are no phones or electricity on that side of the island. Not too many people live there. Those who do, cook on wood stoves and use kerosene lamps for light.

One bad thing about living here is that we get a lot of rain. We have to wear big rubber boots because it's often muddy. When the sun does shine, it makes us feel good.

When we lived in the city we had a dog named Penny. Penny still lives with us. We have other animals, too—twenty chickens, seventeen rabbits, five cats, and two goats. The chickens give us eggs. The rabbits—except for Karen's pet, Parsley—are used

80

for food. The goats give us milk each day. Sometimes Mom makes cheese from the goat milk.

The whole family has to help out on the farm. We feed the animals, gather eggs, and work in the garden. We also clean the barn and chop wood.

Our garden is full of vegetables. But the tomatoes are grown in the greenhouse because it isn't sunny enough to grow them outside. We have to pull the weeds in the garden and keep the bugs off the plants. Dad calls these bugs "green meanies."

Karen and I like to read and write poems and stories. Without a TV, there's plenty of time for that. Dad and Marc play the guitar. Many evenings are spent listening to them play for us.

A doctor visits our island once a week. The dentist comes once a month. If we have to go to the doctor or hospital quickly, we get on a seaplane and fly to another island.

Our house isn't fancy, but we love it because it's cozy. We have a wood stove in the living room. It gives heat for the whole house. We have to chop a lot of wood because it gets pretty cold in the winter.

The snow is exciting for us because there was very little of it where we used to live. Our whole family has a lot of fun skating and sliding, but the cold gets to us. We sleep with our clothes under our pillows so we can get dressed as soon as we get up in the morning. Then we gather around the stove to get warm.

There are things we miss about the life we used to have. When it rains for days and days, we long for the warm, sunny weather we had in the States. Because most of the trees here are evergreens, we don't have many spring blossoms and fall coloring. My mother misses them a lot.

But other things are better. There is very little pollution. Not too many cars rush back and forth on our "street."

Karen says she likes it better here because it's quieter and wilder. She likes to sing one of the songs she made up as she runs up and down the beach. The name of her song is "I'm as Free as the Wind." Do you know what? I think Karen's song describes the way we all feel about our little island.

Understanding What You've Read

1. Why did Lynne and her family move to Malcolm Island?
2. How does the whole family help out on the farm?
3. Name three ways Lynne says life on the island is different from life in the city.

Applying the Skills Lesson

1. Say each compound word below. How many syllables does each word have? Looking for the shorter words in each compound will help you.

   a. seaplane   b. evergreen
   c. starfish   d. greenhouse

2. Say each word below. How many syllables does each word have?

   a. weather   b. circus
   c. chicken   d. doctor

Friendship is important to people. It is a matter of survival to some animals.

SPECIAL FRIENDSHIPS

by Natalie Friendly

There are many different kinds of friendships between animals. No one knows how or why many of these friendships got started.

In certain friendships, some animals behave like "guests." Often a guest will live in another animal's house without helping to build or clean it. The "host" seems willing to do all the work. It just wants to have the pleasure of the guest's company.

In other friendships, "worker" animals do jobs for their "friends." They will clean, feed, or protect their friends. In return, they will receive help that they need.

Workers

The ziczac bird and the crocodile have a strange friendship. Feared by people and most animals, the crocodile has terrible jaws. The jaws are filled with several rows of sharp, pointed teeth. Its body is covered by scales. It has a long, flat tail that could knock you down.

Many crocodiles live in the rivers and swamps of Africa. The swamps and rivers are full of leeches. These strange worms hold onto the inside of the crocodile's mouth. The ziczac bird picks these leeches and other pests from the crocodile's mouth. The crocodile never bites its friend. Yet it would snap up any other bird.

Lookouts and Scouts

Ostriches and zebras help each other in their friendship. They form "teams" to graze together. They protect each other from their enemy—the lion.

The zebra has powerful teeth and a good strong kick. It can defend itself against most animals. However, the sly lion is too much for it. A lion can take a zebra by surprise.

Zebras run very fast. They also have very good hearing. However, they are quite short and cannot see very far.

Ostriches, however, are seven feet tall. They are the tallest birds alive today. They can run faster than horses. They also have keen eyesight.

With the ostriches watching and the zebras listening, they make a good team. They are lookouts in the way that each can do it best.

Guests and Hosts

One of the most ancient animals alive today is the tuatara. This animal can be traced back to the time of the dinosaurs. The tuatara is about two feet long. It has saw-like teeth and very sharp claws. The scales running down its back look like upside-down ice cream cones.

Today tuataras can only be found on a few small islands off the coast of New Zealand. They sleep all day and hunt for snails and insects at night.

Nobody knows how the tuataras became friendly with little gray sea birds called *sooty shearwaters*. Together they have worked out a way to share a burrow-home. The birds build burrows along the cliffs of the island. They spend their days outside looking for food. While they are out, the tuataras sleep in the burrows. At night, the birds come home to rest. Then their friends get up and go out in search of dinner.

Below, the sooty shearwater rests at home. Left, the tuatara goes in search of dinner.

This seems to be a good way of living for both of them. The tuatara is slow-moving and lazy. It does not help to build the home. However, it does the housekeeping. It gets rid of beetles and other insects.

In the winter, the shearwater leaves its home to travel about the sea. It eats fish from the ocean. It even sleeps on the water. While the shearwater is away, the tuatara stays home. It sleeps all winter, just as bears do.

Underwater Friends

There are perhaps more strange forms of life in the sea than can be found anywhere on land. Many of these underwater animals need friends to help them get food and to protect them.

A very beautiful, but dangerous, animal is the sea anemone. It lives in the warm waters of the world. If you saw one, you might say it looks like a beautifully colored flower. In fact it is called the "flower-of-the-sea." But it is an animal. Its tentacles are dangerous.

They can sting with powerful poison. Fish stung by this lovely sea "flower" often die.

Most anemones are not able to move about. They are attached to rocks, shells, or reefs. They wait for the flowing water to bring little fish and other food to them. Then they sting the fish and eat them. If an anemone senses danger, it pulls its tentacles inside a mouth-like opening. Closed up like this, it looks like a tiny tree stump.

Out of the millions of fish living in the ocean, only one is a close friend of the sea anemone. It is the clown fish. Only about three inches long, its body is striped in orange and white. It has black tips on its fins. The clown fish is very bright and easy to see. It is also a very slow swimmer. Its friend, the sea anemone, helps it to stay alive.

The clown fish darts around picking up bits of food. It brings some of this food to the anemone. Sometimes the clown fish draws other fish to its friend. If a bigger fish chases the clown fish, the clown fish leads it into the "arms" of its dangerous pal.

The clown fish makes its nest near its friend. The anemone's tentacles hide the nest.

In order to live, the clown fish must have its friend for protection. And the anemone needs its friend to "bring home the bacon."

For many animals, staying alive often depends upon their friendships with each other. Animals can help each other get food, make a home, move around, and find safety. All kinds of animals need help. This is true for the largest ones right down to the smallest.

Understanding What You've Read

1. How does the ziczac bird help the crocodile?
2. Why do ostriches and zebras make good "teammates"?
3. What habits of the tuatara and the sooty shearwater make it possible for them to share a burrow?
4. How do the clown fish and the sea anemone help each other?

Applying the Skills Lesson

1. Say each compound word below. How many syllables does each word have? It will help you to look for the shorter words in the compounds.

   a. shearwater   b. eyesight   c. lookouts

2. How many syllables does each word below have? Remember that a suffix is usually a separate syllable.

   a. powerful   b. friendly   c. friendship

3. Say each word below. How many syllables does each word have?

   a. company   b. insect   c. burrow

Using Syllables to Decode Words

The following textbook selections have some words you may not know. Breaking hard words into syllables may make it easier for you to say them. The sidenotes will help you look for the syllables in these words.

Using Syllables to Decode Words in Science

Friendship **is made up of a root word (***friend***) and a suffix (***ship***). Say each word part. How many syllables does** *friendship* **have?**

Some plants have a kind of "friendship" with certain animals. They are not really "friends," of course. But they do seem to help each other out. Other plants have a "friendship" with certain plants.

Animal "friends." At certain times some plants have flowers on them. Some flowers have bright colors. The colors attract insects like bees. The flowers also make sweet nectar that many insects like to drink. In return, you might say the insects do a favor

The two consonants together in this word stand for two sounds. Most words like this are divided between the two consonants (*nec•tar***). Say each part of the word. How many vowel sounds do you hear? How many syllables does it have?**

for the flowers. The insects carry pollen from a flower to another flower of the same kind. Pollen is the white or yellow dust made by certain parts of flowers. Pollen is needed by the flowers to make their seeds. What flowers do you know of that attract insects?

One plant, the yucca plant, has a special friend. It is the yucca moth. The yucca flower opens up just once. It opens one evening. It stays open all that night. The next morning it closes, never to open again. Because it stays open only at night, day insects, like bees and butterflies, cannot carry its pollen. But the yucca moth flies at night.

At night the yucca flower, which is white, shines in the moonlight. It also gives off a sweet smell. These things attract the yucca moth. The yucca moth then carries the pollen from one yucca flower to another. At the same time, the yucca moth lays its eggs in the yucca flower. How do you think this is helpful to the eggs of the yucca moth?

—*Exploring Science*
Laidlaw Brothers

How many vowel sounds do you hear in this word? How many syllables does it have?

A compound word can have more than two syllables. How many syllables does this word have?

How many syllables does *helpful* have?

91

Building Skills

Say each word below. How many syllables does each word have?

1. moonlight   2. certain   3. morning   4. flower

Using Syllables to Decode Words in Social Studies

A suffix is usually a separate syllable. The word *explore* has two syllables. How many does *explorer* have?

How many syllables are there in the word *far*? How many are there in *away*? How many are in *faraway*?

Each vowel letter in *Pacific* stands for one vowel sound. How many vowel sounds are in *Pacific*? How many syllables are there?

A Young Explorer

Robin Graham was only sixteen years old when he began an adventure that would frighten most people twice his age. He decided to sail around the world alone. He named his boat the *Dove*. The boat was seven meters long.

Robin came from a family of sailors. His father and mother and his older brother loved the sea. Robin and his family had already sailed to faraway parts of the Pacific Ocean in a small boat. By the time he was thirteen, Robin knew how to find his way by the sun and the stars.

Even so, Robin's journey was an exciting one. It was one of the biggest news stories of the year.

—*People and Ideas*
Silver Burdett

Building Skills

1. Each word below has two consonant letters together. Which word is divided between the two consonants?

   a. mother   b. journey

2. How many syllables does each word below have?

   a. would   b. sail   c. around

Books About Living and Working Together

Going My Way? by Stan Applebaum and Victoria Cox. Harcourt Brace Jovanovich, 1976. The authors tell many interesting facts about animals and plants that live on "hosts."

Stories from the Olympics by Frank and Clare Gault. Walker & Co., 1976. You'll read about some of the winners and losers in Olympic competitions. You can also read charts of winning records.

Art of the Southwest Indians by Shirley Glubok. Macmillan, 1971. Jewelry, rugs, baskets, etc. are shown. These works of art were created by Pueblo, Navajo, and Apache tribes.

A Very Young Circus Flyer by Jill Krementz. Knopf, 1979. This book shows how a nine-year-old boy trains and performs on the high swings in the Ringling Brothers and Barnum & Bailey Circus.

A Prairie Boy's Winter by William Kurelek. Houghton Mifflin, 1973. Through words and illustrations, the author tells about his life during one winter on the prairie in Manitoba, Canada.

Ashanti to Zulu: African Traditions by Margaret Musgrove. Dial, 1976. This book tells about the cultures of more than twenty African peoples.

This Is the United Nations by Miroslav Sasek. Macmillan, 1968. You'll take a colorful tour of the United Nations Building as you read why the United Nations was started and what it does.

Part 2

Tell Me a Story

UNDERSTANDING AND APPRECIATING LITERATURE

Plot

Rita Hammer, the girl in the cartoon, can repair anything. On her way home from her latest job, Rita had a problem. What happened? How did Rita solve her problem? Look at the cartoon pictures above to find out.

What happened in the cartoon is the **plot.** This plot starts with a problem. What is Rita's problem? The first picture shows you. The bridge is out and Rita can't get across. What happens next? What is Rita doing in the second picture? She is taking her cart apart. She is trying to solve her problem. The last picture shows you the solution. How does Rita solve her problem? Rita turns her cart into a boat and sails across the water.

The plot, or what happens, can be stated as follows:

Rita cannot get across the water because the bridge is out, so she turns her cart into a boat. Then she sails across the water.

The plot includes Rita's problem, the actions she takes to solve the problem, and the solution.

Understanding Plot

Stories have plots, too. Many times the plot of a story is a problem and the way the problem is solved. Read the story below. Look for the problem. Then look for the actions taken to solve the problem. Look for the solution.

The Three Goats

Once upon a time, there were three goats named "Gruff." The goats liked to eat the grass on the hill. To reach the hill, they had to cross a bridge. Under the bridge lived a terrible, ugly troll.

When the littlest goat tried to cross the bridge, the troll roared, "Get off my bridge!"

The little goat was afraid and ran back. Then the second goat, who was a little bit bigger, tried to cross the bridge. Again the troll roared, "Get off my bridge!"

The second goat ran back, too. Then came the biggest goat. He was so big that he made the bridge shake.

"Who is shaking my bridge?" roared the troll. "Whoever you are, I'm coming to get you."

The troll came running from under the bridge. But the big goat Gruff was ready—he ran at the troll and knocked it down. The terrible troll ran away as fast as it could. Then all three goats Gruff crossed the bridge to the hill, and they ate to their hearts' content.

The plot of *The Three Goats* starts with a problem. What is the problem? The terrible troll won't let the goats cross the bridge to eat. What happens when the first goat tries to cross the bridge? The troll frightens him away. What happens next? The second goat tries to cross the bridge and the troll frightens him away, too. How do the goats solve their problem? The big goat frightens the troll away. The problem is solved.

In the stories you read, the beginning usually tells you the problem. The actions that people or animals take to solve the problem come next. A solution to the problem usually comes at the end.

So when you read a story, look for the plot. First look for the problem. Look for the actions taken to solve the problem. Then look for the solution. Understanding the plot will help you appreciate the story.

Try This

Read the following story. Look for the plot—the problem, the actions taken to solve it, and the solution.

One day, a turtle was sitting by the water. A sly fox came along and caught the turtle. The turtle was afraid. How could he get away from the fox? He thought for a minute.

"Oh, kind fox," he said. "Whatever you do, please, please don't throw me in the water."

Again and again, the turtle begged the fox:

"Oh, kind fox, you can do anything, but please, please don't throw me in the water."

Finally, the fox grew tired of the turtle's cries. He decided to fix the turtle for good! He threw the turtle right into the river. And the happy turtle swam away just as fast as he could!

1. What is the problem at the beginning of the story?
2. How does the turtle try to solve the problem?
3. What is the solution?

Writing

1. Think of a plot for a story. Write one sentence describing the problem and another sentence describing how the problem is solved.
2. Think about a story you know or have read in which a person has a problem. Write a short paragraph that tells the plot of the story. Tell what the problem is. Then tell what happens and how the problem is solved.

As you read each story in "Tell Me a Story," look for the plot—the problem and how it is solved.

The Princess and the Admiral

by CHARLOTTE POMERANTZ

A very long time ago, there was a small patch of dry land called the Tiny Kingdom. Most of its people were poor farmers or fisherfolk. Their bodies were lean and brown and strong from working long hours in the sun. They built the thatched mud huts in which they lived. They wove the simple earth-colored clothing they wore. And everyone, even the children, helped to plow the fields, harvest the rice, and catch the fish that they ate.

The land of the Tiny Kingdom was as poor as its people. The soil had neither gold nor silver. This was why no country, for as long as the oldest man or woman could remember, had ever made war against them. The people were happy even though their land was poor. It had given them a hundred years of peace.

The ruler of the Tiny Kingdom was Mat Mat, a dark-eyed young Princess, as lean and brown as her people.

One night, almost a thousand years ago, the Princess looked out the window of her Royal Bedchamber at the fishing boats in the harbor below. Then she looked up at the pale sliver of a moon. Sometimes, when the Princess couldn't sleep, she would follow the moon's slow, silent journey upward across the sky into morning.

Tonight the young Princess was too excited to sleep. For this month marked One Hundred Years of Peace in the Tiny Kingdom. As with all other holidays, there would be fireworks and a Carnival. Tomorrow morning, at the Council of Three Advisers, the Princess would choose the date.

There would be all kinds of fireworks: flares and pinwheels that burst into flowers and waterfalls and fishes. Birds and butterflies would flit among trees of green fire. Then at midnight, one — no, three fantastic red dragons would slither and writhe across the night sky.

"Beautiful," sighed the Princess. Her dark eyes were shining.

The next morning, the Princess was the first to arrive at the Council Chamber. The Three Advisers followed. First, the Elder, a man of ninety years. Then, the Younger, a man of eighty years. And finally, the In-Between, who was exactly eighty-five.

The Princess greeted them. "I greet you with joy, my dear Advisers. This month marks One Hundred Years of Peace in the Tiny Kingdom. I think you will agree that this calls for our very best Carnival and fireworks show."

The Three Advisers were strangely silent.

The Elder broke the silence. "Excuse me, Your Highness, but there is no time for a holiday."

"Why not?" asked the Princess.

"There is talk of an attack," said the Younger.

"It looks like war," said In-Between.

The Princess stared at them. She couldn't believe it. "But we have no enemies."

"I fear we do," said the Elder. "We have just had a report from our fishing boats that a large fleet of warships is at this very moment sailing toward our kingdom."

"How terrible!" said the Princess. "How many ships are coming?"

"Our fishing boats report twenty ships of war," said In-Between. "One is the flagship of the Admiral."

103

"How large are the ships?"

"I would judge each to be about five times the size of the Royal Swanboat," said the Elder.

"More like four times the size of the largest fishing boat," said the Younger.

"Oh," said In-Between. "I'd say the truth lies somewhere in the middle."

"Never mind," said the Princess. "How long will it be before the enemy ships reach the harbor of the Tiny Kingdom?"

"Two days, more or less," the Advisers answered in chorus.

The Princess settled herself on her throne. "Let us review our defense," she said, "and make some plans."

The Elder spoke first. "We have no ships of war."

"We have no men or women under arms," said the Younger.

"We do have a large number of fireworks," said In-Between. "Useless at present."

The Princess stepped down from her throne, walked to the window, and looked at the harbor below. "No forts, no soldiers, no weapons," she said quietly. "Clearly, we shall have to use . . . other things." She walked quickly back to the throne. "Call in the Court Astrologer," she said.

The Three Advisers looked at each other. "Beg pardon," said the Younger. "Astrology won't take the place of weapons."

"We shall see," said the Princess.

An old woman tottered into the Council Chamber.

"Your Highness wants me?" she asked. "You haven't sent for me since your grandmother swallowed a chicken neck."

"I wish to know about the position of the sun and moon," said the Princess.

"With pleasure," said the old woman. "When the moon is in its first or third quarter, it's as if she were a stranger to the sun. But when it is a new moon or a full moon, there is a strong attraction. We feel it on earth, in plants and oceans. I often feel it in my bones."

"And what of the moon tonight?"

"Tonight it is a new moon which hangs its fragile lantern over your Tiny Kingdom."

"Interesting," said the Princess. "You may return to your tower."

The Princess asked her three Advisers to come close. "Our course is clear," she said. "As clear as the lantern moon." The four of them huddled together while the Princess whispered her plan.

"And so," she said finally, "the first order of business is to send out a dozen fishing boats to tease the enemy. Their ships are sure to chase ours. If everything goes well, the enemy ships should get here at the right time."

The next day, upon orders of Princess Mat Mat, hundreds of farmers, fisherfolk, and children gathered in a nearby forest to cut down the tallest trees. The strongest men and women sawed through the trunks. The less strong sharpened both ends of the cut trees. And the children stripped off the branches.

Then everyone helped to haul the tree poles to the river bed. Soon the tide had gone down enough for them to drag the poles into the water. Then they hammered them—dozens and dozens of them—into the muddy bottom of the river bed.

The Princess watched from the window of her Royal Bedchamber. When she had counted 253 poles, jutting out of the water like a picket fence, she gave orders for the people to return to their huts.

The next morning, the Princess and her Advisers stood on the Royal Balcony. Not a single pole could be seen.

"I thought the tide would be higher," said the Elder.

"I thought it would be lower," said the Younger.

"Your Highness," said In-Between. "I think you guessed just right."

"It was no guess," said the Princess. "Not after I talked to the Court Astrologer. We know the tides are caused by the attraction of the sun and the moon. When I learned that these two heavenly bodies are close at this time, I knew that the tides would be high. High enough to cover the tree poles." The Princess smiled. "The moon is a faithful friend."

Just then, the first enemy ships were sighted nearing the mouth of the river bed. They were in full chase of the twelve fishing boats that had been sent out to tease them.

The enemy ships sailed up the middle of the river. As they faced the village, fifty more fishing boats appeared from all directions. They closed in around the enemy.

Aboard the enemy flagship, the Admiral gave his order. "Furl sails and drop anchor! Get ready to fight!"

From the Royal Balcony, the Princess looked down at the enemy ships and clapped her hands.

"He did it! The Admiral did just what I hoped he would do!" She tried hard not to jump up and down.

Even the Elder Adviser could not hold back a smile. "Your plan is working," he said.

On the river, the Admiral looked uneasily at all the fishing boats. "It looks as if they are going to climb aboard."

"But, sir," said the Helmsman. "They don't seem to have any weapons."

As he spoke, the fisherfolk began to throw things at the enemy ships. They threw cooking pots, soup ladles, coconuts, oranges, chickens—anything they could find. One tall fisherman took a whole pail of eels and threw it aboard the Admiral's flagship. Then the little fishing boats turned round and quickly sailed past the harbor. The Admiral and his warships were left alone on the river.

The Admiral laughed. "Did they really think they could defeat our mighty Navy with coconuts and cooking pots?"

"It would seem they are a rather primitive people, sir," said the Helmsman.

The Admiral looked at the village and the castle. "No trouble here," he said proudly. "The fishing boats have gone around a bend in the river. Not a living soul on the streets, except for a few chickens and goats. It's clear the natives are badly frightened." He looked down at the water. "The tide is going out, but the middle of the river here is still deep. We'll wait for low tide to make sure we can dock."

Settling into his deck chair, he said, "Tomorrow, first thing, we'll close in around the palace. We must search for and destroy their weapons and take the crown jewels. Then we'll behead the Princess.''

An hour later, as he was napping in his deck chair, a great shout came from below deck. "*Shipping water!*''

"What's that supposed to mean?'' barked the Admiral.

"It means there's a leak,'' said the Helmsman.

From all the other ships came the cry, "*Shipping water! We're shipping water!*''

The Admiral dashed down to the hold. There, a very strange sight greeted his eyes. What appeared to be the trunk of a tree was poking through the bottom of the ship! Even as the Admiral watched, the tree top was slowly coming upward. Then another tree . . . and another . . . and another. By Neptune, more than a dozen were coming through the bottom! And where the wood had broken up around the tree trunks, the water was seeping in slowly but steadily.

"Start bailing and saw off those crazy trees," yelled the Admiral.

"Beg pardon, sir," said the Helmsman. "But if you get rid of the trees, the water will rush through. The trees are like corks. Take away the corks, and we'll all drown."

"Never mind," said the Admiral. "Send a message to the other ships. 'All ships keep on bailing. All Ship Captains to report to my cabin for a Council of War.'"

Some two hours later, the Captains were all gathered aboard the Admiral's flagship. Suddenly the Helmsman stuck his head in the cabin door. "Sorry to break in, sir. The water is draining out of the ships."

"Naturally, you blockhead," said the Admiral. "The men are bailing."

"No, no," said the Helmsman. "It's happening all by itself."

"I'd better have a look," cried the Admiral.

He marched out on deck, tripped over a coconut, then stopped. He stared wild-eyed at the sight before him. All his ships were stuck up on tree poles! The air was filled with loud crackings and bangings coming from the bottoms of all the ships as they settled on the tree trunks. And, of course, the water was drip-dripping out of all the ships' bottoms.

Suddenly everything became clear to the Admiral. He had been trapped. These fisherfolk had used the tide against him. They had put in poles when it was low. His ships had come in when it was high. When the tide went out, he was left stuck up on the poles.

Now he could hear laughing. It came from the farmers, fisherfolk, and children who crowded the river bank and docks.

From around the bend, the little fishing boats returned and closed in around the fleet. At their head was a golden Swanboat. It sailed up alongside the Admiral's flagship.

"Ho, there," said a tall fisherman. "Ready to give up?"

The Admiral looked down and shook his fist. "Never! Just wait till we come on shore."

The tall fisherman smiled. "If you're thinking of sending your men swimming to shore, think again. Because any man found in the water will be hit on the head with an oar."

"Who are you?" thundered the Admiral.

"I'm a fisherman. In fact, I'm the best fisherman around. I gave up a whole pail of eels for the glory of the Tiny Kingdom. So the Princess has given me the honor of taking you to shore to plan the terms of peace."

"Never!" said the Admiral. "I will go down with my ship."

"Your ship isn't going to go down," said the fisherman. "It will stay stuck up there on the tree poles until the ebb and flow of the tides break it to pieces."

The Admiral sighed, climbed down, and settled sadly into the Royal Swanboat. The tall fisherman rowed him to shore.

After the Admiral had changed into dry socks, he was called to the Council Chamber to face Princess Mat Mat and her Three Advisers.

The Princess led the Admiral to the window overlooking the harbor.

"It's a charming sight, isn't it?" she said.

The Admiral turned red. "Charming!" he cried. "It's like a bad dream."

"Try and get hold of yourself," said the Princess.

"How terrible!" cried the Admiral. "To be defeated without a fight." His shoulders fell sadly. "What's the difference. Surely you will chop off my head."

"Certainly we will chop off your head," said the Elder.

The Princess clucked her tongue. She did not agree. "Are you such an old man that you have forgotten the story of the old woman and her chickens?"

"Your Highness," said the Elder, "every child in this Kingdom knows it by heart."

"Perhaps it is time to tell it again," said the Princess. She faced them all and began her tale.

Once upon a time, there was a poor old woman. One day she saw a young man steal into her yard and take two chickens. She knew very well who the young man was, but she did not report him to the Royal Guards. Instead, she waited until that evening, when everyone in the town had gathered in the village square to watch fireworks. The woman called out, "What kind of person steals two chickens from a poor old woman? I'll tell you—a no-good thief with a heart of stone. Shame on this person. Shame! Shame!"

The young man listened and was indeed ashamed. That very night, he stole into the old woman's yard and returned one of the chickens. (He had, alas, cooked and eaten the other one.) The woman saw him and hid. "It is good," she said. "I got back one of my chickens. And the young man did not lose face in the village."

When the Princess had finished her tale, she looked right into the Admiral's eyes and said, "So you see, sir, getting even is not our way. We do not believe that those who have wronged us should be punished any more than is necessary."

"Then you are not going to cut off my head?" asked the Admiral.

"No," said the Princess. "That would be awful."

The Admiral was quite puzzled. "Your Highness, what *are* you going to do?"

"Simple," said the Princess. "I shall give you two guides to take you and your men through the mountains back to your country and your Emperor. I shall also give you food and five water buffaloes to help carry it." The Princess thought a moment. "Of course, we would like for you to return the water buffaloes."

The Admiral knelt down before the Princess and kissed her hand. "Your animals shall be returned. I swear it." He was so thankful his voice shook. "Your Highness, I shall never forget you. Nor shall I ever forget the kind and gentle ways of your Kingdom." Tears filled his eyes. They rolled down his cheeks and spilled onto his chest. "If there is anything I can ever do for you . . ."

"As a matter of fact, there is," said the Princess.

"*Anything*," repeated the Admiral.

The Princess eyed him coolly. She said, "I would ask you to stay at home rather than bother peace-loving people."

That evening, Princess Mat Mat and her Three Advisers stood on the Royal Balcony. There they watched the long, winding line of enemy soldiers and sailors. The water buffaloes pulled carts loaded with food and water. At the front was the Admiral, his nose red from a head cold. He sat on the fattest water buffalo. All along the road winding into the mountains, the farmers, fisherfolk, and children waved them good-by.

"It is good," said the Princess to her Advisers. "We won the battle. And since the Admiral is returning home with all his men, he will not lose too much face with his Emperor." She sighed wistfully. "How close we came to having One Hundred Years of Peace."

"Dear Princess," said the Elder. "What happened this morning could hardly be called a battle. Only one sailor was hurt. And he just got hit on the head by an orange."

"It was more like a skirmish," said the Younger. "But I thought the sailor got hit on the toe."

"That's odd," said In-Between. "I was sure it was a coconut."

"My dear Advisers," said the Princess, "do I understand you to mean that we can still have our celebration?"

The Elder shrugged. "The poor old woman forgot about her chicken. Surely we can forget one small break in a hundred years of peace."

"For the first time," said the Younger, "the three of us agree on the number of fireworks, flares, torches, Bengal lights, Roman candles, and pinwheels. One thousand."

The Princess was thrilled. "Why that's more than I ever dreamed of. And will there be three dragons?"

"Well," said the Elder. "We don't think three is the right number."

"Oh," said the Princess. "How many then?"

"We shall see," said In-Between.

So it came to pass that the Tiny Kingdom celebrated One Hundred Years of Peace (well almost). There was the biggest Carnival and fireworks show in history. Not one, not three, but twelve red dragons slithered and writhed across the night sky.

And of all the happy farmers, fisherfolk, and children in the Tiny Kingdom, not one was happier than Princess Mat Mat.

Understanding What You've Read

1. What was the problem the Princess had to solve?
2. How did the Admiral's ship get stuck?
3. How did the Princess solve the problem?
4. Why did the Princess send the Admiral home?

Writing

1. Pretend you are the Admiral. Write a sentence that tells what problem you faced in the Tiny Kingdom. Write another sentence to tell how you solved it.
2. Write a paragraph about a real or make-believe holiday or celebration. Start with a problem and end with a solution.

Stone Soup

by FAN KISSEN

Cast

Gaston — Second Man
Jean — Second Woman
Mayor — Third Man
First Man — Third Woman
First Woman — Narrator
The Villagers

NARRATOR: This tale is called *Stone Soup*. It is a favorite that is told in different ways in many countries of Europe. Listen and hear how this strange soup was made.

Once upon a time two soldiers were walking along a country road. They had been on leave from their army camp and had spent their time in the big city far from camp. Now they were on their way back. The sun was low in the sky. They were tired and hungry. But both soldiers had spent all their money in the city. They had none left to buy food or to pay for a room for the night at an inn. They wondered what to do.

GASTON: Haven't you any money at all, Jean?

JEAN: Not even one copper piece, Gaston.

GASTON: I'm so hungry I could eat a whole cow!

JEAN: That's the way I feel, too. But even a thick slice of brown bread and a piece of cheese would taste good to me now.

GASTON: I'm so tired I could fall asleep standing up.

JEAN: How good it would feel to stretch out in a nice, soft bed!

GASTON: But first, Jean, a good, hot dinner!

JEAN: Don't keep talking about food, Gaston! It only makes us feel worse. What we can't have, we must do without.

GASTON: (*slight pause*) There's a big barn a little way off the road on this side. Let's go in there. The hay will make a soft bed.

JEAN: Wait, Gaston. The owner of the barn must live somewhere near here. If we can find his house, he might give us a bite to eat and a place to sleep indoors.

GASTON: (*excited*) Oh, look, Jean! There—beyond the barn! There are houses over there!

JEAN: It looks like a small village to me.

GASTON: Let's hurry over, Jean, before it gets dark.

NARRATOR: Now, the farmer who owned the land alongside the road saw the two soldiers walking toward the village. He hurried to spread the news. These

villagers didn't like to share their food with anyone. When they heard that the soldiers were coming, they began to plan how to send them away quickly.

FIRST MAN: Listen, wife! I've just heard that two soldiers are coming down the road toward our village!

FIRST WOMAN: Soldiers! Oh, dear me! They're sure to ask for food. Soldiers eat so much! We must hide our meat!

FIRST MAN: Wrap it in a clean cloth, and I'll hide it in the cellar! Quick, wife! Soldiers walk fast!

SECOND MAN: Oh, dear me! Two strangers are coming— two soldiers! They might ask for something to eat.

SECOND WOMAN: They must not see our food! Help me hide our vegetables and bread!

THIRD MAN: Have you heard the news, wife? Two soldiers are on the way to our village! Let's hide our food!

THIRD WOMAN: More soldiers? Goodness! The last ones asked for some milk. These men might want some, too.

THIRD MAN: We must hide these pails of milk! Help me lower them down into the well! Quickly!

121

NARRATOR: The villagers quickly hid the food they had in their houses. They all decided to try to look as poor and hungry as possible. Soon Gaston and Jean came to the first house at the edge of the village. They knocked at the door.

SOUND: (*light knock on door, slight pause, door open*)

GASTON: Good evening to you. Can you spare a little food for two hungry soldiers?

FIRST MAN: (*sadly*) No, we haven't any food to spare, soldier. We have hardly enough for ourselves and our poor children.

FIRST WOMAN: You'd better go on to the next village.

SOUND: (*door shut with a bang*)

JEAN: Hm! Those children looked pretty healthy to me! Let's try the next house, Gaston.

SOUND: (*knock on door, door open*)

JEAN: Good evening, friend. Can you spare a little food for two hungry soldiers?

SECOND MAN: No, we have no food to spare.

SECOND WOMAN: We haven't eaten anything all day.

SOUND: (*door shut*)

GASTON: Huh! I never saw starving, hungry people look so well fed! Well, let's try the next house.

SOUND: (*knock on door, door open*)

JEAN: Good evening, friend. Can you spare a little food for two hungry soldiers? We haven't eaten all day.

THIRD MAN: No, we have nothing for you. We gave all we could spare to some other soldiers.

SOUND: (*door slammed shut*)

NARRATOR: And so it went. Each door was shut in the soldiers' faces. But as soon as Jean and Gaston had walked away, each villager opened his or her door again to see what would happen at the next house. Soon Gaston and Jean had tried every house, but no one had given them anything to eat. They stopped in the village square and put their heads together to think out a plan. After a while Gaston called out:

GASTON: (*calling loudly*) All you good people at your doors! Come, gather around us!

JEAN: We have something important to tell you!

NARRATOR: The people began to leave their houses and walk to the village square where the two soldiers were waiting. All were curious to know what important thing two hungry soldiers could tell them.

GASTON: Listen, my friends! We asked you for a little food. All of you said you had hardly enough for yourselves. Well, we're very sorry for you. *We'll* give *you* some food. We'll make stone soup for you.

FIRST WOMAN: (*surprised*) Stone soup? I never heard of stone soup!

SECOND WOMAN: Stone soup? How do you make that?

GASTON: (*smiling voice*) I make it with this smooth, round stone I picked up on the road. But any stone will do. First we'll need a large pot — a very large pot that will hold enough soup for all of you.

MAYOR: Soldier, I'm the Mayor of this village. I'll see that you get a big pot. (*calls*) Here! You two big boys! Run across to the town hall and bring us the big pot and the bowls we use for parties.

GASTON: We'll need water to fill the pot. Where can we get that?

MAYOR: Why, from this fountain right here in the square.

FIRST WOMAN: It's good, clear water, soldier. It's where we come to get our water for cooking.

MAYOR: (*smiling voice*) And where you hear the news of the village and talk about your neighbors!

GASTON: (*politely*) Ah! Here come the boys with the big pot. Set it on the edge of the fountain, boys, so that water can flow into it.

SOUND: (*clink of heavy pot on stone, then sound of water flowing into pot*)

JEAN: While the pot is being filled, some of you will have to fetch some wood for a fire.

SECOND WOMAN: Of course! You can't make soup with cold water.

MAYOR: You children! Run and collect some wood.

NARRATOR: Soon a big fire was burning by the fountain in the square, and the big pot was set over it to boil. Then Gaston took the stone he had shown the people and dropped it into the pot.

GASTON: There! You all saw me drop the stone into the water. That's how I make the very best stone soup.

FIRST WOMAN: Good soup, with just some hot water and a stone? I don't believe it, soldier!

GASTON: Well, of course, any soup tastes better if you add some salt and pepper to the water, as you know.

FIRST WOMAN: I'll send my little boy to fetch some salt and pepper from my kitchen.

JEAN: Thank you! Salt and pepper will improve the soup. Now, if we had some carrots, the soup would be even better. But what we can't have, we must do without.

SECOND WOMAN: Well — I have a few carrots at home. I — I think I can spare some. I'll send my little girl to get them. (*in a low voice*) Anna, you saw where we put them. Run and bring as many as you can hold.

GASTON: Ah! Here's the child with the salt and pepper. I'll shake some into the water.

SOUND: (*first Gaston sneezes, then other people sneeze*)

GASTON: Excuse me. It was the pepper. Bless you all! The water is boiling nicely, isn't it?

THIRD WOMAN: That still doesn't look like soup to me.

JEAN: Be patient a little longer, my friend.

GASTON: Here come the carrots! Ah! The nice little girl has even washed them. Thank you, child. I'll slice them into the pot.

JEAN: The soup is beginning to look better already. Don't you agree? Of course, a good stone soup tastes even better with some cabbage and some potatoes added to the stone. But what we can't have, we must do without.

THIRD MAN: I'll send my boy back to my house for some potatoes and cabbage.

JEAN: Thank you, friend. (*a bit louder*) And would any of you good people suddenly remember that you had some meat at home that you could spare?

GASTON: Some meat would make this stone soup just perfect. It would make the soup fit for the King himself. The King asked for just this kind of soup the last time he dined with us. Remember that, Jean?

JEAN: I remember that as perfectly as you do, Gaston.

MAYOR: (*wondering*) You soldiers have eaten with the King? Really? And the King likes this stone soup?

VILLAGERS: They have eaten with the *King*! Imagine that! The *King* likes stone soup!

NARRATOR: Well, the farmers and the villagers brought carrots, and potatoes, and cabbage, and meat to put into the water along with Gaston's stone. The two soldiers stirred the good thick soup while the villagers stared in wonder. At last Gaston called:

GASTON: (*loudly*) The soup is ready, friends. Take a deep breath. Doesn't it smell wonderful?

FIRST WOMAN: (*sniffs*) Mmm! It certainly does!

SECOND WOMAN: And it was made with just a small stone! Imagine!

JEAN: There's enough for all of us, I'm sure. But don't you think we'd all be more comfortable if we had some benches, and perhaps a long table?

MAYOR: We have some we use at our village fairs. Boys, girls, fetch them from the town hall cellar.

THIRD WOMAN: I think this soup would taste extra good if we had some bread to eat with it. Let's each of us send to our home for a loaf of fresh bread.

JEAN: Fine! The *King* likes bread with his soup, too.

GASTON: Yes, we'll eat like kings — and queens!

NARRATOR: It was a wonderful party! The villagers agreed they had never tasted such fine soup. And how cheaply it could be made! All that was needed was a stone, with just a few things added. When they had finished eating, they pushed the tables and chairs to one side and stood talking and laughing among themselves. Then Gaston said:

GASTON: Why not end this party with some dancing? They always have dancing at the King's parties.

MAYOR: A fine idea, soldier! There's the town hall watchman with his violin. (*calls*) Daniel! Give us some music! We'll end this party with some lively dancing!

SOUND: (*folk dance music in, hold briefly, and out*)

128

NARRATOR: At last everyone was tired, though happy. Then Gaston asked:

GASTON: Will someone let us sleep in his hayloft?

MAYOR: What? Let two such fine men as you sleep in a hayloft? I should say not! One of you must sleep at my house. Who will take the other soldier?

VILLAGERS: (*one at a time*) Come to my house! Come with us! I want him!

MAYOR: Good! Let's all say good night now.

NARRATOR: The soldiers slept in soft beds that night. The next morning all the villagers gathered to say good-by to them.

MAYOR: We thank you, soldiers, for what you have taught us. Now that we know how to make soup from a stone, we shall never go hungry.

GASTON: It's all in knowing how, Your Honor. Good-by, friends!

JEAN: Good-by, my friends!

VILLAGERS: Good-by! Good-by!

Understanding What You've Read

1. Name at least four things that went into the stone soup.
2. What was Jean and Gaston's problem? How did stone soup help to solve the problem?
3. What did the people in the village think of Jean and Gaston at the beginning of the play? What did the people in the village think of them at the end of the play?

Writing

1. Write a sentence that tells about a problem you might have making stone soup. Write another sentence or two to explain how this problem could be solved.
2. Write a sentence or a paragraph that tells what happened to Jean and Gaston after they left the village.

Two Fables by Aesop

retold by ANNE TERRY WHITE

The Lion and the Mouse

In the heat of the day a Lion lay asleep at the edge of a wood. He lay so still that a Mouse ran right across his nose without knowing it was a nose, and a Lion's at that.

Bang! The Lion clapped his paw to his face and felt something caught. It was furry. Lazily he opened his eyes. He lifted up one side of his huge paw just a little bit to see what was under it and was amused to find a Mouse.

"Spare me, Great King!" he heard the little creature squeak in its tiny voice. "I didn't mean to do it! Let me go, and someday I will repay you."

"That's very funny," said the Lion, and he laughed. "How can a little thing like you help me, the great King of Beasts?"

"I don't know," the Mouse replied, "but a little creature can sometimes help a big one."

"Well, you have made me laugh," the Lion said, "which is something I seldom do. And anyway, you would hardly make half a mouthful. So ——" He raised his paw and let the Mouse go.

A few days later the Lion was caught in a hunter's net. The woods rang with his angry roaring, and the little Mouse heard him.

"That is my kind Lion!" she cried. "He is in trouble!" As fast as she could, she ran toward the spot from which the roaring came, and there he was. The Lion was thrashing around so in the net that the Mouse didn't dare to come near for fear of being crushed.

"O King, be patient!" she cried. "I will gnaw through the ropes and set you free."

So the Lion lay still while the Mouse worked away with her sharp teeth. And in a short time he was able to creep out of the net.

"You see? I told you I would repay you," the Mouse said happily. "A little creature sometimes really can help a big one."

And the Lion had to admit it was true.

Little friends may prove to be great friends.

The Wind and the Sun

The Wind boasted to the Sun one day: "I am stronger than you by far. Just see how the dead leaves whirl and flee before me!"

The Sun smiled. "You are mistaken," he said quietly.

"Let's see you prove it!" the Wind snapped back.

Just then a traveler came down the road.

"I think I see a way of proving it," the Sun said. "See that traveler down there? Let us agree that he who can make him take off his cloak is the stronger. You may have your turn first."

So the Sun went behind a cloud, and the Wind started to blow. The traveler's cloak flapped wildly. But the harder the Wind tried to tear off the cloak, the more tightly the man drew it around him.

At last the Wind gave up. "Go ahead! Have your try at it," he said.

Smiling, the Sun came out from behind the cloud. He shone in all his glory, pouring his warm beams on the traveler.

"How hot it has suddenly grown!" the traveler said. And he took off his cloak.

Kindness is better than force.

Understanding What You've Read

1. In the first fable, what was the lion's problem?
2. In the first fable, why did the lion think that the mouse would not be able to help him?
3. What was the solution to the problem in the first fable?
4. In the second fable, what did the Wind do to prove that it was stronger than the Sun? What happened?

Writing

1. Pretend that you are the traveler in "The Wind and the Sun." Write three sentences to tell your story. Tell what happened first, what happened next, and what happened last.
2. Write a paragraph or your own fable about a monkey and a tiger to go with one of the following ideas:

   a. Little friends may prove to be great friends.
   b. Kindness is better than force.

More Folktales to Read

More Tales from the Story Hat by Verna Aardema. Coward, 1966. These are African folktales by an author who first heard them told by storytellers in Africa.

Ardizzone's Hans Christian Andersen: Fourteen Classic Tales selected and illustrated by Edward Ardizzone. Translated by Stephen Corrin. Atheneum, 1979. A collection of the most beloved tales.

The Tiger and the Rabbit and Other Tales told by Pura Belpré. Lippincott, 1965. These stories of animals, magic, and adventure reflect the many cultures and the folklore of Puerto Rico.

Old Man Whickutt's Donkey by Mary H. Calhoun. Parents Magazine Press, 1975. This funny retelling of a French fable is about the problems that a farmer and his son have with their donkey.

Molly Mullet by Patricia Coombs. Lothrop, 1975. Molly sets out to rid her village of a terrible ogre.

The Sound of Flutes, and Other Indian Legends told by Lame Deer, Jenny Leading Bird, and others. Edited by Richard Erdoes. Pantheon, 1976. In this book, American Indian storytellers of today retell many old tales of the Plains Indians.

Sweet and Sour: Tales from China retold by Carol Kendall and Yao-wen Li. Drawings by Shirley Felts. Seabury Press, 1979. Twenty-four parables, fables, jokes, and stories are retold in this book.

Part 3

Achieving

Turning to the Dictionary

You may come across words you do not know in the strangest places. You may even find them in a bowl of alphabet soup! Most likely, you'll find them in your reading.

When you do come across a word you are not sure of, you can turn to the dictionary. The dictionary is a useful tool for studying words. It tells you how to pronounce words and what they mean. It also shows you the spelling of a word.

138

Finding Words in the Dictionary

There are hundreds of pages in the dictionary and thousands of words. The words listed in boldface in alphabetical order are **entry words.** How can you find the entry word you want? Usually, you have three guides: the **alphabet,** the **letter tabs,** and the **guide words.** The letter tab tells the letter of the alphabet that the words on the page start with. The guide words tell the first and last entry words on the page.

payroll	peck	P

* **pay·roll** [pā′rōl′] *n.* **1** A list of workers to be paid, with the amounts owed to each. **2** The total sum of money needed to make the payments.
Pb The symbol for the element LEAD. ◆ The Latin word for lead is *plumbum.*
pd. Abbreviation of PAID.
pea [pē] *n., pl.* **peas** or (*rarely*) **pease 1** A round seed, often cooked as a vegetable. **2** A climbing plant that has green pods in which these seeds grow. ◆ The English word for *pea,* whether one or many, was once *pease* [pēz], from the Latin word *pisa.* Because *pease* sounded like a plural, *pea* came into being as its singular form, and now *peas* has largely replaced *pease* as the plural.

pea·nut [pē′nut′] *n.* **1** A vine related to the pea, with pods that ripen underground and hold seeds that are eaten like nuts. **2** The seed or seed pod of this vine.
peanut butter A thick spread for sandwiches, etc., made from ground roasted peanuts.
pear [pâr] *n.* **1** A sweet, juicy fruit, round at the outer end and tapering toward the stem. **2** The tree on which it grows.
pearl [pûrl] **1** *n.* A smooth, rounded, white or variously tinted deposit formed around a grain of sand or the like inside the shell of an oyster or other shellfish. It is valued as a gem. **2** *adj. use: pearl* earrings. **3** *n.* Mother-of-pearl. **4** *adj. use: pearl* buttons. **5** *n., adj.* Pale bluish gray.

Look at the part of a dictionary page shown above. What letter tab is on the page? What are the guide words? Do you see that the letter tab is P and the guide words are *payroll* and *peck*? Would you find the entry word *peach* if you looked at the whole dictionary page? You can use the guide words and alphabetical order to find out.

Look at the word *peach* and the two guide words.

peach   **payroll**   **peck**   (guide words)

Since all three words begin with the same letter, you need to look past the first letter and compare the second letter in each word. The letter *e* comes after the letter *a* in the alphabet. So the word *peach* would come after *payroll*. How many letters do you need to look at in *peach* and *peck* to learn which word comes first?

You can see that the first two letters in these words are the same. Now look at the third letter in these words. Does *a* come before *c* in the alphabet? Yes. Then *peach* would come before *peck*. Since *peach* would come after *payroll* and before *peck*, you know that you would find the entry for *peach* on this dictionary page.

Try This

1. Look at the three words in each group. Put them in alphabetical order. You might have to look as far as the third or fourth letter.

a.	frost	from	freeze
b.	thing	that	thank
c.	boots	both	bag
d.	rock	rope	roll

2. Look at each entry word below. Then look at the guide words next to it. Would you find the entry word on a dictionary page that has these guide words?

Entry Word	Guide Words	
a. jaw	Japan	jelly
b. loud	lot	loving
c. group	grist	ground
d. mew	mew	middle

Locating the Pronunciation Key

You know that a dictionary can't speak. It must use printed symbols to show you how to say a word. It uses letters, dots, and certain marks. Entry words are respelled with these symbols according to the way they are spoken. If you know the sound that each symbol stands for, you can put sounds together to say a word. The more you use the symbols to pronounce words that are new to you, the better you will become at doing it.

Every dictionary has a **pronunciation key,** but the keys are not quite the same. You should always look at the key in the dictionary you are using. It is in the front of the dictionary. Usually a short form of the key is given at the bottom of the dictionary page. A short form of one key is shown below.

* add, āce, câre, pälm; end, ēqual; it, īce; odd, ōpen, ôrder; tŏŏk, pōōl; up, bûrn; ə = a in *above,* e in *sicken,* i in *possible,* o in *melon,* u in *circus;* y͞o͞o = u in *fuse;* oil; pout; check; ring; thin; this; zh in *vision.*

* From the *HBJ School Dictionary,* © 1977 by Harcourt Brace Jovanovich, Inc. Reprinted and reproduced by permission of the Publisher.

Some of the same symbols are used in many dictionaries. Once you get used to the symbols, you may not have to look at the key every time you need help in pronouncing a word.

Studying an Entry Word

Do you know the word *gesture*? By thinking of the sounds the letters stand for, can you be sure of how to say the word? Can you tell its meaning from this sentence?

Mike made a gesture to show he didn't hear us.

The context gives you some idea of what *gesture* means, but not a very clear one. Perhaps you are also still not sure of how to pronounce the word. Does the **g** stand for the first sound in *get* or for the first sound in *gentle*? Let's see how a dictionary can help.

Here is the entry you would find in one dictionary.

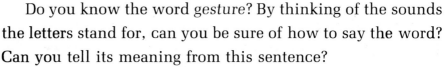

* **ges·ture** [jes′chər] *n.*, *v.* **ges·tured, ges·tur·ing 1** *n.* A motion of the hands, head, or other part of the body expressing or emphasizing some feeling or idea. **2** *v.* To make gestures. **3** *n.* Something done, offered, or said as a formality, courtesy, or for effect: *a polite gesture.*

There are several things to notice.

1. The dot between **ges** and **ture** shows that there are two syllables in the word.

2. Notice how the word is rewritten to show its pronunciation: [jes′chər]. This is called the respelling. Now do you know what sound the letter **g** stands for? It's the same sound as the first sound in *gentle.*

3. The mark ′ after the first syllable in the respelling is an **accent mark.** It tells you that the first syllable is **accented,** or said with greater force than the second syllable.

4. Notice that the letter **t** in *gesture* is pronounced **ch.** The symbol ə in the last syllable is called a **schwa.** It stands for a vowel sound that is spelled in many ways. Look at the pronunciation key on page 141 to find out what sound ə stands for.

Now you can be sure of how to say the word *gesture.* Let's see how the dictionary helps with its meaning. In the entry for *gesture,* the numerals **1, 2,** and **3** show that three definitions are given. You must find the one that is right for the sentence in which you found the word.

Which meaning fits the context? The first one does. You can tell from the sentence that a gesture is something done. You know that Mike did something to show that he didn't hear. You can fit the first definition into the sentence in place of the word *gesture.*

Mike made a motion of the hands, head, or other part of the body to show he didn't hear us.

Many books have glossaries in them. A glossary is a little dictionary found at the back of the book. When a book has a glossary, you can go to it instead of a dictionary. The glossary in this book begins on page 553. It has guide words. It clearly shows where each letter of the alphabet begins. Entry words are listed in alphabetical order. An entry shows how a word is pronounced and gives its meaning.

Try This

1. The words below are respelled. Use the pronunciation key on page 141 to help you pronounce them. What words are they? Make up a sentence using each word.

   a. frō′zən   b. dān′jər
   c. ok′sə·jin   d. ri·mem′bər

2. There are three words in boldface in the sentences below. Look them up in the glossary that begins on page 553. What is the meaning of each word?

   a. A nervous animal may **relax** if a person says something in a soft voice.
   b. Scientists can learn about an animal's **intelligence** by testing the animal.
   c. The team **launched** the rocket.

VOCABULARY STUDY

Greek Word Parts

"Step right up, folks, and speak to Amazo—the machine that talks back. Amazo can explain English words that get their meaning from Greek words. Amazo can—"

"Phooey, Ms. Moneysworth," said Doubting Thomas. "If a machine can do that, then I'm an **astronaut**!"

"Astronaut," said Amazo. "*Astro* comes from a Greek word meaning *star*. *Naut* comes from a Greek word meaning *sailor*. So an astronaut is a star sailor."

"Not bad," said Thomas. He was a little less doubting now. "Mind if I take a **photograph** of Amazo?"

"Photograph," said Amazo. "*Photo* comes from a Greek word meaning *light*. *Graph* comes from a Greek word meaning *writing*. So a photograph is a kind of writing with light."

"Wow!" shouted Thomas. "Ms. Moneysworth, would you and your machine go to Hollywood for a TV **program**?"

"Program," said Amazo. "*Pro* comes from a Greek word meaning *before*. *Gram* comes from a Greek word meaning *writing*. So a program is a kind of writing that is done before—such as a TV schedule!"

"Terrific!" shouted Thomas. "Now how about Hollywood?"

"φαγζάζηφε εδμένα θιαζρήνα."

"What's Amazo's answer?" asked Thomas.

"I don't know," answered Ms. Moneysworth. "But it sure sounds Greek to me!"

Word Play

1. Find the meaning Amazo gave for each word part below.

   naut   *astro*   *photo*   *gram*   *pro*   *graph*

2. The Greek word part *tele* means "far off" or "over a distance." Think of five English words that begin with the word part *tele*.

145

Sometimes a word may look strange to you. Once you hear it pronounced, you may find that you know it. Turn to the glossary in this book or to your dictionary for help with an unfamiliar word.

Saint Bernard dogs have helped people in many places. One Saint Bernard became famous as . . .

Barry: Hero of the Alps

by Bettina Hürlimann *and* Paul Nussbaumer

translated from the German by Elizabeth D. Crawford

Barry was a Saint Bernard dog. He knew well the mountains where he had been born. Almost all year long, snow lay in those high places. As a result, there were many dangers. Often a person could become lost if snow covered the road. Tired travelers could freeze to death if they stopped to rest and fell asleep. Sliding snow could rush down the mountainside and bury anyone in its path.

Barry lived with a group of monks. Their work was to help all those who were in need. Their house was called a hospice [hos'pis]. The monks' only companions were their dogs. People called these dogs Saint Bernards because the mountain pass where they lived was known as Great Saint Bernard.

Though no one guessed it then, Barry was to become a famous Saint Bernard. He became so famous that his story is known in many countries, right down to our time. This is so even though it is more than 150 years since Barry was alive.

Like children, the young dogs had to go to school. They had to be trained to help the monks. There was much to learn. The first thing they had to learn was to obey. For Barry, who liked to play, this was the hardest thing of all.

By the time Barry was a year old, he had learned a great deal. He could run over the snow without sinking into it. He knew how to find a person buried by an avalanche.

Barry grew into a large dog, with sharp eyes and sure movements. He became a good mountain guide.

One day Barry was guiding a group of people
through the snow. As he led them along the
path, it began to snow. Then a thick fog spread
through the mountains. Without warning, down from
the heights above crashed an avalanche. It swept away
three men, burying them beneath it.

Barry knew it was impossible to dig the men out of
the snow by himself. With a great spring, he ran
to the hospice. He led the monks and other dogs back
to where the men were buried.

The men were lucky. Thanks to Barry and the other dogs, they didn't have to lie under the snow long. One by one they were uncovered. Then they were lifted safely onto the sleds. As soon as Barry saw that the men were safe on the sleds, he dashed off.

When the monks arrived home, Barry wasn't there. He had discovered a fresh trail. He followed it and soon came to a lump covered in snow. Barry sensed that it was alive. He poked at it with his nose. It finally stirred and sat up. It was a small girl with a red scarf tied around her neck. She was very stiff with cold. Barry lay on his side close to her, and she held on to him. He was carrying the child back to the hospice when the monks found them.

It wasn't long before everyone on both sides of the Alps was talking about Barry. The little girl told about him in her village when she returned home. The men he had saved spoke of him in the inns of Italy. Soldiers returning from war told their children about him.

In only a few years, Barry helped to save the lives of forty people. Never before had the monks owned a dog so brave or smart.

Even after his death, Barry was not forgotten. At the Great Saint Bernard Hospice, there were always more little Saint Bernards being born. One of them was always called Barry. In this way the first Barry who had helped so many people would always be remembered.

Understanding What You've Read

1. What things did Barry have to learn in school?
2. How did Barry save the girl in the red scarf?
3. Why is there always a dog named Barry at the Great Saint Bernard Hospice?
4. How did so many people get to know about Barry?

Applying the Skills Lesson

1. What two words from the selection are respelled below? The pronunciation key in front of the glossary will help you.

   a. av′ə·lanch   b. kəm·pan′yən

2. Look in the glossary for the following words. Name the guide words on the page where you find each word.

   a. movement   b. guide

Using the Dictionary and Glossary

The dictionary and glossary can help you with words that you meet in your textbook reading. The first selection shows some entries from one dictionary. The second selection shows some different kinds of glossaries. Use the sidenotes to help you understand the entries.

Using the Dictionary

In the respelling, a heavy accent mark (′) is used to show which syllable of a word is said with more force. Sometimes there is also a lighter accent mark (′). It shows which syllable is said with some but not as much force.

Often a picture helps you understand a word. What picture is shown above on the right? How do you know?

The entry word is *jeopardize*. Notice that other forms of this word are also given.

There are two words spelled *lug*. Why is each numbered?

jel·ly·bean [jel′ē·bēn′] *n.* A bean-shaped candy with a hard covering and a gummy center.
jel·ly·fish [jel′ē·fish′] *n., pl.* **jel·ly·fish** *or* **jel·ly·fish·es** A sea animal with a jellylike, umbrella-shaped body and long trailing tentacles that capture and poison its prey.
Jen·ner [jen′ər], **Edward,** 1749–1823, English doctor. He discovered vaccination.
jen·net [jen′it] *n.* A small Spanish horse.
jen·ny [jen′ē] *n., pl.* **jen·nies** **1** A machine for spinning yarn. **2** The female of some birds and animals: a *jenny* wren.
jeop·ard·ize [jep′ər·dīz] *v.* **jeop·ard·ized, jeop·ard·iz·ing** To put in danger; place in jeopardy. ¶3

Jellyfish

lu·di·crous [lōō′də·krəs] *adj.* Causing laughter, scorn, or ridicule; ridiculous; absurd: a *ludicrous* action. **— lud′i·crous·ly** *adv.*
luff [luf] **1** *n.* The turning of a ship closer to the wind. **2** *n.* The foremost edge of a fore-and-aft sail. **3** *v.* To bring the head of a sailing vessel toward or into the wind.
lug¹ [lug] *n.* An earlike part that sticks out, used for holding or supporting something.
lug² [lug] *v.* **lugged, lug·ging** To carry or pull with effort: to *lug* large rocks.

Ludicrous antics

North Pole The northernmost point on the earth; the north end of the earth's axis.

North Sea The part of the Atlantic Ocean between Great Britain and northern Europe.

North Star A bright star that is almost directly above the North Pole; Polaris.

North·um·bri·a [nôr·thum′brē·ə] *n.* An ancient Anglo-Saxon kingdom in England.

North Vietnam See VIETNAM.

north·ward [nôrth′wərd] **1** *adj., adv.* To, toward, or in the north. **2** *n.* A northward direction or location.

north·wards [nôrth′wərdz] *adv.* Northward.

north·west [nôrth′west′] **1** *n.* The direction midway between north and west. **2** *n.* Any region lying in or toward this direction. **3** *adj.* To, toward, or in the northwest; northwestern. **4** *adj.* Coming from the northwest. **5** *adv.* In or toward the northwest. —**northwest of** Farther northwest than: Detroit is *northwest of* Cleveland.

From the *HBJ School Dictionary,* © 1977 by Harcourt Brace Jovanovich, Inc. Reprinted and reproduced by permission of the Publisher.

Maps are often included to show where something is located. What entry is the map helping you to understand?

Sometimes you must look in more than one place to find the information you need. What entry word must you look for to find out about *North Vietnam?*

Building Skills

Look at the dictionary entries above and on page 152 to answer the following questions.

1. Does the dictionary list names of people and places?
2. Are the spellings of plural words (words that mean "more than one") sometimes given?
3. Do some words have just one accent mark?
4. Which lug, **lug**[1] or **lug**[2], fits the context of the following sentence?

They cut the tree down and began to *lug* away the branches.

Using the Glossary

You know that not all glossaries are the same. Some glossaries give more information than others. The sidenotes will help you to understand the sections of different glossaries that follow.

The first glossary section came from a science textbook. However, the definitions used in the glossary were taken from the *Thorndike Barnhart Intermediate Dictionary.*

A Glossary Section from Science

nervous (nėr′vəs), having to do with the nerves, 91

Glossaries give definitions just like a dictionary. What is the definition given for *noise pollution?*

noise pollution, unpleasant or unwanted sounds in the environment, 241

North Star, also known as Polaris, the star that keeps nearly the same position in the northern sky above the North Pole, 187

This number tells on what page the word is found in the textbook.

nuclear (nū′klē ər), having to do with an atomic reaction, 274

This is one way to respell *nucleus.* Which syllable is accented?

nucleus (nū′klē əs), the central part of a cell which controls some of its activity, 95

— Elementary School Science*
Addison-Wesley

A Glossary Section from Health

nucleus (NOO·klee·uhs), controlling part of a cell. The **nucleus** contains "information" that "tells" cells what to do.   7

nutrient (NOO·tree·uhnt), any substance found in food that your body can use for energy, growth, and good health.   165

nutrition (noo·TRISH·uhn), process of eating and using foods.   165

— You Learn and Change: Orange
Harcourt Brace Jovanovich

> This is another way to respell *nucleus.* Capital letters are used to show which syllable is accented.

> Which syllable is accented in this word?

A Glossary Section from Social Studies

natural resource (p. 132). A material useful to people and supplied by nature, such as land, minerals, water, and forests.

North Pole (p. 36). The northern end of the earth's axis. It is located in the Arctic Ocean.

nursery (p. 129). A place where young children are taken care of. Also, a place for growing young trees and plants.

—People and Ideas
Silver Burdett

> This is only a section of the glossary, but the whole glossary looks just like this part. How is this glossary different from the two others shown here?

Building Skills

1. Look back to all the glossary sections to help you answer the questions below.

   a. What things do the glossaries have in common?
   b. Do some glossaries give more than one meaning of a word?

2. Look back to the first two glossary sections. Which definition of the word *nucleus* would you say is clearer? Why?
3. Read the dictionary definition for the entry *North Star* on page 153. Then read the glossary definition on page 154. Do both definitions give you the same information?
4. Tell whether the information listed below can be found in a dictionary, a glossary, or possibly both.

   a. alphabetical order
   b. a page number where the word is found in a textbook
   c. a respelling of a word
   d. the definition of a word

Learning from Graphic Aids

It isn't only in fairy tales that people perform magic. You've probably heard of the spinning wheel. Rumpelstiltskin used one to turn straw into gold. For hundreds of years ordinary people had spinning wheels in their homes. They used the spinning wheels to make yarn. They then wove the yarn into cloth. The picture above shows how the raw wool was turned into yarn. It does seem like magic, doesn't it?

The paragraph on page 157 tells about spinning wheels. If you read it without looking at the picture, you would learn how spinning wheels were used, but you wouldn't know what they look like. Many books you read have pictures in them. If you look carefully at the pictures, you can learn many things that the text alone doesn't tell you.

Diagrams

Read the paragraph below. Use the picture with it to help you understand the text.

The spinning wheel is a very simple tool. You push up and down on the **treadle** with your foot. This treadle makes the **wheel** turn. As the wheel turns, it pulls the **belt** around. The belt moves the **spool,** which twists the wool into yarn. Then the yarn is wound around the spool.

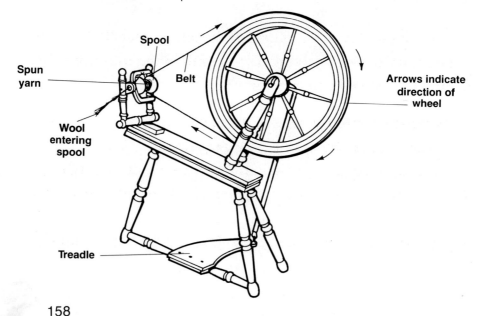

Spool

Spun yarn

Belt

Arrows indicate direction of wheel

Wool entering spool

Treadle

Pictures like the one on page 158 are called **diagrams.** They can be very helpful when you want to know how something is put together or how it works.

Did you notice the words on the diagram? These words are called **labels.** Labels tell about the individual parts of a diagram. The labels on this diagram tell you what the parts of a spinning wheel are called. Each label has a line drawn from it to the part of the picture it names. Do the lines help you to find the right part? The arrows on the diagram show how the spinning wheel works. Do you see that as the wheel turns, the wool moves around the spool?

Reread the paragraph above the diagram. The names of the parts are in boldface. Every time you come to a new part, look for it in the diagram. Using the diagram while you read should help you to "see" the spinning wheel work.

Try This

Use the picture of a spinning wheel on page 157 and the diagram on page 158 to answer the following questions. Use complete sentences to answer.

1. What are spinning wheels made of?
2. Is the treadle above or below the wheel?
3. Do people sit or stand when they use a spinning wheel?
4. What part of the spinning wheel does the yarn wrap around?
5. Does the belt move when the spinning wheel is working?

Graphs

Did you know that there were 33 million fewer sheep on farms in the United States in 1975 than there were in 1900? See how a graph shows this fact.

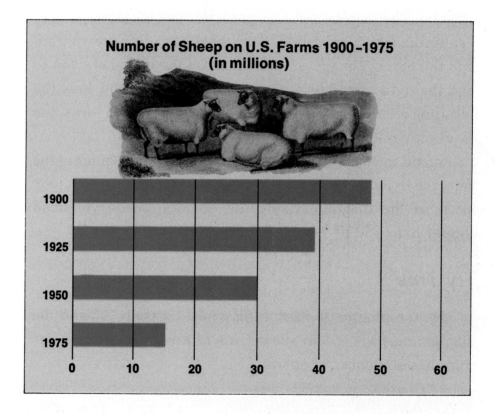

Number of Sheep on U.S. Farms 1900–1975 (in millions)

The graph above is called a **bar graph.** Just by looking at the bars, you can get a sense of the difference between the number of sheep from one year to another. The more you know about how to read a graph, the more you can learn from it. These are the parts of the bar graph you should know.

- The title at the top of the graph tells what the graph is comparing. This graph is comparing the number of sheep in different years. What years does it cover? Note the words *in millions*. Later you will see that they are very important for understanding the numbers along the bottom of the graph.

- The numbers down the side of the graph are the years that are compared. Each bar stands for one of these years. Some graphs might have words down the side. These words name the places or things that are being compared.

- The numbers along the bottom are called the **scale.** The scale in your doctor's office measures your weight. The scale on your ruler or meter stick measures the length of things. The scale on this graph measures the number of sheep.

By comparing the length of the bars with the scale, you can find the number of sheep in each year. The lines that go up from the scale to the top of the graph help you measure the bars. Not all bar graphs have these lines. Look at where the bar for 1975 ends. It is about halfway between the 10 and the 20. Were there 15 sheep in the United States in 1975? You know there weren't. Remember the words *in millions* in the title. Those words tell you that every number in the scale equals that many million. So there were about 15 million sheep in 1975. Now that you know the parts of the graph, see if you can find out how many sheep there were in each year. Then try to compare the years with each other.

Try This

Use the bar graph on page 160 to answer the following questions. Use complete sentences to answer.

1. In which year were there the most sheep?
2. Were there more sheep in 1925 or in 1950?
3. In which year were there the fewest sheep?

Maps

There are many, many kinds of maps. There are ones that will help you find your way in a strange city. And there are ones that can tell you about the weather or the population of different parts of the world. If you know how to read maps, they will help you in your day-to-day life. You can use them to find the right bus to take you downtown or to plan a trip across the state.

The map of Puerto Rico on page 163 shows many important things about Puerto Rico. The box is called the **key** or **legend.** Look at it first to see what the symbols on the map mean. Do you see that ★ means "capital city"? Find the ★ on the map. What is the name next to it? San Juan is the capital of Puerto Rico. The ● is used to show the other important cities. Find the cities on the map. The name of each one is next to the ● . Do you see how the map shows some farming and manufacturing areas? It uses 🌾, 🍍, and 🏭. Find these symbols on the map.

Farming and Industry in Puerto Rico

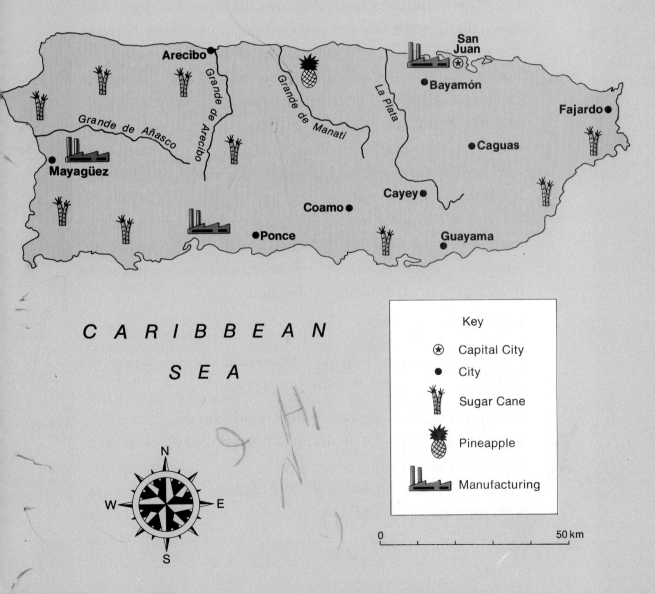

NORTH ATLANTIC OCEAN

Arecibo

San Juan

Bayamón

Fajardo

Grande de Arecibo

Grande de Añasco

Grande de Manatí

La Plata

Caguas

Mayagüez

Cayey

Coamo

Ponce

Guayama

CARIBBEAN SEA

N
W   E
S

Key
⊛ Capital City
● City
Sugar Cane
Pineapple
Manufacturing

0   50 km

Did you notice the black lines on the map? These lines are not in the key. They stand for rivers. Most maps show rivers in this way. Do you see the names of the rivers next to the lines?

Can you find the scale on the map? It is right below the key. The **scale** on a map measures distance. Put your ruler down on the scale. How many centimeters are there between the zero and the 50 kilometers? That's the scale used on the map. The measure 5 centimeters equals 50 kilometers. Once you know this, you can measure the distance between any two points on the map. How far is it from San Juan to Ponce? It's about 70 kilometers.

There is one more thing you should notice about the map. Find the **compass rose** to the left of the scale. It shows direction. The point going straight up shows which way is north. Note the *N* above it. Look for the *S*, *E*, and *W* to see which way is south, east, and west. What direction is Caguas from San Juan? It is south of San Juan.

Try This

Use the map on page 163 to answer the questions that follow. Use complete sentences to answer.

1. What bodies of water surround Puerto Rico?
2. Is San Juan located in the north, south, east, or west of Puerto Rico?
3. How far is it from San Juan to Arecibo?
4. What three cities in Puerto Rico have manufacturing areas nearby?

VOCABULARY STUDY

Multiple Meanings

My Uncle Farnsworth thinks he's funny. He tells jokes based on words with more than one meaning. Here are three examples.

My friend told me about a great ball player who could pitch anything he wanted to. But when he tried to **pitch** a tent, his glove got in the way.

pitch a. to toss or throw
b. to set up or erect

Lucy had a headache. I told her to take a **tablet**. She said she preferred the headache. She never liked the taste of stone.

tablet a. a thin sheet of stone, metal, or wood, with words or designs pressed into it
b. a small flat disk, as of medicine

Sue said the **drill** she did each day helped her to become a great tennis player. That seemed silly to me. What did she need a drill for? Her tennis racket already had holes.

drill a. a kind of instruction based on exercises that are done over and over
b. a tool for making holes

Word Play

1. Look up *pitch* in the glossary. Think of a sentence for each of its five meanings.
2. Find the words *sheet, racket,* and *kind* above. Give two meanings for each of these words.
3. Use each word, *lying* and *slip,* in two sentences. Make the meaning of the word different in each sentence.

The pictures and maps that are included in this selection will help you to understand the adventure better. What can you tell about mountain climbing from the picture on this page?

Mount Everest, 29,028 feet high at its peak, is the highest mountain on Earth. Edmund Hillary and Tenzing Norgay reached its peak on May 29, 1953. They were the first people to do so.

THE DREAM COMES TRUE

by Tenzing Norgay
and James Ramsey Ullman

Hillary and I were left alone. It was then the middle of the afternoon. We were at a height of about 28,000 feet. The top of Lhotse [(h)lōt′sā′], the fourth highest peak in the world, was now below us. Only the top of Kang-chenjunga [kän·chən·jŏong′gə] — far to the east — and the white ridge climbing high into the sky were above.

We started pitching the highest camp ever made. It took us almost until dark. Everything took five times longer because there was so little air to breathe.

At last we got the tent up and crawled inside. There was only a light wind outside and it wasn't too bad. Once inside, we were able to take off our gloves. Hillary checked the oxygen set. I got our little stove going and made warm coffee and lemon juice. Later we had some canned food. Then we got into our sleeping bags.

Lying in the dark, we talked of our plans for the next day. Then we tried to sleep. Even in our bags, we both wore all our clothes. I kept my boots on, too. At night most climbers take off their boots. They believe this helps the circulation in the feet. Yet, at great heights, I prefer to keep my feet warm. Hillary took his boots off and laid them next to his sleeping bag.

At about three-thirty in the morning, we got up. We ate a little of the food left over from the night before. A while later, we opened the tent flap. Everything was clear and quiet in the early morning light.

The first thing that happened was bad. Hillary's boots, lying all night outside his sleeping bag, had frozen. Now they were like two lumps of black iron. For a whole hour, we had to hold them over the stove. We pulled and kneaded them. The tent became full of the smell of scorched leather. At last the boots were soft enough for him to put on. Then we prepared the rest of our gear.

At six-thirty, we crawled from the tent. It was still clear and windless. We had pulled three pairs of gloves onto our hands — silk, wool, and windproof. Then we fastened our crampons to our boots. These iron plates prevent slipping. Onto our backs we slung forty pounds of oxygen sets. That would be the whole load for each of us during the climb.

"All ready?"

"*Ah chah.* Ready."

And off we went.

We drew near the south peak. Suddenly we came upon something we had been looking for: two bottles of oxygen that had been left for us by climbers who hadn't gone to the peak. We scraped the ice off the dials. How good we felt to see that they were still quite full. This meant that they could be used later for our trip down.

We left the two bottles where they were and climbed on. Up until that point, the climbing, if not the weather, had been much the same as I remembered from the year before. But then, just below the south peak, the ridge broadened out into a sort of snow wall. The white wall we were climbing was almost straight up and down. The worst part of it was that the snow was not hard and strong. It kept sliding down, sliding down. And we went with it! Finally I thought, "Next time it will keep sliding, and so will we — to the bottom of the mountain."

This was the one really bad place on the whole climb. Here it was not only a matter of what we did. It was also what the snow under us did. And this we could not control. It was one of the most dangerous places I had ever been on a mountain.

At last we got up this wall. At nine o'clock we were on the south peak. For ten minutes we rested there, looking up at what was still ahead. There was not much farther to go—only about 300 feet. But it was narrower and steeper than it had been below.

Something we had eagerly been waiting for happened on the south peak. We each came to the end of one of our two bottles of oxygen. Now we were able to dump the bottles. That reduced the weight we were carrying by half. Also, as we left the south peak, another good thing happened. We found that the snow ahead of us was hard and strong. This could make a great difference on the stretch that we still had to climb.

From the south peak we first had to go down a little. Then up, up, up. All the time there was danger. The snow could slip. We might get too far out on a heap of ice that would then break away. So we moved just one at a time. The second climber strapped the rope around his ax. He fixed the ax in the snow so that it wouldn't slip.

Hillary now went first. He worked his way up slowly and carefully. Finally he came to a sort of platform above. While climbing, he had to press backward with his feet against the ice heap. I held him with my rope from below as strongly as I could. There was great danger of the ice giving way. We were lucky that it didn't. Hillary got up safely to the top of the rock. Then he held the rope while I came up after.

Finally, we reached a place where we could see the great open sky and brown plains. We were looking down the far side of the mountain upon Tibet. Ahead of us was only one more hump — the last one. It was not hard to get to. The way to it was an easy snow slope. The path was wide enough for two men to go side by side.

A little below the peak, Hillary and I stopped to look up. Then we went on slowly, without stopping. We were there. The dream had come true.

170

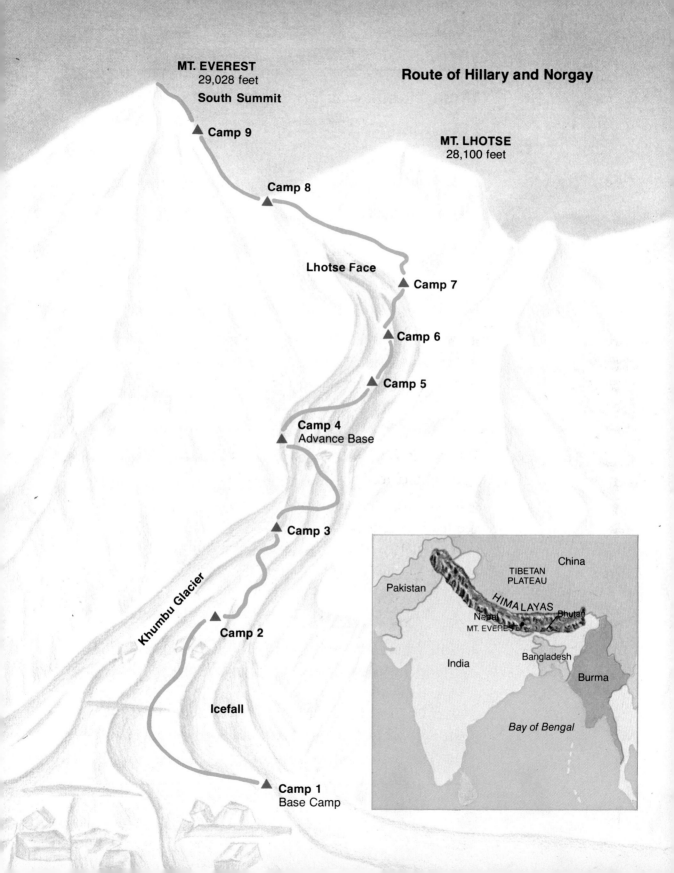

Understanding What You've Read

1. Describe the problem with Hillary's boots. How was the problem solved?
2. Norgay described one place on the mountain as "the one really bad place on the whole climb." Why was this place so dangerous?
3. What was "the dream" that had come true?

Applying the Skills Lesson

1. Look at the smaller map on page 171. Then tell where Mount Everest is located. Choose from the countries listed below.

   a. Pakistan   b. India
   c. Nepal   d. Burma

2. Look at the larger map on page 171. Then answer the following questions.

   a. What is the title of the larger map?
   b. How many camps were made during the climb to the top of Mount Everest?
   c. Which other mountain is shown on the map?

3. Tell whether you found the following information in the text, the pictures, or both.

   a. The men used oxygen masks and oxygen tanks.
   b. At night most climbers take off their boots.
   c. The men used rope and metal ladders.

Newspaper stories often show pictures with captions. Study the pictures in this selection carefully. What information do they give you?

In a different year, on a different day, another person reaches the top of Mount Everest. Read all about it!

The Tokyo News   August 1, 1975

Junko Tabei Conquers Everest

by Chris Welles Feder

May 18, 1975. Junko Tabei rides on the shoulders of her guide, Ang Tsering, after returning from the peak. The woman in the lower right is Hideko Hisano, head of the expedition.

On May 16, 1975, Junko Tabei became the first woman to climb to the top of Mount Everest. Yesterday, Mrs. Tabei agreed to tell the *Tokyo News* how she did it.

Mrs. Tabei lives in Saitama [sī·täm′ə], near Tokyo. She is a small woman of thirty-five and the mother of a three-year-old daughter, Noriko.

Junko attended Showa University. One of her best subjects was music. But her first love was mountain climbing. She joined a mountain-climbing club and spent all her holidays climbing one mountain after another.

Junko and her husband, Masanobu, have climbed the highest mountains in Japan. One year, they went to Europe and scaled the 4,359-meter-high Matterhorn

173

Junko Tabei greets another member of the Japanese all-woman expedition team. This person arrived with supplies at their 6,300-meter camp on Mount Everest on May 1. Fifteen days later, Mrs. Tabei reached the peak of Mount Everest, the first woman ever to do so.

in the Swiss Alps. The Matterhorn is one of Europe's most difficult mountains to climb.

By 1972, Junko was known as one of the best mountain climbers in Japan. A large Japanese newspaper and television company was looking for expert women climbers. The company wanted to send an all-woman team to climb Mount Everest. Hundreds of women wanted to join the Mount Everest expedition. Only fifteen were chosen. One of them was Junko Tabei.

It took the women's team three years to prepare for the Mount Everest expedition. During this time, the women trained on many mountains in Japan. They tested out their mountain-climbing gear. They worked hard so that they would be in top shape for Mount Everest.

At last, the women felt they were ready. Early in 1975, they traveled to Katmandu, Nepal. There they chose nine local people to guide them. The guides showed them the way up Mount Everest. They used the same route Edmund Hillary and Tenzing Norgay used in 1953.

By early May, the women had camped at a height of 6,300 meters. They were resting when an avalanche covered their camp. The women and their guides were almost killed, but they were able to crawl to safety.

Nearly everyone was hurt by the avalanche. There were broken bones and other injuries. Yet the party continued to struggle up the mountain.

Twelve days later, at about 7,500 meters, bad weather set in. At this point, Junko decided to go on alone. The other women were too weak or ill. Junko had been hurt, too. But she was still the strongest member of the team. So Junko took one guide with her, Ang Tsering. They began the final climb to Mount Everest's peak.

Junko climbed for five hours. Shortly after noon, on May 16, she reached the top of Mount Everest. She stood higher than any woman had ever stood before.

Junko doesn't talk about her success as hers alone. She feels that "even one member reaching the top from a good team means the whole group has succeeded."

Understanding What You've Read

1. Why was Junko Tabei one of those chosen to climb Mount Everest?
2. How did the team prepare for the climb?
3. How did Junko Tabei feel about reaching the top of Mount Everest?

Applying the Skills Lesson

1. What information do you get from the pictures that the story does not explain?
2. What information is given in the captions as well as the text?

Look at the pictures on this page. What information do they give?

How can a camera on the moon help us here on Earth? George Carruthers's story helps explain why . . .

THEY LEFT HIS CAMERA ON THE MOON

by Mary Shivanandan

In April 1972, three astronauts set foot on the moon. They had come to do some important tasks. One task was to set up a camera. This machine was made to take pictures that would help people see the air that is above and around our Earth. The pictures would also show very large groups of stars. These stars look like shiny clouds and are called *galaxies.*

First the men set up the camera. Then John Young started it working. No one had to do anything else until all the pictures were taken.

When the men returned to Earth, the camera stayed behind. It was left on the moon. It became the first space observatory ever based on the moon's surface.

From the camera, the men brought back a film tape. The pictures made from this tape showed where certain gases are found above and around the Earth. These had never been seen before. The pictures also showed where bright lights are found in the air at the North and South Poles.

All of this was made possible by a scientist named George Carruthers. He has worked with the space program in Washington, D.C.

George Carruthers was born in Cincinnati, Ohio, on October 1, 1939. He first became interested in space when he was nine years old. He read many books about space exploration. As he grew older, he helped to form clubs for others interested in space. George also became a member of the Chicago Rocket Society. This group was interested in rockets and knew a lot about them.

In college George studied about spacecraft. He also studied ways of seeing and learning about stars and planets.

In 1970, George Carruthers launched a rocket at White Sands, New Mexico. In it was a camera for taking pictures in space. The pictures it took showed gases that had never been seen before between stars. Because his camera was so useful, George Carruthers was given an award for it.

After this success, the Space Administration (NASA) decided to have a space observatory set up on the moon. George Carruthers was the leader of the team that made the camera. The camera was set up by the three astronauts in April 1972.

Since his work on the camera, George Carruthers has talked to many young people about seeking careers in science. He has also kept on trying to improve his cameras so that they take better pictures of stars that are not easy to see.

Understanding What You've Read

1. Why was George Carruthers's camera left on the moon?
2. How did some of the things George Carruthers did when he was younger help lead to his work on rockets and space cameras?
3. Why has George Carruthers kept on trying to improve his cameras?

Applying the Skills Lesson

Say whether the following statements about the selection you just read are true or false.

1. The text describes what the camera looks like.
2. One picture shows what the camera looks like.
3. The text says that the camera took pictures in color.
4. The photograph shows that the camera took pictures in color.

TEXTBOOK STUDY

Learning from Graphic Aids

You find many graphic aids such as pictures, maps, drawings or diagrams, and graphs in your textbooks. These aids often help you to understand more clearly the ideas presented.

Read the following selections and study the graphic aids. The first selection uses a map. The second selection uses a bar graph. The sidenotes will help you understand how to get information from these aids.

Reading Maps in Social Studies

Most of Ghana is low. There are some low hills, but no mountains. The weather is hot most of the year.

Is any of this information shown on the map on page 180?

Study the rainfall map on the next page. Since most of the rain falls in the southwest, that part of Ghana has thick forests. Geographers call that a *rain forest*. It is also called a jungle. The parts with less rainfall are covered with grass and separate clumps of small trees. Geographers call that kind of land a *savanna*.

Does this paragraph tell you where the most rain falls? Does the map show you where the most rain falls?

—*People and Ideas*
Silver Burdett

179

The title under the map tells you what information the map is giving. What does the map show?

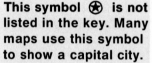

G H A N A

Accra

This symbol ✪ is not listed in the key. Many maps use this symbol to show a capital city.

This legend or key helps you read the map by color. What color shows the most rainfall? What color shows the least rainfall?

AVERAGE YEARLY RAINFALL IN GHANA

	0	50	100	150 miles
	0	50 100 150	200 kilometers	

Inches		Centimeters
Below 40		Below 100
40–50		100–125
50–60		125–150
60–70		150–175
Above 70		Above 175

Building Skills

Read the list of facts below about Ghana. Which two facts did you learn from the text? Which two facts did you learn from the map?

1. There are no mountains in Ghana.
2. The average rainfall in the north of Ghana is below 125 centimeters.
3. Part of Ghana has thick forests.
4. Accra is the capital of Ghana.

180

Reading a Bar Graph in Mathematics

You know that a bar graph compares one thing to another. You get information by "reading" the bars. The notes below the graph will help you understand it. You should be able to answer the questions below the graph.

Steven made a bar graph to show about how long some animals live.

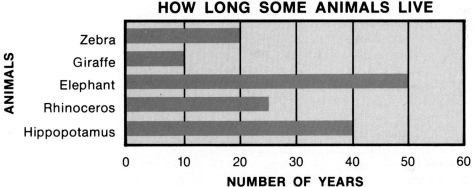

HOW LONG SOME ANIMALS LIVE

- ■ The title tells you what is being compared.
- ■ Look at the words down the left-hand side of the graph. What animals are being compared?
- ■ The numerals below the graph are called a scale. The label below the scale tells what the numerals stand for.
- ■ Look at where each bar ends. Then look down to the scale. The numerals will tell you about how long each animal lives.

1. Which animal usually has the longest life?
2. Which animal usually has the shortest life?
3. Which usually lives longer, a zebra or a hippopotamus?
4. Which usually lives longer, an elephant or a rhinoceros?

— Growth in Mathematics: Orange
Harcourt Brace Jovanovich

Building Skills

1. If the label "Number of Years" did not appear below the scale, would you know what the numerals meant? Why or why not?
2. Look back to the bar graph. Which animal usually lives about forty years?
3. Suppose you made a bar graph to show how fast each animal can go. What might be the *label* on the scale?

SKILLS LESSON

Word Order in Sentences

Sometimes order makes a big difference! In your reading, the order of words can make a big difference.

Here are two groups of words. Which one is a sentence?

Game large there a was crowd the at.
There was a large crowd at the game.

Why is the second group of words a sentence? The words are in an order that expresses meaning. The order of words in a sentence helps you to understand its meaning.

Read these two sentences.

The dog found the girl in the snow.
The girl found the dog in the snow.

Both of these sentences are made up of the same words. Yet each sentence has a different meaning. The order of these words makes the difference.

Does word order *always* make a difference? Read these two sentences.

Pat played tennis every day.
Every day Pat played tennis.

Both of these sentences are made up of the same words. The order of words is different. Do both sentences mean the same thing? You can see that sometimes the meaning stays the same even when the order of words is different.

You have known these ideas for a long time. Think about them again.

- The order of words in a sentence helps to express meaning.
- Two sentences that are made up of the same words can have different meanings.
- In some kinds of sentences, you can change the order of words without changing the meaning.

How will remembering these ideas help you to read better? They remind you that you should read carefully to be sure you get the correct meaning of each sentence.

Try This

Read each pair of sentences. Do both sentences in the pair mean the same thing? Answer *same* or *different*.

1. Last year she was Number One in tennis.
   She was Number One in tennis last year.
2. Carlos swallowed the goldfish.
   The goldfish swallowed Carlos.
3. On top of the mountain grew a giant pine tree.
   A giant pine tree grew on top of the mountain.
4. The frog leaped over the lazy fox.
   The fox leaped over the lazy frog.

Unusual Word Order

Many long sentences are as easy to understand as short ones. Here is a long sentence that is easy to understand.

At the sea aquarium, there were many gray sharks, several black-and-white-striped fish, a baby whale, and lots of funny-looking penguins.

Can you picture the animals at the aquarium? The sentence is easy to understand because you expect to find a list after "there were." The order of words in the sentence does not surprise you.

But sometimes writers use words in unusual order. The word order might surprise you. Then you can get the meaning only after you stop to think about which words go together. Read this sentence.

Out to the field raced the team.

The words are not in the usual order. The sentence is shown in the usual order below.

The team raced out to the field.

The sentence in unusual order may not have given you any trouble. But if it did, you might have asked yourself, "*Who raced?*" The answer, "*The team raced,*" tells you the usual order of the sentence.

Try This

The following sentences have unusual word order. Answer the questions after each one. Then put each sentence in the usual word order.

1. Away from the target swam the shark.
   What swam?
2. Down from the heights above crashed an avalanche.
   What crashed?
3. Into the woods raced the deer.
   What raced?

VOCABULARY STUDY

Antonyms

Traveler: Excuse me. Could you tell me how to get to Pokeville?

Boy: Pokeville? Why, that's easy! Climb to the **heights** of those mountains over there. From the top, you will be able to see into the depths of a valley.

Traveler: Is that Pokeville?

Boy: No. But it's on the way.

Traveler: That doesn't help. Excuse me, ma'am. How do I get to Pokeville?

Woman: Pokeville! Why, I'm very **familiar** with good old Pokeville. It's not strange to me at all. Just sail a boat across the Hoojoob River.

Traveler: And when I do, will I be in Pokeville?

Woman: Well, not quite. But it's on the way.

Traveler: Hmmm. . . . Pardon me, sir. Where's Pokeville?

Man: Gee, whiz. Now let me think. Ah, of course! You'd better get a bicycle. Your traveling will be **reduced**

by six seconds. If you walk, six seconds will be added, and I'm sure you're in a hurry.

Traveler: Yes, I am. But in which direction do I go?

Man: Oh, gee. I don't know.

Traveler: Aw, forget it. Pokeville's too hard to find. I'm giving up and going home. Pardon me, young lady. Is Lughaven far from here?

Girl: Far? Why, it's miles away! You're in Pokeville!

Word Play

1. Antonyms are words that mean the opposite of other words. Find the antonyms in the conversation for *familiar*, *heights*, and *reduced*.

2. Give an antonym for each of these words: *shout*, *fake*.

3. Sometimes a prefix makes a word mean the opposite. The prefix *un-* means "not," as in *unhappy*. Add *un-* to six other words to make their antonyms.

189

The things you've learned about word order can help you to figure out the meaning of sentences.

Soccer is a popular sport all around the world. One of the most famous players comes from Brazil. He is known to millions of fans as . . .

PELÉ: THE KING OF SOCCER

by Clare *and* Frank Gault

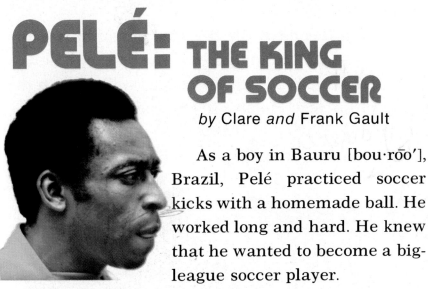

As a boy in Bauru [bou·rōo′], Brazil, Pelé practiced soccer kicks with a homemade ball. He worked long and hard. He knew that he wanted to become a big-league soccer player.

When Pelé was about eleven years old, the mayor of Bauru decided to hold a big match for all the young teams. It was to be played just like big-league soccer.

Pelé and his friends wanted to play, but they did not even have shoes. They had always played soccer in their bare feet. Then a traveling salesman named Joe Milk came forward to help. He was a soccer fan and had heard of the barefoot team. He put up the money for the suits, socks, and shoes. Joe Milk asked that the team be called "Little America." He wanted it named after his favorite team—America—in Rio de Janeiro [rē′ō də zhə·nâr′ō].

191

The boys started to play in their new shoes and suits as soon as they got them. But after only a few minutes, they were unhappy. They had never played in shoes before.

"We can't play with these shoes on," the boys said. "They hurt our feet."

After a few days, the shoes no longer hurt their feet. Pelé soon found that by wearing shoes, he could kick the ball with his toes as well as with the sides of his feet. He also found that the ball went farther.

Sixteen teams came for the Bauru match. Little America won its first game. The team went on to win its second game, too, and its third. The team made the play-off. If Little America won this last game, it would be Bauru's champion.

A huge crowd was there for the play-off. It was a hard, close game, but years of playing together paid off. Pelé was very good that day. He was all over the field, dribbling, passing, shooting.

It was late in the game and the score was tied. One of Pelé's teammates booted the ball over to him. Another player was in Pelé's way. Pelé moved the ball slowly toward the goal. The other player moved in closer to take the ball away. Suddenly, Pelé put on a burst of speed. The other player speeded up, too. Then Pelé stopped cold. He changed direction, still keeping control of the ball with his feet. The other player tried to change direction with him, but he slipped and fell to the ground.

In a flash, Pelé was racing for the goal. Only the goalkeeper was in his way now. Away from the net raced the goalie. Pelé faked a kick. The goalie dove, but the ball wasn't where he thought it would be. Bounce. Bounce. The goalie raced for it, but it went into the net. It was a goal!

The crowd stood and cheered. In a minute, the game ended. Little America had won. The crowd started to shout, "Pelé, Pelé, Pelé." Pelé heard his name being called out. He ran around the field, his arms raised in victory.

Soon after that victory, Pelé joined Valdemar de Brito's team for boys. Valdemar de Brito had been a great soccer player himself.

Valdemar de Brito saw great things in Pelé. He spent extra time with him. He helped Pelé with his passing and kicking. Pelé was a good student. The team was good, too. They were Brazil's junior champions for three years in a row. Pelé was their star.

Pelé's life wasn't all playing ball, however. His family needed his help. They had little money, and everyone who could work had to pitch in. For a while, Pelé went to the railroad station to shine shoes. He was able to make a little money to give to the family.

After coaching for a few years, Valdemar de Brito left Bauru. He went to Santos, a large port city near São Paulo [souN pou'lo͞o]. He talked to the owners of the Santos team. "There's a great young player in Bauru," he told them. "He's only fifteen years old, but he could play on your first team right now."

The Santos team thought de Brito was boasting, but they had to find out. They agreed to give Pelé a tryout with their team.

Valdemar de Brito rushed back to Bauru. He told Pelé's parents about his talk with the Santos team. Pelé's mother and father decided that their son should have a chance.

Pelé went off with Valdemar de Brito for his tryout with the Santos team. The Santos people watched Pelé work with a ball. After only a few minutes, they knew he was a great player.

The Santos people signed him right away. For the first time, Pelé was to be paid for playing ball.

Pelé started with the Santos junior team. After three months, he got a chance to play with the Santos first team. He went into a game as center forward. During the second half, he scored his first goal in a big-league game.

By the spring of the following year, Pelé was a starter with the Santos first team. After just two months of play, Pelé became so well known that he was chosen to be on Brazil's all-star team. He was only sixteen years old.

Pelé played on Brazil's all-star team and World Cup team. In 1975, he joined the New York Cosmos as a center forward. Everywhere he has gone he has been cheered and honored by millions of people.

Understanding What You've Read

1. How was playing soccer on the "Little America" team different from the way Pelé was used to playing?
2. What soccer skills did Pelé use when he played?
3. How did Pelé get to play on the Santos team?

Applying the Skills Lesson

1. Read the following pairs of sentences. Do the two sentences in each pair have the same meaning?

   a. The Santos people watched Pelé work with a ball.
      Pelé watched the Santos people work with a ball.

   b. Everywhere he has gone he has been cheered and honored by millions of people.
      He has been cheered and honored by millions of people everywhere he has gone.

2. Read the following sentence. Answer the questions that follow it.

   Away from the net raced the goalie.
   Who raced?
   How would the sentence above read in the usual order?

The meanings of most sentences in this selection are clear. If you have to stop to figure out the meaning of a sentence, remember what you've learned about word order.

Read to find out how Elaine Zayak became well known as . . .

A Figure on Ice

by Janine Rayce

She wants to win an Olympic figure skating gold medal. Then she wants to become a professional in her own ice show. After that, she wants a career as a movie star.

Maybe all of this will happen one day. But for now, it's practice and more practice for Elaine Zayak, the champion figure skater from Paramus, New Jersey.

Elaine was born on April 12, 1965. When she was three years old, a doctor who treated her for a foot injury said that ice skating would be good for her. Soon Elaine's mother got her into a program called Tots on Ice. It was there that Elaine learned how to skate.

By age five, Elaine had outgrown Tots on Ice. But she was not about to give up skating. Elaine began group lessons when she was six. She took private lessons when she was eight. Elaine was on her way.

She worked hard. When Elaine was ten, she won the North Atlantic Juveniles skating event. From there, she went directly into the Novice Ladies category. In 1978 at the national competition, Elaine came in third.

Information for this story has been obtained from *The Record* of Hackensack, New Jersey and from *Skating* Magazine, the official magazine of the United States Figure Skating Association, by permission. Quotes by Elaine Zayak reprinted by permission of Elaine Zayak.

Elaine didn't stay in the Novice Ladies class for long. She moved right along into the Junior Ladies category. Elaine won the National Junior Ladies event in 1979. Later that same year she came in first in the Junior World Competition in Augsburg, West Germany.

Elaine went from the Junior Ladies category to the Senior Ladies category in 1980. She finished fourth in the national ratings for the Senior Ladies class. She just missed being part of the 1980 United States Olympic team.

Elaine was disappointed at not making the team, but she was still proud of herself. At fourteen years old, she had competed with others who were four and five years older than herself. Coming in fourth was quite good.

By now, Elaine had learned that to skate well is not enough. To win, a figure skater must have style. When talking about her fourth-place finish in the 1980 United States Figure Skating Championship, Elaine said, "Good presentation is very important. I didn't have it then. But I'm working on it."

The life of a skating champion has exciting moments. However, as with any serious athlete in any sport, Elaine's life is almost all work. There is very little time for play. "I just skate. I love to skate. I want to skate all the time. That's all I want to do, and I want to con-centrate on it and do it very well," Elaine says.

In order to "do it very well," Elaine skates from thirty-two to forty hours a week. She can wear out three pairs of skates within a ten-month period. Since each pair of skates costs about $400, keeping Elaine in skates is expensive. But the financial burden on Elaine's family is far greater than this. Besides the skates, Elaine's parents must pay for the music and costumes for Elaine's performances. They must also pay for the plane tickets for Elaine's coach, Peter Burrows, and for her mother, who go with Elaine wherever she competes. The cost can be as high as $25,000 in one year.

But it all seems worthwhile when Elaine steps onto the familiar ice at the rink where she practices. Elaine does her figure-eight drills with care and concentration. But triple jumps are her strong point. She does seven of them in her program, and she does them in a most natural way.

In February of 1981, Elaine successfully finished all seven of her triple jumps to win the senior women's United States Figure Skating Championship in San Diego. According to Elaine's coach, no other woman had ever completed more than two triples in amateur competition.

As a result of her first-place finish in the national competition, Elaine went on to the 1981 World Figure Skating Championship in Hartford, Connecticut. During the short program, which is made up of seven special moves that must be done within two minutes, Elaine made a mistake. She fell while doing a sit-spin. But she was not upset. The next day, when it was time to do her long program, Elaine was confident. In the long program, skaters can choose their own moves. The program must last for four minutes. During those four minutes, Elaine skated with all the confidence that a champion must have. Her skating was close to perfect. The number of people who were cheering mounted as Elaine finished. Elaine's scores were high enough for her to come in second. She won the silver medal.

Being a champion figure skater is fine. But it is not the same as being an Olympic gold medal winner. That is Elaine's next goal. After that, who knows? There are many avenues open to a person with Elaine Zayak's talent and ambition. Having an ice show of her own and becoming a movie star are only two of the things she might do. There are many others.

Understanding What You've Read

1. Why did Elaine start to ice skate?
2. How did Elaine feel when she did not make the 1980 United States Olympic team?
3. What happened as a result of Elaine's first-place finish in the 1981 United States Figure Skating Championship in San Diego?

Applying the Skills Lesson

Read the following pairs of sentences. Do the two sentences in each pair mean the same thing?

1. Maybe all of this will happen one day.
   One day maybe all of this will happen.

2. Elaine had learned that to skate well is not enough.
   Elaine had not learned that to skate well is enough.

3. To win, a figure skater must have style.
   A figure skater must have style to win.

TEXTBOOK STUDY

Understanding Sentences

Word order and punctuation marks can help you to figure out the meanings of sentences. The sidenotes that go with the following selections will help you to understand word order and punctuation.

Understanding Sentences in Social Studies

Technology affects the way people live. At one time, people traveled by horse or in trains. The stable and the railroad station were important places in a town. People bought what they needed in nearby stores. Here the townspeople would meet to talk over the news and trade ideas.

The glossary will help you with this word.

The comma separates the words in the second sentence of the paragraph to make the meaning clearer.

Today there are cars almost everywhere. How did this change life? What happened to the horses, the stable, and the train station? To the places where people bought things?

Several questions are asked before this one. This last question is not a complete sentence. What is this question asking?

How has technology changed the way people live in your community? Talk to some of the people who have lived long enough to see many changes in your town. Find out how they feel about the changes that technology has brought.

—*Planet Earth*
Houghton Mifflin

Building Skills

Read these pairs of sentences. Do both sentences in each pair mean the same thing? Answer *same* or *different*.

1. Technology affects the way people live.
   The way people live affects technology.
2. Today there are cars almost everywhere.
   There are cars almost everywhere today.

Understanding Sentences in Language Arts

Finding Words in a Dictionary

The word *First* can go after the word *however* or at the end of the sentence. The meaning would be the same.

This comma separates the words to make the meaning clear.

This is a *colon*. It means that a list or set of directions will follow. What follows this colon?

A dictionary can help you with many word problems. First, however, you have to find the word that you are having trouble with.

Words are listed in your dictionary in *alphabetical* order. If you remember that, you will save a lot of time looking for a word. Here's another way to save time when you are looking up a word:

With your thumbs, divide your dictionary into three parts. The first part should be **A–F.** The middle part should be **G–P.** The last part should be **Q–Z.** Hold up the middle part. Let the first and third parts lie flat, as you see in the picture.

—*Language for Daily Use:* Orange
Harcourt Brace Jovanovich

Building Skills

Read the following pairs of sentences. The first sentence in each pair comes from the selection you just read. The second sentence shows a different order of the same words. Do both sentences mean the same thing?

1. With your thumbs, divide your dictionary into three parts.
   With your dictionary, divide your thumbs into three parts.

2. Here's another way to save time when you are looking up a word.
   When you are looking up a word, here's another way to save time.

SKILLS LESSON

Understanding Antecedents of Pronouns

If you don't know to whom someone is referring, you may not understand what that person is saying. When you meet **pronouns** as you read, you need to know what they refer to.

Some pronouns are words like *he, they, she,* and *it.* These words stand for the names of people or things. The words in boldface in the following examples are all pronouns. What does each pronoun refer to?

1. When John saw the ship, **he** waved wildly.
2. The girls played tennis. **They** played a hard match.
3. Dr. Clark trained a shark. **She** taught **it** to ring a bell.

In example 1, **he** refers to John. In example 2, **they** refers to the girls in the first sentence. In example 3, **she** refers to Dr.

Clark and **it** refers to the shark. Both were mentioned in the first sentence.

You know many other pronouns. **You** use **them** all the time. And **you** have no trouble understanding sentences with pronouns in **them,** if **you** know the word or words the pronouns stand for. (The words in boldface in the paragraph you have just read are all pronouns.)

Sometimes a pronoun is not close to the word it stands for. Then you may have to "hunt" for its meaning. In the sentences below, the pronoun *she* appears several times. What does *she* mean each time?

Eugenie studied sea life for many years. **She** went to several colleges in New York. **She** visited many labs that study sea life. **She** knew that one day **she** wanted to have a marine lab of her own.

In the sentences above, you know that *she* refers each time to Eugenie. However, in a group of sentences, you may find that different pronouns are used to refer to different people or things.

Read the following sentences.

Elephant's ear is the name of a plant. **It** grows where the weather is warm. The leaves of this plant are very large. **They** look much like the ears of elephants.

The pronoun *it* in the second sentence refers to the elephant's ear plant. What does the pronoun *they* in the fourth sentence refer to? *They* refers to the leaves.

Try This

Read the following sentences. What does each pronoun stand for?

1. The baby shark had been born at the lab. **It** was quite tame. **It** could be petted and fed by hand.
2. Dr. Clark had proved that sharks could be trained to do simple tasks. Now **she** wanted to test **their** eyesight.

Pronouns That Stand for Ideas

Pronouns often stand for names of people or things. In addition, some pronouns, such as *this, that,* or *it,* may stand for a word or group of words that expresses an idea. You may have to think a bit before you can say what these pronouns stand for.

Read the following sentences.

We don't all have the same sense of taste. **That** is probably why some people you know just can't stand lemon. You may think **it** is the most delicious of all flavors.

It in the third sentence clearly refers to lemon. The pronoun *that* in the second sentence stands for the whole idea of the first sentence ("We don't all have the same sense of taste."). *That* relates the idea in the first sentence to the second sentence.

In the example on the next page, can you tell what the pronouns in boldface refer to?

Miss Liberty's dedication was set for October 28, 1886. **It** was a cold, rainy day. But **that** did not keep away the thousands of people who lined the streets to watch the long parade.

The pronoun *it* in the second sentence refers to the date, *October 28, 1886,* in the first sentence. The pronoun *that* in the third sentence refers to the idea of *a cold, rainy day* in the second sentence. In each case, the pronouns relate one sentence to another.

Try This

Don't let pronouns confuse you. Study each group of sentences. Then answer the questions.

1. Was working with live sharks possible? No one had ever tried **it.**

   What does the pronoun *it* in the second sentence refer to?

2. "A monument should be built to celebrate American freedom," cried Laboulaye. He got up from his chair. "**It** should be built by the work of both countries."

   What does the pronoun *it* in the third sentence refer to?

3. People can sometimes go up in an airplane and make rain. They can take dry ice and spread **it** on the clouds. **This** is called seeding the clouds.

   What does the pronoun *it* in the second sentence stand for?
   What does the pronoun *this* in the third sentence refer to?

VOCABULARY STUDY

Suffixes

"Tell me the problem," said Detective Izzy A. Clod to the suffixes *-al* and *-tion.*

"We're missing our words!" they cried.

"Give me the facts," said Clod. "Just the facts."

"Certainly," said *-al.* "I mean 'having to do with,' as in **natural**, 'having to do with nature.' (The *e* is dropped from *nature* before I'm added to the end of *nature*.)"

"And I mean 'the act of,' as in **graduation**, 'the ceremony in which people graduate,' " said *-tion.* "(When I'm added to the end of *graduate*, the *t* and *e* are dropped.)"

Clod sat and thought for a moment. Then he reached into his desk. He pulled out two sentences.

"I always keep some sentences around, just in case," he said. "I think you'll find the words you need in these."

1. I know a bear that lives in a (**nation**) park.
2. A (**celebrate**) was held to honor a new three-liter bottle of shoe polish.

"But those sentences don't make any sense," cried the suffixes.

"They will, if you know where you belong," said Clod. "Next case."

Word Play

1. Look at sentences 1 and 2 above. Add the suffix *-al* or *-tion* to the words in boldface. Tell what each word means. Note that the spelling of one word changes when the suffix is added.
2. Add the suffix *-al* or *-tion* to the following words:
   suggest   music   sign   connect   monument   select
   Give a sentence for each word.

Be sure to look for the things or ideas that the pronouns stand for. This will help you to understand the selection better.

What rare and wonderful fish live in the seas of the world? Is it possible to work with live sharks? Dr. Eugenie Clark found the answers to these questions and others.

The Woman Who Trained SHARKS

by Chris Welles Feder

Eugenie Clark's interest in the sea began when she was six years old. Every Saturday morning, she went to the New York Aquarium. There, Eugenie spent hours looking at the many different fish. Some were beautiful. Some were strange. Some didn't look like fish at all. Eugenie never tired of looking at sea life. Because of her interest, she decided to become an *ichthyologist* [ik'thē·ol'ə·jist]. This is a scientist who studies fish.

Eugenie studied sea life for many years. She went to several colleges in New York. She visited many labs that study sea life. She knew that one day she wanted to have a marine lab of her own.

Dr. Clark Gets Her Lab

By 1955, Eugenie Clark was a doctor of ichthyology. She was also a wife and mother. Family life kept Eugenie busy. However, she did not give up her dream to have her own lab.

One day, Dr. Clark got a wonderful offer. Some people wanted to start a marine lab near Sarasota, Florida. The area was rich in sea life. It was just the spot for an ichthyologist to work. Would Eugenie move to Florida and run the lab?

Dr. Clark talked it over with her husband. He had just become a doctor. He liked the idea of working in Florida. He wanted Eugenie to go on with her work, too. So, in January 1955, the family moved to Florida.

Within just a few weeks, Eugenie Clark's lab was under way. It was called the Cape Haze Marine Laboratory. Dr. Clark thought her first job would be to get samples of fish.

However, before she could start that job, she got a phone call. It was to change her life.

A doctor was doing some work on cancer. He needed shark livers for his work. Could the Cape Haze Laboratory get him a shark? Eugenie had never caught one before. Nevertheless, she promised the doctor she would try to help him.

Eugenie hired some people to catch a shark. They set up a line far offshore. The line stretched for about 100 meters. On it were about 100 hooks, spaced evenly along the line. The line worked very well. It caught twelve sharks in just one week!

Now Dr. Clark had a pile of dead sharks at the lab. It was a good chance to study these dangerous fish. At that time, no one knew very much about them. No one was certain why they attacked people.

Dr. Clark tried to learn all she could about sharks. This would not be easy. If people understood sharks better, they might be able to protect against shark attacks.

Studying dead sharks raised more questions in Dr. Clark's mind. She wanted to find the answers to these questions. But there was one big hitch. To get the answers she wanted, Dr. Clark would have to work with live sharks.

Was working with live sharks possible? No one had ever tried it. Dr. Clark decided to take her chances. She had an underwater pen built at the lab. The pen had wire netting around it.

Dr. Clark had two live sharks put in the pen. They were called "lemon sharks" because of their pale color.

Getting the dead sharks ready for study in the lab.

In those days, people thought sharks could not learn anything. Dr. Clark wanted to find out if this was true. She planned to give the sharks a test. Her idea was to see if they could learn to do a simple task.

Testing the Sharks

Dr. Clark made an underwater "target" to test the sharks. The target was a square piece of wood. The wood was hooked to an underwater bell. When the wood was pushed, the bell rang.

Every day, Dr. Clark stood on the feeding stand for twenty minutes. She dropped the wood into the water. Then she put some food on a string right in front of the wood. At first, the sharks seemed afraid. They would not come close enough

Testing a shark. The shark pushes the wood target with its nose, which sets off an underwater bell. Then Dr. Clark lowers the food.

to take the food. Then, little by little, the fish became bolder. Finally, one swam right up to the wood. To get the food, it had to push the piece of wood with its nose. This set off the bell.

Day after day, Dr. Clark made the fish do the same thing. After six weeks, she gave them the big test. She put the wood in the water. But this time, she didn't lower any food. Would the sharks still make the bell ring? If they did, it would show they had learned to connect two ideas—ringing the bell and getting food.

Dr. Clark held her breath and waited. One shark rushed at the wood with its mouth open. When it saw there was no food, it swam away. Another minute passed. The fish swam back again. It looked at the piece of wood. The shark did this eight times. Then, to Dr. Clark's delight, it pushed the wood with its nose. Quickly, Dr. Clark dropped food into the water. It was a big moment.

This big, dangerous fish had learned to ring for its dinner!

Scientists and other visitors came to see what the sharks had learned. These people could not believe their eyes. No one had ever thought that sharks could be trained at all. The fact that they could learn to ring bells was very surprising to everyone.

Dr. Clark then wanted to test a shark's eyesight. Many people believed that sharks had poor eyesight. Was this true? The answer could be very important. It would help in planning ways to protect against shark attacks.

Dr. Clark ran some tests using two targets. One was a white square. The other was a red circle. In time, the sharks learned that if they pushed the white square, they got food. If they pushed the red circle, nothing happened. Soon they stopped pushing the circle. Young sharks stopped pushing the circle sooner than the older ones did. This and other tests

A shark swimming with a pilot fish.

proved that these fish could see well enough to tell the two different targets apart.

Dr. Clark knew that sharks swim with black-and-white-striped pilot fish. One day, she hit on the idea of using black-and-white-striped targets. She thought such stripes must be easy for sharks to see. She was right! They learned to use striped targets faster than any other kind. After running these tests, Dr. Clark talked to a friend. "If you're going to be swimming near sharks," she said, "don't wear a black-and-white-striped suit."

More Tests, More Success

Dr. Clark ran the Cape Haze Laboratory for about ten years. During this time, her work with sharks became known around the world. She was seen as a leading expert in her field.

One of the best moments in Eugenie Clark's career came in the summer of 1965. She was invited to visit the Crown Prince of Japan. It was proper to bring a gift to the Crown Prince. Eugenie gave Prince Akihito [ä·ki·hē′tō] one of her trained baby sharks.

Standing beside Prince Akihito, Eugenie Clark thought of all the years of work that had gone into this moment. Then she thought of all the work ahead of her. There was still much to learn about sharks. However, some very important questions had been answered. The work of Dr. Eugenie Clark was a big step forward in understanding sharks.

Understanding What You've Read

1. How did Eugenie Clark become interested in ichthyology?
2. How did a phone call change Dr. Clark's life?
3. What three things did Dr. Clark discover about sharks?

Applying the Skills Lesson

What does each pronoun in boldface in the following sentences refer to?

1. Some people wanted to start a marine lab near Sarasota, Florida. The area was rich in sea life. **It** was just the spot for an ichthyologist to work.
2. In those days, people thought sharks could not learn anything. Dr. Clark wanted to find out if **this** was true.

If you have trouble understanding a sentence that has pronouns in it, look for what the pronouns stand for. Remember: A pronoun is not always near the word or words it stands for.

What famous lady is taller than a twelve-story building and stands over New York Harbor? Read to find out about . . .

The Lady in the Harbor

by Natalie Miller

It was a summer evening in 1865. Auguste Bartholdi, a young French sculptor, was at the home of Edouard de Laboulaye. Laboulaye was well known for his writing. Bartholdi listened to the other guests talking about France and the United States. Both countries loved liberty. The French had helped the Americans fight for their freedom.

"A monument should be built to celebrate American freedom," cried Laboulaye. He got up from his chair. "It should be built by the work of both countries." All the guests agreed.

Bartholdi's heart beat fast. Perhaps he would be chosen to make such a monument. After all, he was known all over France for his statues. Bartholdi did not speak out that night. He decided to wait for the right moment. He wanted to talk with Laboulaye alone.

Before the right moment came, France was at war with Prussia. Bartholdi went away to fight in the army.

After the war, Bartholdi visited Laboulaye. They talked over Bartholdi's idea. Laboulaye suggested that Bartholdi go to America. He could find out what the people there thought about such a gift from France.

The Idea Becomes Real

On the morning his ship arrived in New York, Bartholdi went on deck to catch his first sight of the city. Before him spread a busy harbor. Guarding the entrance was tiny Bedloe's Island. It is now called Liberty Island.

"That is where I want my statue!" cried Bartholdi. "On that island. I shall call her 'Liberty Enlightening the World'!"

Suddenly he knew exactly how she should look. He hurried to his cabin for his drawing pad.

By the time the ship docked, he had drawn a calm, proud lady. She wore a long robe, and on her head was a crown. In her right hand, she held high a torch. In her left, she carried a tablet. The date, July 4, 1776, was carved into the tablet.

Bartholdi remembered the quiet strength his own mother had always shown. "Who could be a better model?" he thought.

Bartholdi showed his drawings to many important Americans. Everyone was eager to have a monument to liberty built by the two countries. France would give the statue. America would build the base on which it would stand.

When he returned to France, Bartholdi's friend, Laboulaye, invited many important people to his house. Bartholdi told them all about his trip to America. He showed them a clay model of his statue. The people liked the plans. They decided to raise the money. Bartholdi could go ahead with his idea.

The French people were happy to give money for a gift to the United States. School children gave their small coins. Rich people gave large sums.

Happily, Bartholdi had his studio made larger so that he could build the lady right there in Paris. He asked his friend Alexandre Eiffel to make a framework for her. She had to be strong enough not to tip over in a storm.

Work in Progress

One day a man visited Bartholdi. He was one of the people helping to raise money for the statue. The man said, "America will be 100 years old next year. There will be a big celebration in Philadelphia. Do you think you can finish Miss Liberty in time?"

Bartholdi shook his head sadly. He pointed to the rough model of the statue. It was already taller than most of the houses near it. "The real Miss Liberty will be four times as large as this one," he said.

"I understand," said the man. "It cannot be finished."

"I will try to have the arm holding the torch ready," said Bartholdi, "That will be taller than this statue. It would show the Americans that we are really getting our gift ready."

The man left smiling.

In August 1876, the arm arrived in Philadelphia. When the arm was put together, 900,000 people stopped to admire it. They couldn't believe its size. Miss Liberty's fingers were taller than a person.

Since the arm had been finished, Bartholdi had his workers begin on the Lady's head. Many people came to watch. They were amazed. The workers were like tiny elves next to the Lady's lips and hair.

Miss Liberty's head was finished in time to go to the Paris World's Fair in 1878.

Mr. Eiffel's workers built the framework for the rest of the Lady on a big platform in Bartholdi's courtyard. Soon Miss Liberty began to rise above the housetops.

By 1884, she was finished. She stood looking down on the roofs of Paris, waiting to go to her new home. But her home was not ready for her.

America Accepts the Gift

The people in America did not understand that Miss Liberty was a gift to all the Americans. They thought she was a gift only to New York. So they didn't want to pay for her base.

At that time, Joseph Pulitzer was editor of the *World* newspaper. He wrote stories that asked people to give money to help pay for Miss Liberty's base. Pulitzer asked his friends who worked at other cities' newspapers to help. Soon the country knew that Miss Liberty was a gift for everyone. The people sent money. At last there was enough money to build the base.

In Paris, the huge statue was taken down piece by piece. She was carefully packed in 214 boxes. In June 1884, she left for America.

When Miss Liberty's ship arrived in America, ninety boats greeted her with flags flying. They went with her into New York Harbor.

The base, which had to be very big and solid to hold the Lady, was not finished. So Miss Liberty was stored on Bedloe's Island.

When the last stone of the base was put in place, the workers showered coins from their pockets into the wet mortar. They were very happy.

Next came the hard task of putting Miss Liberty together. The people on shore watched each day as the framework rose higher into the sky. Then came the copper "skin."

The World Greets Miss Liberty

Miss Liberty's dedication was set for October 28, 1886. It was a cold, rainy day. But that did not keep people away. Thousands came to watch the parade. Bartholdi, standing next to President Cleveland, enjoyed every bit of it.

At last it was time to go over to the island. At two o'clock, Bartholdi climbed the steps to the top of his "Statue of Liberty Enlightening the World." He watched for the sign to pull the cord that dropped the flag from her face. Finally, he pulled the cord. Hundreds of ships in the harbor tooted their whistles. Bells rang. Cannons boomed. Bands played.

Miss Liberty began as a sign of the friendship between two countries. Since that time, she has come to mean freedom for the whole world. People coming to live in America look upon her as a friend. She shows them the way to the land of freedom and the chance to make a good life.

Understanding What You've Read

1. Why did Bartholdi build his statue?
2. What ideas about the statue did he get when he first went to America?
3. What has the statue come to mean? Why?

Applying the Skills Lesson

Read the sentences below. Each pronoun in boldface refers to people or things in another sentence. What does each pronoun refer to?

1. Bartholdi's heart beat fast. Perhaps **he** would be chosen to make such a monument.
2. After the war, Bartholdi visited Laboulaye. **They** talked over Bartholdi's idea.
3. Bartholdi pointed to the rough model of the statue. **It** was already taller than most of the houses near **it.**
4. Thousands came to watch the parade. Bartholdi, standing next to President Cleveland, enjoyed every bit of **it.**

Understanding Antecedents of Pronouns

You come across many pronouns in your textbook reading. In reading the following selections, pay close attention to the pronouns. Use the sidenotes to help you understand them.

Understanding Antecedents of Pronouns in Science

Science in Your Life

You know that there is fresh water and salt water. Every day you hear and read about these waters being polluted. What does this mean to you?

The pronoun *you* stands for the reader.

The word *this* refers to the idea in the second sentence.

Every year there are more people living on the earth. This means more water is needed. More and more food, in the coming years, may come from the oceans. The oceans may be "farmed." The pollution of the oceans must stop.

Whenever a river, lake, or ocean is polluted, you cannot use it. Where will you be able to swim or fish? Animal life is hurt by pollution, too. Any animal that lives on or near water can suffer.

The word *it* might stand for any of three things mentioned in this sentence.

—*Understanding Your Environment*
Silver Burdett

227

Building Skills

Read the second paragraph of the selection again. What does the word *this* in the second sentence refer to?

Understanding Antecedents of Pronouns in Health

Todd and Marta went on a hike. Todd's older sister, Kate, went with them. The trail was steep. Marta slipped and fell. Her arm hurt.

The word *them* stands for two people. Which two people?

"Don't move," said Kate. "Your arm might be broken. Moving it might hurt it more."

Todd, Marta, and Kate are the three people in this story. Which name does *your* stand for?

First Kate wrapped Marta's arm in a towel. Then she tied two straight sticks to Marta's arm. How will the sticks help? Kate made sure the ties were just tight enough to hold the sticks in place. If the ties are too tight, the blood might stop flowing through Marta's arm. What could happen if the ties are too loose?

Does *she* stand for Marta or Kate?

Next Kate put Marta's arm in a sling. Then she tied a band over the sling. The band will keep the joints on both sides of the injury from moving. Which joints are those?

The word *those* refers to "the joints on both sides of the injury." Those joints are the shoulder and elbow joints.

— *You Learn and Change:* Orange
Harcourt Brace Jovanovich

228

Building Skills

1. The following sentences are from the selection you have just read. What do the words in boldface stand for?

   a. "Don't move," said Kate. "Your arm might be broken. Moving **it** might hurt **it** more."

   b. Next Kate put Marta's arm in a sling. Then **she** tied a band over the sling.

2. Which pronoun might stand for these people or things? Match the pronouns in column 1 with the people or things in column 2.

1	2
them	broken arm
it	Todd and Marta
she	Todd
he	Kate

229

Books About Achieving

Nightmare World of the Shark by Joseph J. Cook. Dodd, 1968. You'll find information on different types of sharks and legends about sharks.

Columbia and Beyond: The Story of the Space Shuttle by Franklyn Branley. Collins, 1979. This book tells many interesting facts about the space shuttle and the uses it will be put to on earth.

Illustrated Soccer Dictionary for Young People by James B. Gardner. Harvey, 1976. Cartoons and text explain the rules and skills of soccer. There are short biographies of Kyle Rote, Jr. and Eusebio da Silva Ferreira, two famous soccer players.

Making Your Own Sculpture by Harry Helfman. Morrow, 1971. Nine projects—using such things as plastic cups and drinking straws—are explained.

How to Photograph Your World by Vicki Holland. Scribner, 1974. The author talks mostly about the beauty of photography. Many photographs are shown.

Kids Camping by Aileen Paul. Doubleday, 1973. You'll find information about camping, including planning, equipment, and backpacking.

Superpuppy by Jill and D. Manus Pinkwater. Seabury, 1974. This is a guide to puppy care and training.

Women Who Win by Francene Sabin. Random, 1975. This book has short biographies of fourteen women athletes from the United States.

Part 4

Songs Without Music

UNDERSTANDING AND APPRECIATING LITERATURE

Poetry

HIGGLEDY, PIGGLEDY, POP.
THE DOG HAS SWALLOWED THE MOP.
THE CAT'S IN A HURRY,
THE PIG'S IN A FLURRY.
HIGGLEDY, PIGGLEDY, POP.

Understanding Humorous Poetry

You hear poetry every day. The songs you sing are poems. Jump-rope rhymes, like the one in the cartoon, are poems. Can you think of a poem that you've heard or read?

Read the poem in the cartoon. It is a **humorous** poem. It makes you laugh. What words are especially funny? "Higgledy, piggledy, pop" are silly words that have no meaning. What else makes this a funny poem? The things the animals are doing are funny. These poems are just for fun.

Understanding Lyric Poetry

There are different kinds of poems. Some poems are humorous. Other poems tell you how the poet feels. These are called **lyric** poems. Read this poem:

March

by ELIZABETH COATSWORTH

A blue day,
A blue jay,
and a good beginning.

One crow,
melting snow —
spring's winning!

What has the poet described? She has described a day in March. Is this a happy poem or a sad poem? Which words tell you that it is a happy poem? "A good beginning" and "spring's winning" sound happy. The poem also tells you how the poet feels about spring. She is glad that it is March and spring is coming.

Understanding Narrative Poetry

Another kind of poem is the **narrative** poem. A narrative poem tells a story. Read this narrative poem.

Under a Toadstool

by OLIVER HERFORD

Under a toadstool
Crept a wee elf
Out of the rain
To shelter himself.

Trembled the wee elf
Frightened, and yet
Fearing to fly away
Lest he got wet.

To the next shelter   Tugged till the toadstool
Maybe a mile!   Toppled in two,
Sudden the wee elf   Holding it over him
Smiled a wee smile,   Gaily he flew.

"Under a Toadstool" is a narrative poem. It is a poem that tells a story. What is the story in this poem about? It is about an elf who gets caught in the rain without an umbrella. How does the elf keep from getting wet in the rain? The elf keeps from getting wet by using a toadstool for his umbrella.

Understanding Rhyme and Stanzas

Humorous, lyric, and narrative poems may have things in common. All of them may **rhyme.** When a poem rhymes, two or more lines end with words that have the same sounds. The three poems you just read have rhyming words. Look back at "Higgledy, Piggledy, Pop" on page 232 and find some rhyming words.

Any poem may have stanzas. If the lines of a poem are grouped into parts, the parts are called **stanzas.** Which of the three poems you just read are divided into stanzas? "March" and "Under a Toadstool" are. How many stanzas are in each? The lyric poem has two stanzas. The narrative poem has four.

Humorous poems are just for fun. Lyric poems describe how a poet feels. Narrative poems tell you a story. Poems may rhyme and have stanzas. But all poetry is written for you to enjoy.

Try This

Read the following poem. Then answer the questions.

I Meant to Do My Work Today

by RICHARD LeGALLIENNE

I meant to do my work today—
    But a brown bird sang in the apple tree,
And a butterfly flitted across the field,
    And all the leaves were calling me.

And the wind went sighing over the land
    Tossing the grasses to and fro,
And a rainbow held out its shining hand—
    So what could I do but laugh and go?

1. How many stanzas are there in the poem?
2. Is it a rhyming poem? Which words rhyme?
3. Is the poem humorous, lyric, or narrative?
4. What three things keep the poet from doing work?
5. How does the poet feel?

Writing

1. Write a four-line humorous poem that rhymes and begins with the following line:

    I have a dog that's big and gray.

2. Write your own lyric poem.

As you read "Songs Without Music," notice how poets use words to create humorous, lyric, or narrative poetry.

These poems are humorous. Notice the different ways each poet makes you laugh. Decide what is funny in each poem.

Ickle Me, Pickle Me, Tickle Me Too

by SHEL SILVERSTEIN

Ickle Me, Pickle Me, Tickle Me too
Went for a ride in a flying shoe.
"Hooray!"
"What fun!"
"It's time we flew!"
Said Ickle Me, Pickle Me, Tickle Me too.

Ickle was captain, and Pickle was crew
And Tickle served coffee and mulligan stew
As higher
And higher
And higher they flew,
Ickle Me, Pickle Me, Tickle Me too.

Ickle Me, Pickle Me, Tickle Me too,
Over the sun and beyond the blue.
"Hold on!"
"Stay in!"
"I hope we do!"
Cried Ickle Me, Pickle Me, Tickle Me too.

Ickle Me, Pickle Me, Tickle Me too
Never returned to the world they knew,
And nobody
Knows what's
Happened to
Dear Ickle Me, Pickle Me, Tickle Me too.

Eletelephony

by LAURA E. RICHARDS

Once there was an elephant,
Who tried to use the telephant—
No! No! I mean an elephone
Who tried to use the telephone—
(Dear me! I am not certain quite
That even now I've got it right.)

Howe'er it was, he got his trunk
Entangled in the telephunk;
The more he tried to get it free,
The louder buzzed the telephee—
(I fear I'd better drop the song
Of elephop and telephong!)

Helping

by SHEL SILVERSTEIN

Agatha Fry, she made a pie,
And Christopher John helped bake it.
Christopher John, he mowed the lawn,
And Agatha Fry helped rake it.
Zachary Zugg took out the rug,
And Jennifer Joy helped shake it.
And Jennifer Joy, she made a toy,
And Zachary Zugg helped break it.

And some kind of help
Is the kind of help
That helping's all about.
And some kind of help
Is the kind of help
We all can do without.

Lost and Found

by LILIAN MOORE

LOST:

A Wizard's loving pet.

Rather longish.

Somewhat scaly.

May be hungry or
upset.

Please feed daily.

P.S. Reward.

FOUND:

A dragon

breathing fire.

Flails his scaly

tail

in ire.

Would eat twenty LARGE meals

daily

if we let him.

PLEASE

Come and get him.

P.S.   No reward necessary.

The Engineer

by A. A. MILNE

Let it rain!
Who cares?
I've a train
Upstairs,
With a brake
Which I make
From a string
Sort of thing,
Which works
In jerks,
'Cos it drops
In the spring,
Which stops
With the string,

And the wheels
All stick
So quick
That it feels
Like a thing
That you make
With a brake,
Not string. . . .

So that's what I make,
When the day's all wet.
It's a good sort of brake
But it hasn't worked yet.

Have you heard of the man
   Who stood on his head,
And put his clothes
   Into his bed,
And folded himself
   On a chair instead?

TRADITIONAL

243

Understanding What You've Read

1. How many stanzas are in "Ickle Me, Pickle Me, Tickle Me Too"? Find some rhyming words in each stanza.
2. In the poem "Eletelephony," what words make the poem humorous?
3. One line in "The Engineer" gives the poem its humor. Which line is it? Why does it make you laugh?

Writing

1. In "Eletelephony," word parts are combined in a humorous way. Write your own funny sentence or poem using nonsense words.
2. Write a short rhyming poem with a surprise ending that makes the poem funny.

Poets often paint pictures with words. In these poems, the poets describe nature in new and unusual ways. Their descriptions can also tell you how the poets feel about nature.

Spring Song

by AILEEN FISHER

A meadow lark came back one day
and searched beneath the faded hay
out in the rocks, beside a cleft,
to find a song that he had left.

He found it. And he tried it out.
He tossed the melody about,
and not a note was hurt a bit
by winter drifting over it.

The River Is
a Piece of Sky

by JOHN CIARDI

From the top of a bridge
The river below
Is a piece of sky—

    Until you throw
    A penny in
    Or a cockleshell
    Or a pebble or two
    Or a bicycle bell
    Or a cobblestone
    Or a fat man's cane—

And then you can see
It's a river again.

The difference you'll see
When you drop your penny:
The river has splashes,
The sky hasn't any.

I Like Weather

by AILEEN FISHER

Weather is full
of the nicest sounds:
it sings
and rustles
and pings
and pounds
and hums
and tinkles
and strums
and twangs
and whishes
and sprinkles
and splishes
and bangs
and mumbles
and grumbles
and rumbles
and flashes
and CRASHES.

Songs of Thunder

NAVAJO CHANTS

Thonah! Thonah!
There is a voice above,
The voice of the thunder.
Within the dark cloud,
Again and again it sounds,
Thonah! Thonah!

Thonah! Thonah!
There is a voice below,
The voice of the grasshopper.
Among the plants,
Again and again it sounds,
Thonah! Thonah!

_____

The voice that beautifies the land!
The voice above,
The voice of the thunder.
Within the dark cloud
Again and again it sounds,
The voice that beautifies the land.

The voice that beautifies the land!
The voice below:
The voice of the grasshopper.
Among the plants
Again and again it sounds,
The voice that beautifies the land.

249

A narrative poem tells a story. "The Wind and the Moon" tells a story about how the Wind felt about the Moon and how the Moon fooled the Wind.

The Wind and the Moon

by GEORGE MacDONALD

Said the Wind to the Moon, "I will blow you out;
      You stare
      In the air
    Like a ghost in a chair,
Always looking what I am about;
I hate to be watched; I will blow you out."

The Wind blew hard, and out went the Moon.
      So, deep
      On a heap
    Of clouds to sleep,
Down lay the Wind, and slumbered soon—
Muttering low, "I've done for that Moon."

He turned in his bed; she was there again!
        On high,
        In the sky,
    With her one ghost eye,
The Moon shone white and alive and plain,
Said the Wind, "I will blow you out again."

The Wind blew hard, and the Moon grew dim,
        "With my sledge
        And my wedge
    I have knocked off her edge!
If only I blow right fierce and grim,
The creature will soon be dimmer than dim."

He blew and he blew, and she thinned to a thread.
        "One puff
        More's enough
    To blow her to snuff!
One good puff more where the last was bred,
And glimmer, glimmer, glum will go that thread!"

He blew a great blast and the thread was gone.
    In the air
    Nowhere
  Was a moonbeam bare;
Far-off and harmless the shy stars shone;
Sure and certain the Moon was gone!

The Wind he took to his revels once more;
    On down,
    In town,
  Like a merry-mad clown,
He leaped and hallooed with whistle and roar—
"What's that?" The glimmering thread once more!

He flew in a rage; he danced and blew;
    But in vain
    Was the pain
  Of his bursting brain;
For still the broader the Moon-scrap grew
The broader he swelled his big cheeks and blew.

Slowly she grew, till she filled the night,
      And shone
      On her throne
    In the sky alone,
A matchless, wonderful, silvery light,
Radiant and lovely, the Queen of the night.

Said the Wind, "What a marvel of power am I!"
      With my breath,
      Good faith,
    I blew her to death—
First blew her away right out of the sky—
Then blew her right in; what strength have I!"

But the Moon she knew nothing about the affair;
      For high
      In the sky,
    With her one white eye,
Motionless, miles above the air,
She had never heard the great Wind blare.

Understanding What You've Read

1. Sometimes authors describe one thing by comparing it to something else. Why does John Ciardi call a river "a piece of sky" in his poem on page 246?
2. How do you think Aileen Fisher feels about weather in her poem on page 247? Give two reasons for your answer.
3. You know that a narrative poem tells a story. What happens in "The Wind and the Moon"? What does the wind try to do? Why isn't the wind successful?

Writing

1. Describe something familiar in a new way. You may use one of these:

   bird, sunset, tall building, bridge,
   dark road at night, traffic light, school bus

2. Write your own narrative poem. Divide your poem into stanzas. You may wish to retell a story you have read as a narrative poem.

A lyric poem tells you how the poet feels. Through description, a poet can share a feeling with you. As you read these lyric poems, notice the feelings that each poet expresses.

Butterfly Wings

by AILEEN FISHER

How would it be
on a day in June
to open your eyes
in a dark cocoon,

And soften one end
and crawl outside,
and find you had wings
to open wide,

And find you could fly
to a bush or tree
or float on the air
like a boat at sea . . .

How would it be?

255

The Sidewalk Racer

by LILLIAN MORRISON

Skimming
an asphalt sea
I swerve, I curve, I
sway; I speed to whirring
sound an inch above the
ground; I'm the sailor
and the sail, I'm the
driver and the wheel
I'm the one and only
single engine
human auto
mobile.

By Myself

by ELOISE GREENFIELD

When I'm by myself
And I close my eyes
I'm a twin
I'm a dimple in a chin
I'm a room full of toys
I'm a squeaky noise
I'm a gospel song
I'm a gong
I'm a leaf turning red
I'm a loaf of brown bread
I'm a whatever I want to be
An anything I care to be
And when I open my eyes
What I care to be
Is me

Stopping by Woods on a Snowy Evening

by ROBERT FROST

Whose woods these are I think I know.
His house is in the village, though;
He will not see me stopping here
To watch his woods fill up with snow.

My little horse must think it queer
To stop without a farmhouse near
Between the woods and frozen lake
The darkest evening of the year.

He gives his harness bells a shake
To ask if there is some mistake.
The only other sound's the sweep
Of easy wind and downy flake.

The woods are lovely, dark and deep,
But I have promises to keep,
And miles to go before I sleep,
And miles to go before I sleep.

A piñon tree is a small pine tree found in the Southwest;
a piñonero is a blue jay that eats the nuts of this tree.

Oh! Piñonero!

by MARY AUSTIN

Oh! Piñonero!
Now you are back in the piñon tree,
It means snow on the mountain
And school for me,
Piñonero!
And I wish I had nothing else to do
Than flit about in a coat of blue
Eating piñon nuts,
Like you,
Piñonero!

260

Understanding What You've Read

1. In "Oh! Piñonero!" what does the return of the little bird mean to the child? How does the child feel about the piñonero?
2. "Stopping by Woods on a Snowy Evening" is a rhyming poem. Find the words that rhyme in each stanza.
3. Robert Frost describes the wind and the snow in an unusual way in "Stopping by Woods on a Snowy Evening." How do you think he feels about the wind?
4. How do you think George MacDonald feels about the wind in "The Wind and the Moon"? Compare it with the way Robert Frost feels in "Stopping by Woods on a Snowy Evening."

Writing

1. Write a lyric poem about something that makes you feel happy, sad, or some other way. Choose your words carefully.
2. It might be fun to fly like a bird, or to be a kitten, or even a fire engine. Tell in a rhyming poem what you would like to be and why. Begin your poem this way:

    I dreamed I was a . . .

More Poems to Read

My Black Me: A Beginning Book of Black Poetry compiled by Arnold Adoff. Dutton, 1974. These poems are about the feelings and hopes of many black poets.

Rhymes About Us by Marchette Chute. Dutton, 1974. This book is full of poems about children and the things they think about and do every day.

Moments: Poems About the Seasons edited by Lee Bennett Hopkins. Illustrated by Michael Hague. Harcourt Brace Jovanovich, 1980. A collection of fifty poems about the four seasons by well-known and modern poets.

Songs of the Dream People: Chants and Images from the Indians and Eskimos of North America edited by James Houston. Atheneum, 1972. These songs and chants come from many Native American cultures.

Out Loud by Eve Merriam. Atheneum, 1973. These poems are all about sounds that beg to be read out loud.

Where the Sidewalk Ends by Shel Silverstein. Harper & Row, 1974. These funny and thoughtful poems are all illustrated with line drawings by the poet.

A Great Big Ugly Man Came Up and Tied His Horse to Me compiled by Wallace Tripp. Little, 1974. You'll find all kinds of nonsense verses here, including some chants and limericks.

Part 5

Communicating

Understanding the Topic of a Paragraph

Which of these groups of words tells what the picture above is about?

my dog and I   *my house*   *cats and dogs*

If you picked *my dog and I*, you found the **topic** of the picture. A topic is what something is about. You can find topics in what you read, too.

264

Writers put their thoughts into sentences. They put sentences together in paragraphs. In many paragraphs, all the sentences—or almost all of them—are about one topic. In some paragraphs, every sentence tells or asks something about the topic.

Read the paragraph below. What is each sentence telling you about?

Some dolphins live in oceans. Other dolphins live in rivers. All of them swim fast. Dolphins have long beaks. They have many sharp teeth lining their jaws. Dolphins eat fish. Dolphins are also very smart. They are friendly to people, too.

What is the topic of the paragraph you just read?

fish   *dolphins*   *oceans*

The topic of the paragraph is *dolphins*. Every sentence tells something about dolphins.

Now read the next paragraph. As you read the paragraph, ask yourself this question: "What are all or most of the sentences telling about?" The answer will help you find the topic of the paragraph.

Of all the animals in the world, the cheetah is the fastest. It is faster than a racehorse or an antelope. This speedy animal is found in Africa and Asia. Its legs are thinner and longer than the legs of a lion or tiger. When hunting, the cheetah can run at a speed of as much as 112 kilometers an hour.

What is the topic of the paragraph?

the racehorse   *the antelope*   *the cheetah*

The racehorse and the antelope are only mentioned in one sentence. But every sentence in the paragraph tells something about the cheetah. So the third choice is correct. The topic of the paragraph is *the cheetah.*

266

Try This

1. Read each of the paragraphs below. Study the words below each one. Which word best states the topic?

   a. Libraries have many things to offer. They have books, of course. They also have magazines and newspapers. Many libraries lend records or tapes that you can listen to. Others show movies. Some libraries have storytellers. Sometimes libraries even hold art shows.

   libraries   *books*   *magazines*

   b. Ants do some of the things that people do. Ants live in groups. They build cities. They dig tunnels. They build roads. Some kinds of ants plant gardens. Ants do some other things, too. They even fight wars. Did you know that ants do all these things?

   people   *ants*   *gardens*

2. Read the following paragraph. What is the topic? Remember to think of what all the sentences are telling about.

   Have you ever seen a sea horse? A sea horse's head and neck look a little like those of a real horse. Sea horses range in size from about five to thirty centimeters long. Their skin is bumpy. Although the sea horse doesn't look at all like a fish, it really is a fish.

VOCABULARY STUDY

Homophones

I say, Sir Francis. It's quite terrible out here. How long will we have to <u>wait</u> for the rain to stop?

Eh, what? Did you say the <u>weight</u> of the rain is terrible? I don't notice anything especially heavy about it.

No, no, Sir Francis. I said *wait,* "to stay until something happens." I didn't mean *weight,* "the amount something weighs." *Wait* and *weight* are *homophones.* They sound the same, but they don't mean the same thing. They're not spelled the same way either. There are lots of homophones.

Quite so, old chap.

What does it matter—<u>nights</u> or days. Foggy, damp weather is never very good.

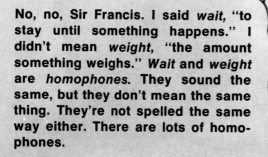

You see, this foggy, damp weather is no good for our <u>knights</u>. It's bad for their armor, you know. Stiffens it.

Word Play

1. Choose the correct homophone to fit the meaning of each sentence below.

   a. Please tell me the (wait, weight) of this package.
   b. I have twenty-five (sense, cents) to spend at the store.
   c. I fell asleep early (for, four) (nights, knights) in a row.

2. Give a homophone for each word: *see, no, flower.*

3. Think of as many pairs of homophones as you can.

As you read, look for the topics of paragraphs. Thinking about the topics will help you understand what you read.

Through our senses we learn about the world.
Here is a chance for you to learn more about . . .

YOU AND YOUR SENSES

by Jeanne Bendick

Always, every minute, without even thinking, you are asking yourself questions and answering them. What do I see? What do I hear? What's that smell? Does this taste good? Am I warm enough?

Suppose you had to learn everything about the world, all by yourself, right from the very beginning. Suppose you had no one to help you and no books to tell you. How would you learn what the world was like?

You would use your senses. The more carefully you use your senses, the more you learn about the world. But using your senses well takes a lot of practice and thinking.

These Are Your Senses

Seeing, hearing, smelling, tasting, and feeling are your **outer senses.** They tell you what is happening in the world around you, outside your body. You see through your eyes and hear through your ears. You smell through your nose. You taste through your tongue and your nose.

You have feeling senses, too. You are using your sense of touch when you rub a smooth apple or feel the wind on your face. Your sense of pressure is like touch, sometimes harder, sometimes softer. You can feel your sweater touching you. If it is too tight, it presses. You can also feel when the pressure changes.

Your **inner senses** signal messages from inside your body. They tell you when you are feeling pain from inside, like a stomach ache. They tell you when you are thirsty, hungry, or tired.

Your muscle sense is an inner sense. It tells you where each part of your body is and what it is doing. It guides your hands and feet and head and every other part of you. You don't have to think about all the motions you make every day. But suppose you're learning a new sport— maybe how to ski or swim. Then you have to think about what you want your muscles to do.

Your sense of balance is also an inner sense. It tells you if you are straight up or upside down, tipping over or getting dizzy.

Stand on one leg and start leaning sideways. Do you know right away when you've leaned as far as you can without tipping over? Your sense of balance is a big help here. No matter how you move, it tries to keep you right side up.

Understanding Messages from Your Senses

To help you get the messages your senses send, you need **experience.** Your experience is made up of every single thing you have ever done in your life and everything that has ever happened to you. It is everything you have ever seen or heard or smelled or tasted or felt.

Experiences don't have to be nice. Smelling a rotten egg is an experience just as much as smelling a pine tree. Eating a blueberry is an experience. So is taking medicine. Riding a merry-go-round is an experience. So is falling down stairs. You have a hundred different kinds of experiences every day.

If you had never seen a horse or a picture of a horse, how would you get the message "A horse" when you saw one? If you were eating a blueberry for the first time, your senses could tell you, "It's small and sweet." But your experience could not tell you "A blueberry!" The more experiences you have, the better you can tell someone else what you are seeing, hearing, tasting, touching, or smelling.

We often tell about things by comparing them to other things. Suppose you wanted to tell about a yellow daisy. You might say, "The flower is like sunshine." Or you might say, "The flower is the color of a fried egg." To tell about the noise inside a sea shell, you could say, "It sounds like cheering." You could also say, "It sounds like the ocean." Whatever kinds of experience you have, they help you to understand things and to tell about them.

Paying Attention to Your Senses

Your senses keep sending you messages about the world around you. Your experience helps you to figure out what the messages mean.

"I see the leaves falling from that tree" is a message from your eyes. "I hear a fire siren" is a message from your ears. "I smell dinner cooking" is a message from your nose.

But then what happens? You ask yourself, in your mind, what the message means. "I see the leaves falling. *What does that mean?* It must be autumn." "I

hear a fire siren. *What does that mean?* There's a fire near here." "I smell dinner cooking. *What does that mean?* It must be time to stop playing and go eat."

Is the answer you give yourself always the right answer? Have you made the right guess? "I see the leaves falling, so it must be autumn" could be the right answer. But "The tree is sick" could be an answer, too.

Can you depend on your senses? Usually you can, if you pay attention to them and learn to use them well. But if you're not paying attention, they don't work as well as they should. First, you

275

have to ask yourself, "What am I trying to find out?" You may find out by looking, listening, smelling, feeling, or tasting.

When you don't use your senses and your mind, it's like living in a tunnel. When you do use them, everything is more exciting and more fun. You're living in the whole world.

Understanding What You've Read

1. How could you learn about the world if you had no person or book to tell you?
2. What are your outer senses? Your inner senses?
3. What is experience? How does experience help you to understand new things?

Applying the Skills Lesson

1. What is the topic of the first paragraph in the left-hand column on page 272?

   a. your ears   b. seeing   c. your outer senses

2. What is the topic of the first paragraph in the left-hand column on page 274?

   a. your life   b. your experience   c. messages

3. What is the topic of the second paragraph in the left-hand column on page 274?

   a. experiences that are fun
   b. experiences that are not fun
   c. different kinds of experiences

Look for the topic in each paragraph. Ask yourself, "What are all the sentences about?"

Is there one "language" that everyone understands? Read about . . .

SIGNS AND SYMBOLS

by Winifred *and* Cecil Lubell

Anywhere you go you will see all kinds of signs. Many signs have words, but there's another kind of sign without words. It's a picture sign. It tells you something without spelling it out in letters.

Think about some picture signs you see each day. A clock face is a picture sign. It tells you the time. A traffic signal is also a sign without words. Green says "GO." Yellow says "WAIT." Red means "STOP."

One Language for Everyone

That's the idea behind a sign without words. It's a way of giving information to people who come from different countries and who don't all read or speak the same language.

We already have many signs and symbols that mean the same things in different parts of the world. For example, everyone knows what arrow signs mean. You see them everywhere, in all kinds of shapes and sizes. And everywhere in the world they mean the same thing.

Suppose you went to every zoo in the world. In any language this sign means the same thing: "This way to the elephants."

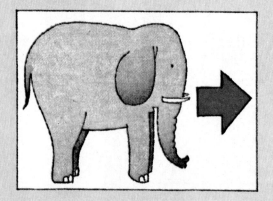

Even people who can't read can understand an arrow. It's a useful sign. It gives you quick, easy directions such as: "GO AROUND THE BEND," "TURN RIGHT," and "TURN LEFT."

Musical notes mean the same thing everywhere, too. It doesn't matter what language people speak or read. When the notes printed on a sheet of music are played, they sound the same all over the world.

Signs Are Shortcuts

Many signs and symbols give us directions or information without using letters and words. Some signs are used *with* letters, words, or numerals. And remember, letters themselves are symbols. Letters stand for the sounds we put together to make words. A question mark (**?**) doesn't stand for a sound the way the letter signs ABC do. Yet the question mark gives information. It tells us that the words in front of this mark should be read as a question.

There are many other signs that are used with letters and numerals. Do you know some of these signs?

Of course, signs like these are useful only if everyone agrees on what they mean. For example, everybody had to agree that the sign + means "plus" and that the sign = means "equals." People also had to learn the numerals **1** through **10.** Then, if we write **6 + 3 = 9,** everybody knows it means "Six plus three equals nine."

You can see that signs and symbols are shortcuts for saying something quickly. That's the reason they are used a great deal on roads.

Signs for Drivers

It's often hard to read a word sign when you're driving fast on a highway. If the words are not in your own language, you may not be able to understand the sign at all. What you need is a clear sign without words. Here is such a sign.

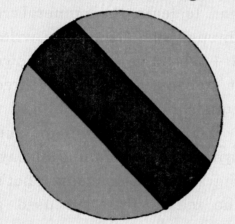

This sign is easy to see. Anyone in the world can understand it—once he or she is told what it means.

The thick black line stands for something crossed out. A black line in a red circle is used in many parts of the world as a traffic sign. It means: "NO!" or "DON'T GO THIS WAY!" Here are some other road signs you may know:

Winding road ahead.

Bicycle path.

School   Crossing.

Other Signs and Symbols

Signs and symbols are used in many other ways as well. Airports have picture signs to tell where things are. Shopkeepers hang picture signs to show what they are selling.

Flags and animals are used as symbols. Some flags are put out as danger signs. They warn people about strong winds out on the ocean. They warn people that ice on ponds may be too thin to skate on. Other flags are symbols for countries. Animals are used as symbols for groups in sports and government, and for makes of cars.

Are Signs Enough?

Signs without words can tell us a lot. But picture signs cannot take the place of words altogether. With words we can express ideas and thoughts. We can't do that with just signs.

For example, thousands of years ago people did not know how to write. They left picture signs on the walls of the caves in which they lived. But these pictures can tell us only a little about the lives of the people who made them. They cannot tell us anything at all about their thoughts.

So you can see why we need more than just pictures to express ideas. If we want to find out about history, or tell other people what we are thinking and feeling, then we need words and language.

Understanding What You've Read

1. How do signs with pictures rather than words help people who are in a strange country?
2. What are symbols?
3. In what ways are signs "shortcuts"?
4. Why can't picture signs take the place of words altogether?

Applying the Skills Lesson

1. What is the topic of the second paragraph in the right-hand column on page 278?

   a. picture signs   b. musical notes   c. language

2. State the topic of the second paragraph in the left-hand column on page 281.

TEXTBOOK STUDY

Finding Topics

Paragraphs in textbooks usually have topics. When you read your textbooks, think about the topic of each paragraph. Ask yourself the question, "What are most of the sentences telling about?" As you read the following selections, use the sidenotes to help you understand the topics of the paragraphs.

Finding Topics in Language Arts

How Our Language Grows

Sports-World Words

Sports fans often make up or borrow words to describe a player's position or actions. Many of these are lively, exact words. For instance, a baseball fan would not call a player sent to bat for another player a *substitute*. That player would be a *pinch hitter*.

> **Every sentence in this paragraph tells something about sports words. *Sports words* is the topic of the paragraph.**

When a term like *pinch hitter* is very popular with fans, it may spread outside of the sport. Someone who takes the place of another in any pinch may be called a *pinch hitter*.

A football game is started with a *kickoff*. Many people use this term to describe the beginning or the start of

> **What one thing are the sentences in this paragraph telling about?**

283

anything. You might hear about the *kickoff* of a charity drive. *Kickoff* is a much more exciting word for a beginning than *start*.

— *Language for Daily Use:* Orange
Harcourt Brace Jovanovich

Building Skills

1. Read the second paragraph of the selection again. What is the topic of the paragraph?
   a. sports fan
   b. the term *pinch hitter*
   c. popular sports

2. Read the third paragraph of the selection again. What is the topic of the paragraph?
   a. the word *kickoff*
   b. football
   c. the word *start*

Finding Topics in Social Studies

The topic of this paragraph is *animal helpers*. See how every sentence tells how people have used animals to help them.

Ever since the first people tamed wild dogs to help them hunt, living things have helped us do things. They have carried loads, pulled carts, and helped us run our tools. They have helped carry our messages and grow our food.

Often this is called the "Age of Machines." It seems as if people no longer need other life-forms to help in their technology. Buses, cars, and trains have replaced the family horse. Soldiers today dash into battle in tanks instead of on galloping horses. Many Eskimos now use snowmobiles instead of dog teams. In the desert, jeeps are replacing camels. In much of the world today, plows are pulled by tractors instead of oxen and horses. Rather than riding on horseback, cowboys may use helicopters and jeeps to round up cattle.

What do all the sentences in this paragraph tell about?

You know that hammers and saws are tools. So are all the machines used for doing work.

But many of our tools still depend on life-forms to work. The coal, oil, and gas that run our tools all come from things that once were living. Even tools that use electricity may depend on life-forms. Much of our electricity is generated by burning coal or oil.

—Planet Earth
Houghton Mifflin

Building Skills

1. What is the topic of the second paragraph of the selection you just read?

   a. how machines replaced animals
   b. how horses help people
   c. how jeeps help people

2. What is the topic of the third paragraph of the selection?

   a. coal   b. animals   c. tools

SKILLS LESSON

Understanding the Main Idea
of a Paragraph and Using Details

Look at the pictures above. They are both about the same thing. Each picture tells you something about kittens. So *kittens* is the topic of both pictures.

The first picture shows you that the kittens are drinking milk. The second picture shows you that they are playing with yarn. Each picture tells you something different about the kittens. The thing each one tells about the kittens is the main idea of the picture. "The kittens are drinking milk" is the main idea of the first picture. What is the main idea of the second picture? "The kittens are playing with yarn" is the main idea.

Understanding the Main Idea of a Paragraph

Many of the paragraphs you read have main ideas. The **main idea** is the most important thing the paragraph says about the topic. The topic of the paragraph below is *dogs*. Can you find the main idea?

Dogs make good pets. Dogs are fun to play with. They like being around people. Dogs are also rather smart. They can learn many tricks.

What one thing does every sentence have in common? Do you see that each one says something about why dogs make good pets? "Dogs make good pets" is the main idea. Reread the paragraph. Notice that the main idea is stated in the first sentence.

Now read the following paragraph. Try to find the topic and the main idea.

Taking care of a dog is a big job. You have to feed a dog. You also have to be sure it gets exercise. If your dog gets sick, you have to take it to a doctor. And don't forget, you have to love your dog and play with it. That's part of the job, too.

This paragraph is also about dogs. But the main ideas of the two paragraphs about dogs are different. The first sentence in the paragraph above states the main idea: "Taking care of a dog is a big job."

The main idea is often stated in the first sentence of a paragraph. But sometimes it is stated in another sentence. You can find the main idea by following two steps. First look for the topic. Then ask yourself this question: "What is the most important thing the paragraph says about the topic?"

Read the following paragraph. Can you find the sentence that states the main idea?

The aardvark has a snout like a pig's. But its ears aren't like pigs' ears. They look like a rabbit's ears. The tail isn't like a rabbit's, however. It's long and heavy. The aardvark also has a funny, long tongue, which it uses to catch ants. Yes, the aardvark is a very strange-looking animal!

Did you see that every sentence tells you something about the aardvark? The topic of the paragraph is *the aardvark*. What is the most important thing the paragraph says about the topic? It's stated in the last sentence. "Yes, the aardvark is a very strange-looking animal" is the main idea.

Try This

Read the following paragraphs. Answer the questions that follow each paragraph. Use complete sentences to answer.

1. Dolphins can be taught to do many tricks. Some dolphins can blow horns. Some can leap through hoops. Others can jump out of the water to ring a bell.

   a. What is the topic of the paragraph?
   b. Which sentence states the main idea of the paragraph?

2. Aesop wrote a fable about a fox and some grapes. He also wrote one about a tortoise and a hare. He wrote a few about mice, too. Some of Aesop's other fables have lions, dogs, and even a grasshopper in them. In fact, most of Aesop's fables are about animals.

   a. What is the topic of the paragraph?
   b. Which sentence states the main idea of the paragraph?

Using Details

Read the paragraph about caring for a dog on page 288 again. The first sentence is very important. It states the main idea. But the other sentences are important, too. These sentences give details about the main idea. Each **detail** is a small piece of information. It tells you something about the main idea.

What details would you expect to find in a paragraph with this main idea?

Here are some ways to make your leg muscles strong.

You could expect to find details that tell you how to make leg muscles strong. Some of these ways might be by running, swimming, and jumping rope. The main idea gave you a clue to the kinds of details that might follow.

Now read the following paragraph. The main idea is stated in the first sentence. The other sentences give details that explain the main idea.

The camel is well suited to desert life. First, it has padded feet that help it walk through burning desert sands. Second, it has an extra stomach for storing water. So it can go a long time without becoming thirsty. Third, the shape of its eyes and nose makes it easy to keep out blowing sand. Fourth, it stores fat in its hump. On long trips, it can get energy by burning up this fat.

The main idea is "The camel is well suited to desert life." Four details explain the main idea: (1) padded feet, (2) extra stomach, (3) shape of eyes and nose, and (4) stored fat in hump. Each detail is a fact about the camel's body. All these facts are reasons why the camel is well suited to desert life.

Try This

Read the following paragraphs. Find the main idea in each one. What details explain the main idea?

1. People enjoy many different kinds of hobbies. Some people enjoy crafts like weaving or pottery-making. Other people like to grow flowers and plants. Others like to build things. Still others make a hobby of cooking or baking.
2. Many English names come from other languages. Rex and Patrick are both from Latin. Jean is French, as is Louise. Sarah, Thomas, and John all come from Hebrew.

VOCABULARY STUDY

Compound Words

"Wait until you see my circus act!"

"Sorry. We're not hiring new acts."

"But listen to this. I start out with a trained **jellyfish.** You know, the fish that looks like a blob of jelly. I feed the jellyfish a **blueberry.** . . . ."

"Does that berry have a kind of bluish-purple color?"

"That's the one. Anyway, the blueberry will give the jellyfish strength."

"Why does it have to be strong?"

"Why, to walk across the **tightrope**!"

"A jellyfish is going to walk across a thin rope that's stretched tight above the ground? That's the silliest thing I've ever heard!"

"You haven't heard the more important part. The jellyfish will work for free! So you only have to pay one of us."

"Correction. I don't have to pay either of you. The jellyfish gets the job, but I'm afraid you're out of luck."

"But we're a team! The jellyfish needs me!"

"Oh, that's right. I forgot. You'd better leave your box of blueberries."

Word Play

1. A compound word is made of two or more short words. Think of a sentence for each compound word in boldface.

2. With each short word below, make three compound words.

   any   ball   out   eye   under   berry   light

3. Imagine your own circus act and write a paragraph describing it. Use at least three compound words.

In many of the paragraphs in this selection, the main idea is stated in the first sentence. If it is not, see if another sentence states the main idea.

When you want to tell someone something, you can use more than words. Read how . . .

ACTIONS
SPEAK LOUDER THAN WORDS

by Kathlyn Gay

Without speaking a word, you can "say" all kinds of things by using your face and your body. The way you move your eyes and mouth can speak for you. You can "talk" by moving your hands and arms. The way you hold your head, walk, sit, or stand sends messages to the people looking at you. When you use different parts of your body, moving separately or together, you are "speaking" body language.

294

Using Body Language

Almost everyone begins very early in life to communicate with body language. In fact, each of us learns body language as well as spoken language. We don't even think about it. As children we learn that moving the head up and down means "yes." We learn that moving the head back and forth means "no."

You may not be aware of the body language you use. You may scratch your head to show you are puzzled. If you bend your index finger toward you, you may mean "Come here." Clap your hands or pat your lap and your dog might come running up to you. You may use your thumb and finger to form a circle. You're saying "Great!" or "Job well done!"

Have you ever had to give someone directions on how to get to a certain place? It's very hard to do this without using your hands and arms. Suppose you want to describe a monster movie. Could you do it without using body language? Try talking about an exciting football game or a carnival ride. As you talk, you'll use body language in dozens of ways.

Understanding Body Language

Sometimes body language helps to show what spoken words mean. A hug from someone who tells you, "I'm sorry you were hurt," helps you know that the person really means it. In the same way, a frown along with harsh words from someone makes it quite clear that the person is angry.

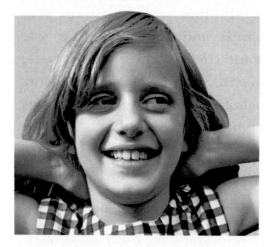

Sometimes the same body language sign can mean different things. You know that a police officer's raised hand means "Stop." But a raised hand in your classroom has a different meaning. There it tells the teacher you want to either ask something or answer a question.

A smile can also mean different things. Often a smile means a person is feeling happy. But some smiles mean "I'm embarrassed." Other smiles mean "I'm shy." A fake smile says, "I don't think that's so funny."

Body Language at Work

Lots of workers use body language to do their jobs. Have you ever watched a building being built? The workers use their arms and hands to send messages. Much of the time the noise of the machines makes it impossible for them to talk or yell loud enough to be heard.

Do you know anything about sports? You may know what it means in baseball when umpires jerk their thumbs over their shoulders. It means "You're out."

Often people who perform on TV know when to do something or say something by watching the stage manager's arm and hand signs. These signs let the performers know things like "Half a minute is left in the show."

Special Body Language

Have you ever watched deaf people use sign language? If so, you know how important arm and hand signs are to those who can't hear. In the sign talk of the deaf, quick hand and arm movements near different parts of the face have certain meanings. Unless you understand sign language, you cannot tell when one sign ends and another sign begins. They all seem to run together. Some deaf people "sing" songs in sign language or make up poems. They also tell funny stories and jokes in sign language.

Body Language in Your Life

To become aware of body language, watch the people around you. Watch your friends, family, classmates, and others. You can

297

also think about what you do with your own body. What movements do you make? How do these movements communicate to others?

Many times body language alone can tell you whether your friend is feeling silly, sad, tired, lonely, happy, angry, or worried. You know without thinking about it, because you have learned many things about your friend over a period of time.

Silent signs and signals are used every day, everywhere. You'll see them used in religious services, in sports, at family gatherings, and so on. Think about the ways each part of the body can talk so that you can tell whether you are correctly reading a silent message.

Understanding What You've Read

1. What is body language?
2. What examples of body language used in people's work are given in the selection?
3. Why is it important to understand body language?

Applying the Skills Lesson

1. The topic of the second paragraph on page 296 is a *smile*. What is the main idea?

   a. A smile can also mean different things.
   b. Often a smile means a person is feeling happy.

2. Read the paragraph on page 294 again.

   a. Which is the topic of the paragraph, *body language* or *giving directions*?
   b. Is the main idea stated in the first sentence or the last sentence?

At a special school in Washington, D.C., all the students are deaf or hard-of-hearing. There they learn to talk out loud as well as to "talk" with their hands and bodies.

My Mother Teaches Deaf Children

by Todd Baker *with* Donna Chitwood

My mother, Annette Baker, can talk with her hands! The children she teaches at Kendall School can't hear. So they have to be able to *see* what she says. She uses **sign language** as she talks to her class of deaf ten- and eleven-year-olds. In sign language, people move their hands and arms to "say" words.

Kendall School is a national demonstration school for deaf boys and girls. The teachers, many of whom are also deaf, work out methods of teaching the deaf. These methods are used to help deaf pupils all over the United States. The school has classes for deaf children up to the age of fifteen.

Kendall is on the grounds of Gallaudet [gal′ə·det′] College in Washington, D.C. Mom told me that Gallaudet is the only liberal arts college for deaf people in the world. Kendall School, a high school, a college, and a graduate school are all on the same

299

grounds. There are about 160 deaf boys and girls at Kendall. There's a total of about 1,500 students in all the schools at Gallaudet.

My family and I live in a townhouse in Columbia, Maryland. There are twenty-eight of us in my class in Columbia. But there are only five children in Mom's class. She says that's because she must watch all her pupils when she is teaching. She must make sure they are watching her, too.

I can look away from my teacher and still hear her. But Mom's pupils can't look away. They won't know what she is saying. Mom can't just say, "Class, pay attention." She has to turn the lights on and off a few times.

Mom's class starts each day with a hearing aid check. The students at Kendall wear hearing aids. That way they can learn to use any sounds that they are able to hear. That doesn't mean that they can understand what people are saying, even with their hearing aids on. But they might be able to hear enough sound to give them clues about speech or about what is going on around them.

Mom's class spends a lot of time studying language and reading. Some of the children at schools for the deaf come from homes where no one is able to talk to them. Most of us learn language by listening to and copying others' speech. But when people can't hear, they can't learn to talk or understand speech that way. Deaf children have to try to catch up on what they missed. They may have experienced many things before coming to school. But they don't know how to name these things. They never heard the words.

For example, they have seen the sun. They know that it rises and sets. But they may not know what to call it or how to explain what it does. Their teachers have to try to get the children to remember the things they have seen. Then they can use these things to help them build a system of language.

The American manual alphabet of the deaf.
Each position of the hand shows a different letter.

301

Mom's class also studies other school subjects. There is time for sports, too. Her classes are fun. She uses a lot of films and pictures of what she is talking about. Her class watches special shows on a color TV set. Kendall has a television studio. The twelve-, thirteen-, and fourteen-year-olds at Kendall produce their own news show once a week. Classes watch the show every Monday.

I have learned how to *finger-spell* just as Mom's pupils do. I use the American manual alphabet of the deaf. There are certain ways to hold your hand to make each letter. Sometimes there is no sign for a word. Sometimes people can't remember a sign. But they can always spell the word on their fingers.

If I tell my name to someone in my mother's class, I say it and spell it at the same time. Then the person can read my lips and see the letters, too. It's hard to tell just from lip reading whether a

person is saying *Baker* or *maker.* Lots of words in English look alike when you move your lips without speaking aloud.

Mom uses *Total Communication* in her classes. That means using speech and lip reading, sign language, and finger-spelling. It also means using gestures, pantomime, and "body language." Mom wants her pupils to use them all.

Mom has been working at Kendall for many years. She has also helped families to understand about being deaf, and she has worked with their deaf children at home. Mom says that involving the families of deaf children is very important.

Kendall helps hearing people learn to understand and talk to deaf children. Mom says that there is no reason why her deaf pupils can't do all the things hearing children do.

Understanding What You've Read

1. Why must deaf children always watch their teachers?
2. How do hearing people learn language?
3. What is finger-spelling?
4. Why does Annette Baker use Total Communication in her classes?

Applying the Skills Lesson

1. Read the second paragraph in the left-hand column on page 299. The main idea is given in the first sentence. What are the details?
2. Read the first paragraph in the left-hand column on this page. What details help you understand the main idea in the first sentence?

Notice how in some paragraphs in this selection the details follow the main idea. Notice how in other paragraphs the details come before the main idea.

One of the most beautiful ways to express an idea or feeling is through the language of music. One person who does this is singer . . .

VIKKI CARR

by Al Martínez

When Vikki Carr sings, her lovely voice quiets a noisy nightclub audience. When Florencia Bisenta de Casillas Martínez Cardona speaks, people listen. Being able to command attention through the beauty of her music or her ideas is important to Vikki and Florencia. But to be talented is not in itself enough. One must also help others. Vikki and Florencia have both these qualities. In fact, they're the same person.

Vikki Carr was born Florencia Bisenta de Casillas Martínez Cardona in 1942 in El Paso, Texas. She was the eldest of seven children. She remembers the hard times of her childhood.

The family moved to southern California when Florencia was a baby. There, she made her musical debut at the age of four. She sang a song in Latin for a holiday program.

In high school Florencia signed up for all the music courses she could take. She also took part in many music programs. On weekends she sang with local bands. Upon graduation, she joined Pepe Callahan's Mexican-Irish Band as a soloist. From there, she went on to become one of the world's leading female pop singers.

As a singer, Vikki Carr has been a very busy person. She is both a recording star and a TV star. Once she had two albums and two singles among the nation's top one hundred records—at the same time! She has also appeared on many TV variety shows. She has taped TV specials in London and Mexico City, as well as in the United States. She has performed before the President of the United States and before the Queen of England. She has starred in concerts around the world from Holland to Australia.

Yet even with all her fame, Vikki Carr makes it a point to remember that she is Florencia Bisenta de Casillas Martínez Cardona.

Vikki Carr surrounded by some of the winners of her scholarship award that helps outstanding Mexican-American students to attend college.

305

In 1971, Ms. Carr began what was to be a yearly scholarship award to help one outstanding Mexican-American to attend college. But instead of one student, she chose eight the first year. Then in 1972 she chose nineteen students. In 1973, she again chose nineteen students. She has also worked on behalf of the Office of Economic Opportunity, the March of Dimes, VISTA, and the Tuberculosis Association. Because of these things, Vikki Carr is as well known for helping others as she is for her beautiful voice.

Understanding What You've Read

1. How old was Vikki Carr when she made her musical debut?
2. What things did Vikki Carr do in high school and upon graduation that helped her to become a leading singer?
3. Name three ways in which Vikki Carr has shown that she cares about people.

Applying the Skills Lesson

1. Read the second paragraph on page 305. Which sentence states the main idea? How many sentences contain details that explain this main idea?
2. Do the details in the paragraph at the top of this page come before or after the main idea? What is the main idea?

TEXTBOOK STUDY

Finding Main Ideas and Details

Looking for main ideas can help you understand what you read in your textbooks. Thinking about details is important, too. The details help explain the main ideas. As you read the following selections, use the sidenotes to help you find main ideas and details.

Finding Main Ideas and Details in Science

The Pacific Ocean is vast. It washes against our west coast from northern Alaska to southern California. From our coast, the Pacific Ocean stretches very far west.

> **The topic of this paragraph is *the Pacific Ocean.* What is the main idea?**

In the Pacific Ocean are enormous numbers of living creatures, of many different kinds. Among the animals, there are the simplest animals, made up of just one cell. There are animals made up of many cells: sponges, worms, and relatives of the jellyfish, some of which look like beautiful flowers. There are also crabs and lobsters of many kinds, and clams and other animals with shells. (One kind of clam is larger than a child and may weigh 10 times as much.) There are octopuses and squids.

> **The topic of this paragraph is *life in the Pacific Ocean.* What is the main idea?**

> **This sentence contains details that explain the main idea. How many other sentences give details?**

Then there are the fish. There are thousands of kinds of fish in the Pacific Ocean. Among them is the salmon.

—*Concepts in Science:* Orange
Harcourt Brace Jovanovich

Building Skills

What is the topic of the last paragraph of the selection? What is the main idea?

Finding Main Ideas and Details in Mathematics

In math problems, details are very important. The details give you information you need to know in order to answer the problems.

Problem Solving

1. Ajax the Strongman can hold up three men. Their weights are 86 kilograms, 79 kilograms, and 68 kilograms. How much weight is Ajax holding?

You need the details given earlier in the problem in order to answer this question. What are they?

2. The white horse weighs 760 kilograms. The tiger weighs only 383 kilograms. How much more does the horse weigh?

What details do you need to know in order to answer this question?

3. The daring tightrope walker is 54 years old. He has been with the circus for 29 years. How old was he when he joined the circus?

Why is the present age of the tightrope walker important in this problem?

4. 785 people saw the afternoon show and 883 people saw the evening show. How many more people saw the evening show?

Read math problems carefully. Suppose you overlooked the word *more* in the last sentence. What mistake would you make in your answer?

5. In problem 4, how many people in all saw the show?

— *Elementary Mathematics*
D. C. Heath

Building Skills

Read problem 5 of the selection again. What details would you need to answer this problem?

SKILLS LESSON

Time Order

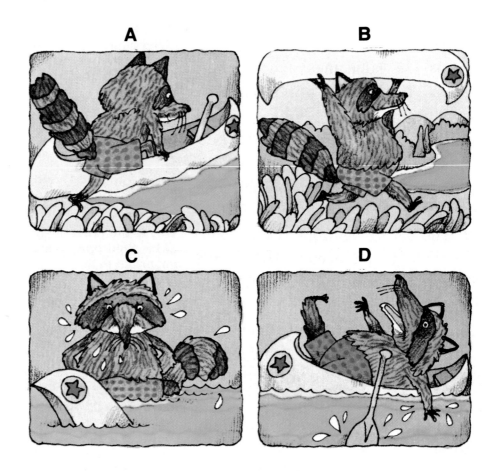

The four pictures above are from a comic strip. Do you notice anything wrong with the order? The pictures have been mixed up in **time order.** Time order is the order in which events happen.

Now look at the pictures again. How should they be arranged to show what happened first, what happened second, and so on? You can see that the order should be *B, A, D, C.*

Clues to Time Order: Time Words

Sometimes writers want to tell about events according to the order in which the events happened. They can use clue words to help the reader understand the order of events. Words such as *first, second,* and *third* can be time clues.

Read the following paragraph. Look for clues to help you follow time order.

We hired some workers to build our garage. The first day, they made the floor by pouring wet cement into wood frames that look like long, narrow boxes. The second day, they nailed thick boards together to make the walls and the roof. The third day, they put the siding on the walls, shingled the roof, and hung the big door.

In this paragraph, *first day, second day,* and *third day* are time clues. They help you understand when the events happened. Did the workers make the walls or the floor first? You can tell from the time clues in the paragraph that the workers made the floor first.

Many other words can also be used as time clues. Some of these words are *before, after, next, then,* and *finally.* Use them to help you follow time order as you read.

Try This

1. Read this paragraph about landing a jet plane. Use the clues to help you follow time order.

   Before beginning the landing, the pilot listens for directions from the control tower. Then the pilot brings the plane down into the correct path. After the plane touches down on the runway, the pilot puts the engines into reverse. This slows the plane down. Finally, the pilot taxis the plane to the unloading area.

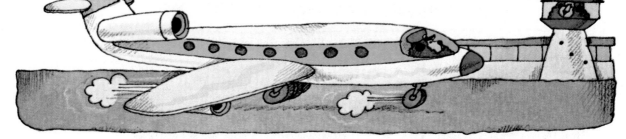

2. Listed below are the events you just read about. They are mixed up in time order. Put the sentences in the right time order to make a paragraph that tells about landing a jet.

   a. The pilot puts the engines into reverse.
   b. The plane touches down on the runway.
   c. The pilot listens for directions.
   d. The pilot taxis the plane to the unloading area.

Dates

One of the best clues to time is a date. You often find dates in your reading. Sometimes they are written as numerals: **1981.** Sometimes they are written as words: **Fourth of July, December, Tuesday.** A full date names a month, a day, and a year: **May 29, 1953.** What are the dates in the following sentences?

The year was 1969. On July 20, people landed on the moon for the first time.

The United States will be 300 years old on the Fourth of July, 2076.

The dates are 1969, July 20, and the Fourth of July, 2076.

Try This

1. Read the following paragraph about mail service in the early American colonies. Look for words and numerals that show the time order. Name those time clues.

   The first post office was set up in 1639 in Massachusetts. Three years later, in 1642, mail service was started between Boston and New York. Post riders made that trip once a month. Toward the end of the 1600's, there was weekly mail service from New Hampshire to Delaware. The riders stopped at Boston, New York, Philadelphia, and other important towns along the way.

2. Below is a list of some events from the paragraph about mail service. They are mixed up in time order. Put the events in the right time order.

   a. There was weekly mail service from New Hampshire to Delaware.
   b. The first post office was set up in Massachusetts.
   c. Mail service was started between Boston and New York.

VOCABULARY STUDY

Synonyms

Latoose Tralec here. Yes, I'm back with some more of my great paintings. I just know you'll like them. And here they are!

"The <u>Enormous</u> Eagle." This bird is quite large. In fact, it's huge. I wouldn't want to run into one. But it does make a fine painting.

"The Harsh Harmonica." You wonder how a little instrument like the harmonica can make rough or unpleasant sounds? Just listen to my friend play it. Or rather, don't!

"The <u>Sturdy</u> Stoplight." This strong, firm traffic signal is quite interesting, don't you think? What? You don't? Well, maybe you'd prefer my sculpture!?

Word Play

1. Synonyms are words that mean the same thing. Find two synonyms for each underlined word above.
2. Give at least one more synonym for each underlined word.

Could a man, on his own, invent a written language? One man who did was Sequoyah. He gave his people . . .

THE TALKING LEAVES

by Cynthia Benjamin

A man sat at his workbench under the shade of a large tree. The man had been a brave warrior. Now he was a fine painter and silversmith. But he was not drawing pictures at his workbench. He was not making beautiful silver buckles. He was carving strange signs on a piece of bark.

The sun rose higher. Still the man worked. His friends came to watch him. They stood over him and looked at the signs he made. They shook their heads and moved away.

316

"He is wasting his time making those signs," they said. "He would do better to make silver buckles."

But the man paid no attention. He kept working under the shade of the large tree. The man's name was Sequoyah.

Sequoyah and His People

Sequoyah was a Cherokee. The Cherokees were one of the great Indian nations that lived in North America. They farmed the land that is now Tennessee, Alabama, and Georgia. They raised corn and wheat on their farms, and kept pigs and cattle.

Cherokee parents taught their children all they had learned about farming. In this way the Cherokees could pass their knowledge on to their grandchildren. But the Cherokees did not have a way to write down their thoughts.

Sequoyah called some pages of writing he had seen "talking leaves" because the paper was thin as a leaf. He knew that people could "talk" to each other with written words.

Sequoyah never learned to speak, read, or write English— the language of the words on these "talking leaves." Yet he knew their great power.

"I think that a word is like a wild animal," he said to his friends. "Many people have learned to catch these animals, to tame them, and to put them on paper. Soon the Cherokees will be able to do the same thing."

In 1809, Sequoyah set out to find a written language for his people. He was a man who lived for a dream.

In time, Sequoyah no longer made silver belt buckles or took care of his farm. He spent his days at his workbench, making the signs that one day would be read by other Cherokees. He worked all day and far into the night, making marks with pebbles, with charcoal, and with sticks.

A Divided Nation

Within a few years, much of the Cherokee land had been taken away through treaties. After Sequoyah's farm was taken away, he and his family went further West. Soon the Cherokee nation was divided. Half remained in the East. The rest of the Cherokees went West. More than ever before, they needed a written language to bring them together.

At his new home in what is now Arkansas, Sequoyah built

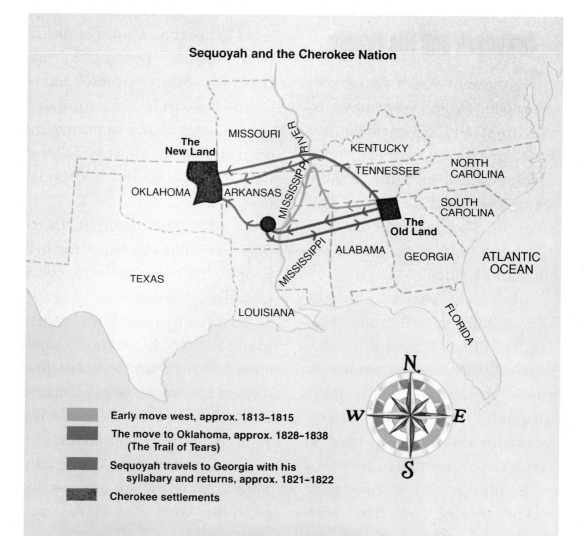

Sequoyah and the Cherokee Nation

MISSOURI

The New Land

OKLAHOMA ARKANSAS

MISSISSIPPI RIVER

KENTUCKY

TENNESSEE

NORTH CAROLINA

SOUTH CAROLINA

The Old Land

MISSISSIPPI

ALABAMA GEORGIA

ATLANTIC OCEAN

TEXAS

LOUISIANA

FLORIDA

N · W · E · S

Early move west, approx. 1813–1815

The move to Oklahoma, approx. 1828–1838 (The Trail of Tears)

Sequoyah travels to Georgia with his syllabary and returns, approx. 1821–1822

Cherokee settlements

a hut where he could work on his writing. For years he had been making over a thousand different signs or pictures. Each picture stood for a different word in the Cherokee language. At first he had drawn pictures of birds and wild animals. Later he had made up his own signs for the different Cherokee words.

But there were so many words! Sequoyah wondered how anyone could remember all the different signs he would have to make up. But he worked on.

Sequoyah Creates a Syllabary

Quite often Sequoyah's six-year-old daughter, Ahyoka [ä·yō′kə], visited the hut to watch her father work. She talked to him for many hours. She told him all the news from the village.

One afternoon, Sequoyah listened more carefully to his daughter. Suddenly he laughed out loud. After twelve long years, in 1821, he had found the answer to his problem. He asked Ahyoka to talk more and more.

Listening to her talk, Sequoyah found that the Cherokee language was made up of different combinations of sounds. These combinations of sounds are called **syllables.** Sequoyah decided to make up one sign for each syllable.

Instead of a language with over one thousand signs, Sequoyah found he could make all the Cherokee words by using just eighty-six signs. Each of these signs stood for one syllable. These syllables were then arranged in different combinations to make new words. To make these different signs for the syllables, Sequoyah took the letters that he had seen on the "talking leaves." For example, the letter *k* stood for the Cherokee syllable *tso*. The letter *z* stood for the syllable *no*.

There were not enough letters for all the signs that

Sequoyah needed. So he set to work again. He made up more signs. He also used signs from the Greek and Hebrew alphabets. Soon Sequoyah had the eighty-six different signs that he needed.

The Big Test

At last it was time for Sequoyah's work to be put to a test. The Cherokee chiefs stood in a circle. They spoke to Sequoyah, and he carefully copied down their words on paper. Then Sequoyah's young daughter was brought to her father. Sequoyah had already taught her the different signs. Now he showed her the words he had written.

Everyone was very still. They all watched as Ahyoka read back the signs to her father. The chiefs shook their heads. They could not believe what they heard. They knew the young girl could not possibly have heard what they had told her father to write down.

The chiefs decided to test her again. Sequoyah wrote down more signs for his daughter to read. Again, Ahyoka read her father's message.

It was true! Sequoyah had really developed a written language for his people.

A Nation Joined Again

The chiefs all wanted to learn how to read the signs. In just a few days, they were all reading the Cherokee language.

Within a few months, everyone was learning to read and write. They learned in the open fields or under the shade of a tree or in log cabins. Some Cherokees learned while they cared for their farms. Others studied in their free time. Mothers and fathers taught their children. Sometimes children even taught their grandparents.

The Cherokees in Arkansas felt closer together than ever. Now they wanted their people

who were still in the East to learn their written language.

The chiefs wrote a message. Sequoyah set out with it on a long journey back to Georgia.

After Sequoyah had taught the Cherokees in the East to read and write, he went back to Arkansas. For the first time, the Cherokees in the West could write to their families in the East. And their families in the East could answer them. The Cherokees could never be divided again.

In 1828, the first Cherokee newspaper, the *Cherokee Phoenix*, was printed. Later, the laws of the Cherokee people were also written down.

It was around this time that Sequoyah and many other

Cherokees moved to what is now Oklahoma. Wherever he went, Sequoyah was loved and honored.

Today there is a small log cabin in Oklahoma that has become a monument. It is a monument to the wise man who lived for a dream and saw his dream come true. The great sequoia tree in California has been named for this man. He will never be forgotten by his people.

Understanding What You've Read

1. Why did Sequoyah call pages of writing "talking leaves"?
2. What did Ahyoka do that surprised the chiefs?
3. Why was Sequoyah's invention useful to the Cherokees?

Applying the Skills Lesson

Some events from the selection are listed below. They are mixed up in time order. Put them in the right time order. If you need help, look back to the selection for time words and dates. They are the time clues.

1. Sequoyah created a written language for the Cherokees.
2. Sequoyah went back to the East with a written message for the Cherokees there.
3. The first Cherokee newspaper was printed.
4. Sequoyah began working to develop a written language for the Cherokees.

The author of this selection relates events in her life that led up to her becoming a writer. Look for words that help you understand the time order.

Stories are a special form of communication. What makes some people want to communicate in this special way? Find out in . . .

A STORYTELLER'S STORY

by Jane Yolen

Why I Became a Writer

To some people, writing and writers are a mystery. That was never true for me. I come from a family of writers. My mother wrote short stories and crossword puzzles. My father wrote for a newspaper. He was president of the Overseas Press Club.

Writing was as much a part of my life as breathing. Is it any wonder that I always wanted to be a writer? It was a plan that lasted through dreams of dancing, horseback riding, and becoming a lawyer. To write for a newspaper, I thought, would be the best thing of all.

I saw writing as an activity with many rewards: good friends, a good living, and a way of getting the world to listen to my ideas. But I didn't know until later that writing is also hard work.

How I Began Writing

I wrote and wrote. In grade school, I wrote my first play with music. All the actors played vegetables. I was the chief carrot. The final big number was a salad!

My brother is about four years younger than I. When we were young, we put out two issues of the *Yolen Gazette*. I wrote it and drew the pictures for it. He gave me the news. That meant he reported back all interesting things going on in our apartment building. We sold copies at ten cents a paper. When we had made almost a dollar each, we quit. Or rather, my mother, who typed it and made the copies, quit.

In high school, I wrote for the school newspaper. In college, I wrote both newspaper stories and poems.

Illustration (page 324) by David Palladini from *The Girl Who Cried Flowers and Other Tales* by Jane Yolen.

I thought about writing for a newspaper when I grew up. Or maybe I would write poems. In all that time, I never thought about telling stories for a living.

Something happened that led me to story-writing. My father was writing a book about kites. I was his assistant. He had written movies, plays, and newspaper and magazine stories. Yet he had never written a book before. He wanted to write about kites because he was once the World Kite Flying Champion. He called his book the *Young Sportsman's Guide to Kite Flying.*

As I worked on the book with him, I tried to write about kites in a new and exciting way. I made things that happened long ago in China and Egypt sound as if they were happening right now. I took strange old tales and tried to make clear what was real — and not real — about them. I wrote stories.

Suddenly I was in love: with fiction, with story-telling, with tales of adventure.

I did not become well known from my father's book. But I learned some very important things from working on it. I learned that writing is work — hard work. Words I had written often had to be changed. Perhaps a sentence could be clearer. Perhaps several sentences could fit together better. Sometimes I had to write things over several times. But to me, writing was still the most wonderful work in the world.

Writing My Own Books

At last I knew it was time for me to start writing books on my own. How old was I then? Just twenty-one. I had been writing all my life. Yet I was just starting.

I began with what I knew best. I based my writing on things that had really happened. But I tried to write about them the way a storyteller writes. My goal was to make hard, cold facts come alive. My first book, *Pirates in Petticoats*, was about women pirates. I went to the library and found a lot of facts about them. Then I used those facts as the seeds of my story.

Soon I began to write fantasy and fairy tales. Here I could mix my love of fiction and my sense of poetry. Every once in a while, I still write true stories. The newspaper reporter in me does not want to let go. Nevertheless, children seem to love my fairy tales best.

Where My Stories Come From

My fairy tale stories sound like old folk tales. However, I make them up out of my head—and my heart. They are really about my life.

My stories mix many things I have known. My grandfather was a storyteller. His tales came from a single source: the Russian-Jewish tradition. I did not grow up with that tradition. I heard English nursery rhymes as a child. And American folk tales and fairy

Illustrations (pages 326 and 327) by Leonard Vosburgh from *Pirates in Petticoats* by Jane Yolen.

327

Illustration above by David Palladini from *The Girl Who Cried Flowers and Other Tales* by Jane Yolen.

tales from other countries — Russia, China, Hungary, Egypt, Ireland, Spain — kept me busy for hours. I heard the stories from *A Thousand and One Arabian Nights*. I read about the Greek and Roman gods and goddesses. I learned about King Arthur and his knights. I watched Mickey Mouse on the first TV set in our neighborhood. All these things later influenced my stories.

My grandfather and I had different sources for our stories. Yet many things about our stories are the same. We both knew that tales are a way to explain things. All storytellers know this. My grandfather used his stories as long-ago rabbis did, to explain a point of law or to teach something. I use my tales to explain myself.

What Stories Can Do

In stories, people often find characters who are like themselves. The way a character handles a problem may give the readers ideas about how to handle their own problems.

Perhaps one of my tales may touch some hidden part of you. It may give you an answer to a question you never had to ask. It may make you laugh if it is a funny story. It may touch your heart. However it touches you, it makes us partners—you and me. It is my gift to you. It is a part of me that you will own—always.

Understanding What You've Read

1. What are some of the sources of Jane Yolen's ideas?
2. Why do you think Jane Yolen wanted to become a writer?
3. What does Jane Yolen say stories do for some people?

Applying the Skills Lesson

Read the first three paragraphs under the heading "How I Began Writing" on page 325. Then put the following events in the right time order.

1. Jane wrote for the high school newspaper.
2. Jane wrote her first play with music.
3. Jane wrote newspaper stories and poems in college.
4. Jane and her brother wrote the *Yolen Gazette*.

TEXTBOOK STUDY

Recognizing Time Clues

Time order is important in your school reading. You have learned to watch for words and dates that tell time order. In the following selections, look for time clues to understand the order of events. Use the sidenotes to help you.

Recognizing Time Clues in Social Studies

Another way to say *Until the 1850's* is "Before 1850." What was travel between California and New York like before 1850?

Travel has changed. Until the 1850's the fastest way to go from New York to California was by ship. People had to sail all the way around South America to get there. That trip took almost three months. Today you can make the trip by plane in about five hours.

What word in this sentence is a time clue?

Ships were fastest for long journeys because railroad trains made only short trips. Good roads were unknown in most parts of the country. But after 1850, the railroads began to grow rapidly. They soon became the fastest and best way to get from one place to another and to move goods.

Soon is a time clue. But it is not exact, like a date. You cannot tell the exact year that railroads became the best way to travel.

What happened in 1869?

In 1869, the first railroad line across the continent was finished. Then other **transcontinental** lines were built. It no longer took three months to go from New York to California. It took only a little more than a week.

Around 1900, the first "horseless carriages" began to appear on our city streets. Those first automobiles were noisy and slow. They often broke down. At first, few people thought the auto would ever take the place of the horse.

This clue refers to the time mentioned in the first sentence—around 1900.

The Wright Brothers flew their first plane in 1903. Most people paid little attention. Surely, they thought, a machine that flew through the air could never be a safe way to travel.

When did the Wright Brothers fly their first plane?

Now cars move on **superhighways** at high speeds. Airplanes fly along at 600 miles (960 km) an hour. Yet only seventy-five years ago, people were afraid of a "horseless carriage." It could only go 20 miles (32 km) an hour. It's hard to believe!

Seventy-five years ago refers to the time clue two paragraphs back— around 1900.

—*People and Ideas*
Silver Burdett

Building Skills

The list of events below are from the selection you have just read. Put the events in the right time order. Look back at the dates in the selection if you need help.

1. The first railroad line across the continent was finished.
2. The first "horseless carriages" began to appear on our city streets.
3. The fastest way to go from California to New York was by ship.
4. The Wright Brothers flew their first airplane.

Recognizing Time Clues in Language Arts

The following selection tells about a famous author, Henry David Thoreau. Use the sidenotes to help you understand the time order. The sidenotes may also help you with some hard words.

Thoreau lived during the nineteenth century. At this time, our country was entering the Machine Age. Many people believed that machines would bring progress and a better way of life. But others, like Thoreau, thought that industrialism would cause people to lose touch with nature.

A *century* means 100 years. The *nineteenth century* means 1801–1900. What happened during the time 1801–1900?

The context helps you with this word. Look for clues in the sentences above. What is *industrialism*?

In 1845, Thoreau left society to live alone by Walden Pond. He built a house for himself, grew his own vegetables, hunted, and fished. He lived like a hermit for two years to prove that a person could still live off the land without machines. You can read his ideas in his book called *Walden*.

When you say this word you may know it. The context also helps you. What is a *hermit*?

How long did Thoreau live alone? Look for the time clue.

— *Language for Daily Use:* Orange
Harcourt Brace Jovanovich

Building Skills

Use the time clues in the selection and the sidenotes to help you decide if the following statements are true or false.

1. The Machine Age began around 1900.
2. The year 1845 is part of the nineteenth century.
3. Our country began entering the Machine Age before Thoreau went to live by Walden Pond.

Following Directions

It was easy. I just followed the directions.

The girl in the picture was able to build the model sailboat by following the written directions. Directions can help *you* to make something, too. They can also help you to do many other things. What are some of those things?

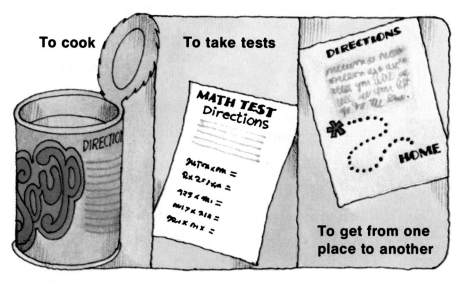

To cook

To take tests

To get from one place to another

When you want to follow a set of directions, it is important to first read carefully through *all* the directions. This will help you to get a general idea of what you will be doing. It will help prevent you from falling into a trap of doing too much, too little, or the wrong thing.

Read and follow the directions below. Don't get caught in a trap!

1. Take out a piece of paper.
2. Write your name on the paper.
3. Under your name, print the names of two people in your classroom.
4. Do not do directions 1–3.

Did you get caught? If you even took out a piece of paper then you were caught. You can see how reading *all* the directions first is important!

Following Directions to Make Something

In following directions, be sure you pay attention to details. It is important not to leave out any steps. It's also important to do each step in the right order.

Some directions that tell how to make things are numbered and some are not. Often, directions also use time words to help you know the right order. Pay attention to such time words as *first, next, then, before, after,* and *until.*

The following set of directions tells how to make a papier-mâché head. The sidenotes will help you understand some of the information that directions give you.

How to Make a Papier-Mâché Head

Many directions begin with a list of materials you'll need. Read the directions through. You will find out how much water and flour you'll need. You will also find you need a mixing bowl.

This sentence gives more information about how much water to add.

One step was not included in these directions. The writer did not say "Blow up the balloon." If you had read the directions through first, you would know that you must do this. Which step makes it clear that the balloon should have been blown up?

Materials:

1 large balloon
flour
water
newspapers
paint

1. Tear the newspaper into long, narrow strips. Make the strips about five centimeters wide by thirty centimeters long.
2. Make the paste. Put one half cup of flour into a large mixing bowl. Add water and stir. Use enough water so that the paste feels like mud.
3. Soak a strip of newspaper in the paste. Then place the strip on the balloon. Smooth the paper out so that there are no air bubbles. Continue soaking strips, covering the balloon, and smoothing the strips until there are about eight layers covering the entire balloon.

4. When the layers are dry, poke a pin through the layers in order to pop the balloon. The head will keep its shape only if the layers are dry enough.

5. Now you are ready to paint the head.

Notice that you are not given directions for painting the head. Does the picture give you an idea of what to do?

Try This

1. Read the directions below and follow them. Then answer the question that follows.

Number Fun

How old are you? Write your age on a piece of paper and multiply it by 3. Add 6 to that number. Divide your answer by 3. Subtract 2. What number is left? It should be your age.

If you did not come out with the right answer, go back over the directions. What detail did you miss?

2. Read paragraph *a* below. Then read what happened and answer the question that follows. Do the same thing with paragraph *b*.

a. Empty a package of lime gelatin into a bowl. Add one cup of boiling water and stir until dissolved. Then add one cup of cold water and stir again. Chill the mixture for an hour, or until the gelatin begins to get firm. Stir in one half cup of orange pieces. Chill again until the salad is firm.

Hilda put the gelatin and the hot and cold water into a bowl. Then she added the oranges and put the bowl in the refrigerator for an hour. When she took it out, the oranges were in a layer on the bottom. What detail had Hilda missed?

b. Walk east from Indian Rock to Log Bridge. Cross the bridge. Sight the fire tower on Thunderbird Mountain directly to the south. Walk south five kilometers to the edge of Pine Meadow. At the south edge of the meadow is a stone marker. Smuggler's Cave is two hundred meters south of the marker.

Jean's patrol walked east to Log Bridge, then sighted a fire tower to the south. They walked five kilometers south and found themselves at the edge of Fern Swamp. What detail did they miss in the directions?

VOCABULARY STUDY

Getting Meaning from Context Clues

Are you tired, bored, or a little worn out? Then Rutherford's Riddles are for you. You can have some fun by using context clues to help you guess the answers.

I can hold a number of things
within my see-through tank.
I'm filled with water, fish, and
    plants
found near a riverbank.
What am I?

an aquarium

I am a message of a secret kind.
When I'm opened, you don't know
    what you'll find.
It sometimes takes many letters
    to make me.
In order to get me to work, you
    must break me.
What am I?

a code

I can tell you many things
And never make a sound.
When I use my arms and hands
and move them all around,
I can make you laugh and cry
And let my feelings show.
I don't use sounds,
I don't use words—
Just watch and you will know.
What am I?

a pantomime

Word Play

1. Give a definition for the words *aquarium, code,* and *pantomime,* using the context clues in the riddles above.

2. Write a riddle and ask a friend to solve it later.

Look for the important details as you follow the directions. The details will help you to have fun in a secret way.

Can you read this message? 9 8–1–22–5 1 19–5–3–18–5–20. You can if you know the code that was used to write it. Learn this code and others in . . .

SECRET MESSAGES

by Herbert S. Zim

People have been writing secret messages for about 4,000 years. They have done it in many ways. Some have used invisible ink. Some have added words to messages to mix them up.

Some people have used **codes** or **ciphers** to hide their secrets. In a code, one letter, number, word, or sign stands for a whole word or group of words. In a cipher, one letter, number, or sign stands for a letter in the alphabet.

Here is one code.

FATHER EATING APPLES	
CODE	**MEANING**
APPLES	PLEASE MEET ON ARRIVAL
EATING	WILL LEAVE BY FIRST PLANE
FATHER	GENERAL OF THE AIR FORCES

In this code, one word stands for a group of words. FATHER EATING APPLES would have a very different meaning to someone who knew it was in code and who had the book that told what each word means. It would mean: GENERAL OF THE AIR FORCES WILL LEAVE BY FIRST PLANE PLEASE MEET ON ARRIVAL.

Here is another code.

In this example, each sign stands for one letter in the alphabet. Once you know what each sign stands for, you can read the message.

A ▭	H △	N ◯	T
B ⊡	I ⟁	O ⊖	U ⯊
C ⬒	J ⟁	P ⊘	V ⬓
D ⊟	K ▽	Q ⊕	W
E ⊞	L ▽	R ⊙	X ✕
F ◿	M ▽	S |	Y ⊔
G ◺			Z ⊔

You can see the difference between the two codes. The second is really a cipher. However, most people talk about codes when they really do mean ciphers.

That is all right. The word *code* is not as correct, but it is used more often. It will be used here also.

A Number Code

An easy code to learn and use is a number code. It uses **numerals** for letters.

A 1	H 8	N 14	T 20
B 2	I 9	O 15	U 21
C 3	J 10	P 16	V 22
D 4	K 11	Q 17	W 23
E 5	L 12	R 18	X 24
F 6	M 13	S 19	Y 25
G 7			Z 26

The nice thing about this code is that you can make a copy of it at any time. If you don't remember that **O** is **15** and **W** is **23,** write down the alphabet. Then number the letters from **1** to **26.** In using this code, put a dash between numerals. This way a **21** and a **2–1** clearly mean two different things. Using this number code, can you read this message?

8–1–22–5   1   8–1–16–16–25   2–9–18–20–8–4–1–25

When you *read* a message in code, you are **decoding** the message. When you *write* a message in code, you are **encoding** the message.

Writing a secret message can be fun. But you must take enough time to do it correctly. Here are a few things you need to know when you start. The best paper to use is ruled paper. You should have some sharp pencils. When you write, use only capital letters. Print each one large and clear. Use all the space you need. Three or four words to a line are enough.

To encode a message, first copy it on your paper. Use capital letters. If you need more than one line, leave a space of four lines before you go on. When you have finished writing the message, go back to the beginning. Write each code numeral directly under each letter in the message.

Here is how a short message might be encoded.

```
M E E T        M E      A T      T H E
13-5-5-20      13-5     1-20     20-8-5



D R I N K I N G        F O U N T A I N      A T       T W O
4-18-9-14-11-9-14-7    6-15-21-14-20-1-9-14  1-20      20-23-15
```

After you are finished, write the coded message on another piece of paper. Make sure you have everything correct. Then throw away your worksheet.

A Position Code

Anyone can make up a code using the alphabet. But the code must be easy to remember if it is to be useful.

In one kind of code, it is the position of letters that counts. Letters and dots are put in certain places in diagrams.

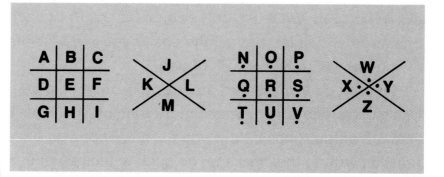

In the position code above, **A** is ⌟ , **B** is ⊔ , **C** is ⌞ . The shape of the lines around each letter in the diagram is the key. So ＞ is **K**, ⋁ is **J**, ＜ is **L**.

You can see that the shapes of the lines for the last half of the alphabet are the same as for the first half. So dots are added to make them different. ⌟ is **A**, but ⌣ is **N**. ⊔ is **B**, but ⊡ is **O**, and so on. Unless a person knew the diagrams, it would be very hard for her or him to guess the code.

Use the diagrams above. Can you decode this message?

⌐⌐⌐⌞ ⊔⊡⊐⊐ ⌐⌞ ⌐⌟⊡⊐

There are many other kinds of codes. You may have seen some. You may have heard some. Knowing about a code is one thing. Knowing a code is quite something else. It means practice, lots of it. But the practice can be fun. All you have to do is use the code. And that is what codes are for.

After you have encoded and decoded many messages, you will be able to use the code quickly and with very few mistakes.

Understanding What You've Read

1. Name three ways people have written secret messages to each other.
2. What is the difference between encoding and decoding a message?
3. Why would it be hard for someone to guess the position code?

Applying the Skills Lesson

1. Use the number code on page 342. Decode the message in the sentences that lead into the title of the selection on page 340.
2. Follow the directions in the first and second paragraphs on page 343. Encode the message "CALL ME AT HOME." Use any one of the codes given in the selection.
3. When is a pig like ink? Decode the answer:

   23–8–5–14   25–15–21   16–21–20   9–20   9–14
   1   16–5–14.

This selection has several experiments using sound. You will need to follow directions to be able to do the experiments. Don't miss any important details!

When people talk, you hear the sounds they make. You also hear many other sounds around you. Have you ever thought about . . .

What Makes Sound?

by John M. Scott

When you hear the buzz of a bee, do you ever wonder how it makes that sound?

It does it by moving its wings back and forth. This moving back and forth is called **vibrating.** The vibrating wings of the insect push the air and make it move.

The beginning of all sound is something that vibrates, or moves back and forth. When you pound a drum, or ring a bell, you are making things move back and forth. Objects that move back and forth fast enough make sound.

When you talk, your tongue, vocal cords, and lips move back and forth. They cause the air to move. They even make your head rattle and shake. To prove it, place your hand firmly on top of your head. Then talk loudly, or sing. You will feel your head shake, or vibrate.

Vibrations That You Make

You can feel the vibrations set up in the air when you talk by using an empty coffee can or oatmeal box.

Hold the empty can or box so that your finger tips are touching the bottom or closed end of it. Place the open end of the can or box next to your mouth. Now talk into it. As the air carrying your sounds hits the bottom of the can

or box, it will vibrate. You will feel these vibrations with your finger tips.

You can find out that things which vibrate make sound by making your own simple string telephone.

Get two empty coffee cans. Ask a grown-up to punch a hole through the bottom of each can with a small nail and a hammer. Get a piece of heavy string or cord

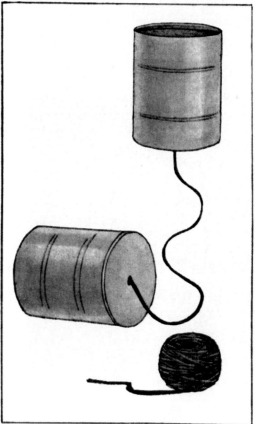

about fifteen feet long. Push one end of the string through the hole in one of the cans. Tie a big knot at the end of the string so it can't pull out. Push the free end of the string through the hole in the other can. Knot it in the same way.

Ask your friend to pick up one can by the rim. Have your friend walk away from you until the string is pulled tight. Hold your coffee can. Speak into it while your friend holds the coffee can next to his or her ear.

When you talk, the sound of your voice makes the bottom of the can vibrate. This motion is passed on to the string, which, in turn, makes the listening can move back and forth. The vibrating metal of the listening can sets air into motion so that your friend hears your voice.

Vibrations That You Hear

Now think about the bee again. This insect can make sounds by moving its wings back and forth. Perhaps you may wonder why you can't make sounds by moving *your* arms back and forth.

To find out why, get a thin wooden or plastic ruler. Place one hand firmly on one end of the ruler against the top of a table. Let most of the ruler stick out over the edge of the table. With your other hand, hit the free end

of the ruler. Most likely you will see the free end moving back and forth. And you will hear it.

Now move more of the ruler back onto the top of the table. Make sure the end sticking out over the edge is shorter.

Hit the free end of the ruler again. This time you may be able to see it move a little, and also hear it. The sound you hear will be higher, or have a higher **frequency.** The frequency is the number of times in one second that an object moves back and forth. (To find out how long a second is, you will need a watch or a clock with a second hand.)

The human ear cannot hear anything that vibrates less than about twenty times in one second. You just cannot move your arms back and forth faster than twenty times a second. Now you know why you can't hear your arms when they move!

Vibrations All Around You

Much of your learning and your joy in life will come to you by sound. You will hear the voices of those you love. You will also listen to songs and shows on radio and TV. On a beautiful summer day you may stand by a big fountain in a park. You can listen with joy as the big, sparkling drops of water splash into pools.

Understanding What You've Read

1. What is a vibration?
2. Suppose a person moves his or her arms back and forth the way a bee moves its wings. Why won't the person's arms make buzzing sounds?
3. What are some of the vibrations that are all around you?

Applying the Skills Lesson

The last paragraph in the right-hand column on page 348 and the first paragraph in the left-hand column on page 349 give directions for making and using a string telephone. What are the five things you need to make the telephone? What are the steps described for making the telephone?

Following Directions

In many of your textbooks, directions are given to make something, to study something, or to do an experiment. The following selections have directions to do or make something. The sidenotes in the first selection will help you understand the important details.

Following Directions in Science

Something to Do

All the details are important here. Only one little detail isn't as important as the others—the "four or five" in the first sentence. You could choose any number of sounds.

With several classmates, think of four or five common sounds. They should be sounds that everyone has heard many times. Tape-record your sounds. Do this where the rest of your class cannot hear you.

Play your recording for the class. Ask them to try to identify the recorded sounds.

Be careful to make recordings that do not change the sounds. Each recording should sound just as it does in real life.

If you didn't follow these details, what might happen when you played the sounds?

Which sound was easiest for the class to identify? Which was hardest? Why?

Questions are often asked after you do something. They are really the main idea of the whole experiment.

TO THINK ABOUT

If you were blindfolded, do you think you could identify a sound that you never heard before? Why?

— Elementary School Science
Addison-Wesley

Building Skills

1. Suppose you didn't pay attention to the last detail in the first paragraph, and the class heard you recording the sounds. Why wouldn't the experiment work as well?

2. How do the pictures help explain the details in the first paragraph?

Following Directions in Language Arts

There are no sidenotes for this selection. Read it carefully. Then answer the questions that follow.

Making Puppets

There are many kinds of puppets. Perhaps you have already made some. If not, here is one kind that is easy to make.

Clothespin Puppets

1. Paint faces on the heads of wooden clothespins.

2. Make arms by attaching wire or pipe cleaners to the body. Cover with cloth or twisted paper. Bend the arms in the position you want.

3. Make clothes from paper, cardboard, aluminum foil, or heavy cloth. Attach to clothespins with glue or tape or by sewing.

4. Paste on wool or colored string for hair.

5. Make the puppets move by holding them at the bottom by another clothespin.

Use your imagination in designing puppets' faces and clothes. Just make certain your puppets are sturdy.

— *Language for Daily Use:* Orange
Harcourt Brace Jovanovich

Building Skills

1. Why do you think it might be a good idea to read the whole selection through before you start to make your puppets?

2. What choices do the directions offer you in step 3?

3. If you read direction 5 before direction 1, would it make sense? Why or why not?

4. What important detail is told in the last sentence of the selection?

Books About Communicating

Communication by Irving and Ruth Adler. John Day, 1967. The history of communication is the subject of this book. It even includes a chapter on communication with other worlds.

Understanding Body Talk by Thomas Aylesworth. Franklin Watts, 1979. This book tells you the meaning of body motions and expressions on faces.

Before You Came This Way by Byrd Baylor. Dutton, 1969. Native Americans in the Southwest communicated with rock pictures thousands of years ago. This book tells about those prehistoric pictures.

Science Experiments with Sound by Harry Sootin. Norton, 1964. Fifty experiments help you understand the basic nature of sound.

Windows on the World by Anne Terry White and Gerald S. Lietz, M.D. Garrard, 1965. This book explains how our senses bring us important information about the world.

Anna's Silent World by Bernard Wolf. Lippincott, 1977. Photographs tell most of this story about the active life of Anna, a young deaf girl.

Codes and Mystery Messages by Cameron Yerian. Childrens, 1975. This fun book tells how to create different kinds of codes, such as hobo signs, touch talking, flag signals, and so forth.

Part 6

Fresh Starts

UNDERSTANDING AND APPRECIATING LITERATURE

Characterization

Barney Fisk is the kindest boy in Duckville.

The picture above tells you about a character named Barney Fisk. Characters are the people or animals in stories or cartoons. How do you find out what a character is like? In the picture above, you learn about Barney in three different ways.

One way you learn about Barney is from the cartoonist's words at the bottom of the picture. What does the cartoonist's description tell you about Barney? You learn that he is the kindest boy in Duckville.

A second way you learn about Barney is from other characters. One character can tell you about another character. What does the horse in the picture say about Barney? It tells you he is always being kind.

A third way you learn about Barney is by his actions. What is Barney doing? He is helping ducks. Barney is being kind. Now you know that Barney is a kind character.

Understanding Characterization

Characters in a story may be people, animals, or other things. You learn what characters are like in three important ways.

One way you learn about a character is through the author's description. Read the paragraph below. Look for what the author tells you about Ramón.

In a small village far away, there lived a generous boy named Ramón. Ramón always thought about others. Whatever Ramón had, he shared with the children.

What is Ramón like? The author describes Ramón as "generous" and tells you that he shares with the children. You learn what Ramón is like from the author's description.

The second way you learn about a character is from what other characters say. Read the conversation on page 360. Look for what Ramón's friends say about him.

"Do you know what Ramón did this afternoon?" asked Tommy. "He took me to the library!"

"Really?" said Maria. "But Ramón had a baseball game this afternoon. I know Ramón is generous, but that's really nice."

What does Tommy say about Ramón? He tells you that Ramón took him to the library. What does Maria say about Ramón? She tells you Ramón is generous. You learn about Ramón from what other characters say.

The third way you learn about a character is from what the character does and says. Read the paragraph below. What Ramón does and says tells you what he is like.

Ramón broke his only peach in half. "Here you are," he said as he handed a piece to Tommy. "We'll share."

The author doesn't say that Ramón is generous. How do you know that Ramón is generous? What does Ramón do? He gives half of his peach to Tommy. What does Ramón say? Ramón tells Tommy that he will share. Ramón's words and actions tell you that he is generous. The author has shown you what Ramón is like by what Ramón says and does.

Knowing about the characters helps you to enjoy a story. You find out about a character in three ways—from what the author says about the character, from what other characters say about the character, and from what the character does and says.

Try This

Read the paragraphs and answer the questions.

Doris wanted to learn how to skate. She fell down often, but she didn't quit. Doris was not the kind of person to give up easily.

"I don't care how long it takes," she said. "I want to learn."

"When you want to learn something, Doris, you really stick with it," her brother Max said.

On Saturday Doris practiced by herself all day long. That evening she ran inside.

"Hey, Max," she said happily. "Do you want to see me skate?"

1. How does the author describe Doris?
2. What does another character say that tells you about Doris?
3. What does Doris do and say that tells you what she is like?

Writing

1. One way you learn about characters is through the author's description. Write one or two sentences that describe your favorite cartoon or story character.
2. Write a paragraph describing a hero or other brave character.

As you read "Fresh Starts," you will learn about the characters by what they say and do and by what is said about them. Look for these ways to learn about the characters.

362

Coyote Cry

by BYRD BAYLOR

It is night.

A boy and an old man sit beside their campfire, listening, listening . . . waiting.

Finally, from somewhere across the hills, from some rocky ledge, from some steep ravine comes the high windy cry of a coyote.

At first they hear only one. But from other hills and other ledges and other ravines coyotes answer. Ay-eee. Ay-eee.

In the darkness, far back from the small, flickering campfire, coyotes sing and yip and howl and whine.

The boy, Antonio, stiffens.

He does not like that sound, that wailing, that yapping. And anyway, Coyote is his enemy. Antonio never forgets that, even at the end of a day, when he is almost ready for sleep.

"Coyote is my enemy," he says. "And I am his."

But the old man, the grandfather, has no enemies. Sometimes he even makes excuses for Coyote.

He says, "It is hard to enjoy a supper of rocks and sand, and so Coyote does what he must to stay alive."

"Even so, he is my enemy."

"He is our neighbor, our *compañero*," the grandfather says. "We share the same rocky land."

"Even so, he is my enemy."

The grandfather and the boy have nothing else to do now that the sheep are quiet in their night pen, now that the beans and green chiles and tortillas and wild honey have been eaten, now that the stars are out.

So they listen to coyotes.

"They have a different song tonight," the grandfather says after awhile. "It tells you there will be rain. Not tonight. Maybe not tomorrow either. But soon. Coyote feels a change in the air."

Antonio listens. He feels only the still dry summer night, yet he knows that his grandfather hears many

things in the coyote's voice that he himself has not yet learned to hear.

The old man tries to teach the boy these things.

"Sometimes," he says, "Coyote sings for the coming of winter. Sometimes he sings for hunger or for thirst. Sometimes for his mate. Some people even say they know by his song whether he runs free in the hills or whether he fears traps and hunters."

"Let him fear *me*," Antonio says.

Sometimes Coyote seems to be laughing, not afraid of anything at all.

The old man has seen coyotes gathered together for company. He is sure of that.

"And they play games—those coyotes—chasing each other until they have to lie down, panting. I have looked at tracks that ran around and around. I almost think that on those nights Coyote dances."

But Antonio does not wish to think of Coyote dancing on some sandy ledge. Coyote is his enemy. He only thinks of him *that* way.

"He won't be dancing after he meets me. Then he'll be running. *Cuidado*, Coyote. *Cuidado*. Watch out for me."

It is like this every night.

The old man and the boy lie there on the ground, each with his blanket wrapped around him. They lie pressed as close to the earth as any of the wild creatures up in the hills. And when they sleep, they close their eyes, still listening to the coyotes who have been hidden all day and now will walk their trails by moonlight.

Antonio and his grandfather cannot let themselves sleep soundly.

They sleep—they even dream—still half listening for the sheep they must take care of day and night.

Now, of course, the sheep are quiet. But their pen is no more than a wide circle of branches that Antonio and his grandfather cut from scrub oak and manzanita and sycamore trees. It is not high enough or strong enough to keep all other animals out.

If a wildcat prowls, if a night bird screeches, if a coyote comes close, the sheep will run in fear. If the sheep move, the old man always wakes first, faster than Antonio, and he runs to the pen. He runs, calling out to calm his sheep. And his eyes peer into the shadows to find what it is they fear.

Too often it is Coyote he finds there. And Coyote must be kept away from the summer lambs, which still run, playing and jumping in the pen long after their mothers are quiet.

Usually, the long-haired yellow collie Blanca sleeps where she too can guard the sheep.

Like the old man, this dog's whole life, as far back as Antonio can remember, has been caring for that flock of sheep . . . herding them across the valley to graze, bringing them back in the evening, keeping them safe all through the night.

But now Blanca does not run beside the old man when they go down the trail in the morning. Neither does she stay beside the sheep at night, because she has four new pups hidden under a manzanita bush not far from the glow of the campfire. There, the small branches twist down and touch the earth, and the pups lie curled together among the shadows, pale and soft.

They are still too young to open their eyes. They don't even have names yet . . . and they have no need of names. They have never left the manzanita branches that keep them hidden from the rest of the world. They have never been far from their mother's warm fur.

But now in the first gray half-light of dawn, the pups stir. One of them stretches and yawns and rolls away from the others until he lies beyond the shelter of the manzanita branches.

The old man, too, moves restlessly in his sleep. Even in sleep, he seems to know that something is not as it should be. Without opening his eyes, he lifts his head to listen.

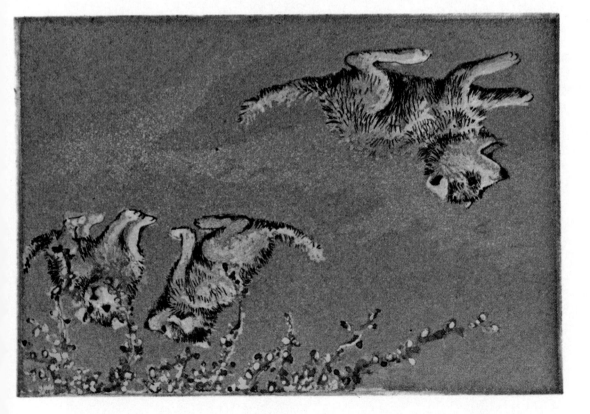

There is nothing but silence—silence and crickets. He drifts back into sleep. . . .

It is the wild barking of the dog Blanca that rouses Antonio and the grandfather at sunrise. They leave their blankets and go running toward the manzanita, where Blanca is sniffing the ground, circling back and forth, growling.

Antonio kneels beside the pups, stroking them, whispering to them. "But you are all right. Nothing is wrong here. . . ."

And then he sees that one of the pups is gone.

"Coyote!" he screams out. "Coyote was here."

And he is right. Already the grandfather is bending over coyote tracks in the sand.

The tracks circle the manzanita bush. They tell of one coyote, alone, quiet as a shadow.

Antonio is angry, and his anger is loud. He fills the dawn with his shouts, with his threats. He wants every coyote in the hills to hear him.

"I'll get you, Coyote. Cuidado, Coyote. Watch out, Thief."

Even though it is still too dark to see far beyond the light of their lantern, they both search for the pup. Perhaps, after all, he has just crawled away. Perhaps the coyote tracks mean nothing.

But the grandfather says, "The pup made no tracks. No tracks at all."

He looks off toward the hills, shaking his head, wondering. . . .

There is only one hope—to find where these coyote tracks lead. This will be Antonio's job.

While the old man takes the sheep to pasture, the boy follows the tracks from the small twisting tree, past the sheep pen, along the damp sandy creek and up toward the first hills. But now the earth becomes rocky. Time after time, Antonio sits down on the ground and studies the faint footprints, trying to decide which way to turn. Often the ground is too hard to hold a footprint. Or grass may hide it. Or there may be only rocks.

Antonio stops to listen. Even the slightest voice could tell him something. But the wind carries no coyote sounds today, no pup sounds. Only quail flutter from the tall shadowy grass as he walks by. Only jack rabbits watch him from the far hills.

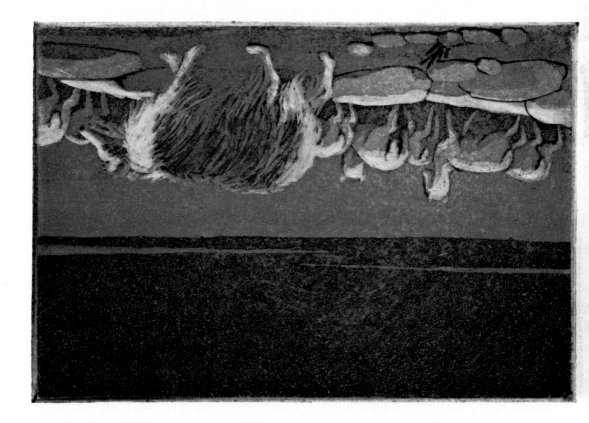

And when he calls out "I'll get you, Coyote!" there is only an echo of his own small voice in the ravine: "I'll get you, Coyote."

But he does not get Coyote. All that afternoon, he does not even see Coyote.

Instead, he walks slowly back to meet the grandfather as he brings the sheep to their evening watering place in the shallow creek. The old man doesn't have to ask. He sees Antonio's face and he knows.

For a long time, they don't talk about it at all. They simply go about the business of caring for the sheep. And then Antonio chops wood while the grandfather cooks beans on the open fire.

It is not until night, when once more they lie on the ground, wrapped in their blankets, that Antonio can talk about it.

And then the grandfather says, ''Of course, it is possible that the little one was not harmed.''

But Antonio will not be comforted. ''Coyote is mean,'' he says. ''He is my enemy and I am his.''

''Remember,'' the grandfather reminds him, ''we saw no sign that Coyote killed the pup.''

Antonio shakes his head in the darkness. ''I saw enough, I know.''

It is always this way at night now. When the coyotes wail softly in the far hills, the old man and the boy lie beside the last glow of their campfire and talk about how different it would have been if only one of them had been awake when Coyote came creeping into their camp . . . or they talk about what the tracks looked like that morning, circling the manzanita's lowest branches.

''By studying those tracks,'' the old man says, ''I know that Coyote was a female, small and light herself.''

They think this over.

''Then why didn't she have pups of her own? Why wasn't she taking care of them instead of stealing another one? Why did she leave her den?''

They can only wonder about these things. Night under the summer stars is a time for wondering.

During the days, when they are out with the sheep they do not speak of it, but each one knows that they both half believe they will find the answer somewhere in one

of those dry ravines, or in some grassy flat, or along some quiet trail.

Every day Antonio thinks, we could find that answer any day, this day, tomorrow. When?

Now it is morning—another morning.

Antonio and his grandfather have taken the sheep a different way this time, along the other side of the creek. They have just walked across a little hill and they stop to rest near the bottom of the slope.

There has been rain and the air is cool and the far blue mountains seem closer. The grandfather bends down to look at a cactus flower blossoming pink and white from a crack in the rock.

Just below them at the foot of the hill, the rock juts out and forms a shelter, a small overhang not large enough to call a cave. The boy and the old man stand for a minute here on the slope of the hill, looking down. They are not in a hurry.

Something moves. They see a flash of yellow fur among the tall weeds. Antonio hardly breathes. The grandfather is as still as a rock or a tree. They wait.

Below them the small furry thing moves back into the rock shelter and then again comes bounding into the sunlight.

Now they are sure. It is the pup . . . Blanca's pup. Antonio wants to run to it at once. But the old man puts out his hand to stop him. They stay there, watching.

Now something else comes into sight. A coyote—a mother coyote—puts her forepaw against the pup and plays with him the way any mother dog plays with her own babies. The pup rolls and nips and jumps. The coyote watches him. She turns her head from side to side whenever the pup moves.

When the pup is tired and flops down in the sand to rest, she licks its fur and nuzzles it. The pup makes its small contented sounds.

But Antonio's hands are tight. His eyes blink. He cannot believe what he is seeing. It is as if the hills he has walked all his life had turned suddenly into a strange and unknown land.

"Coyote," Antonio whispers, "Coyote. . . ."

Antonio does not wait to see what the grandfather wants to do. He goes leaping across the rocks to the bottom of the hill.

At the first sound, the coyote and the collie pup both run toward the rock shelter. There, the pup has been carefully taught, is safety. But Antonio is beside him in an instant. He grabs the pup up into his arms.

The coyote looks at the pup but there is nothing she can do to hide him now. She turns and runs, and Antonio, holding the pup tightly against him, sees the coyote look back before she disappears in the low brush. The pup whines and tries to twist loose, but Antonio says, "No, stay with us. You're no coyote."

The old man is there now. Together they look at the coyote's den, the damp earth, the grass bent to fit the creatures that lay there, the rocks that almost hid them from sight.

From far away there comes a coyote's cry. The pup turns its head and yelps.

The coyote sound comes once more, farther away, as lonely as any sound you ever heard. Antonio keeps it in his mind even after it has stopped.

They take the pup and turn back to the sheep, and all that day Antonio keeps the pup with him. His mind whirls with his own thoughts, with the sharp puppy barks beside him, with the memory of that voice.

"Why?" he keeps asking the grandfather as they walk beside the sheep. "Why did that coyote take Blanca's pup if not to kill him?"

The old man, of course, can only guess. "Maybe some-thing happened to her own pups. Maybe she kept looking for them. Maybe she kept wishing for another one."

"She must have been afraid when she came to our camp."

The old man nods. "But Coyote does what it must. It does what its bones say to do."

Late in the afternoon, they bring the sheep back to the creek for water and then up the bank to their pen.

Antonio runs ahead and takes the pup to Blanca. Blanca sniffs the pup and bristles and walks around him, looking at him carefully. She smells the touch of coyote on her pup and it puzzles her. Like Antonio, Blanca has been at war with coyotes for a long time. Yet, finally, she decides to take the pup back and she pushes it toward his brothers.

The pups no longer stay under the manzanita branches. Now they are old enough, strong enough, to come out into the world, to explore, to taste, to blink in the sunlight, to jump at Antonio.

Antonio watches the pup he has just carried home from the coyote's den. It is a dog again, not a coyote. Yet he wonders. . . . When it grows up will it remember anything of those days? Will the sound of a coyote cry mean anything to him? Will he remember a den hidden among the rocks?

The old man and the boy listen carefully at night. Who knows whether the coyote will come back? Perhaps she is waiting in the shadows. Perhaps she will try to take the pup again. . . .

But that night passes. And another. And another. And they put it out of their minds.

Then one cool dawn—still dark but with the first
streaks of orange in the night sky—the old man lifts his
head from his blanket. He sees two shining eyes. It is
Coyote. He reaches over and touches Antonio, and puts
his fingers to his lips. "Shhh."

They make no sound.

Now they see the pup moving toward the spot where
Coyote stands. Coyote comes no closer. She waits. The
pup peers into the darkness to make sure. Then he goes to
the coyote and they touch noses. That is all. Just that. The
pup goes back to his sleeping brothers.

When they look again, Coyote is gone.

She does not come back.

They know her tracks now, and every day they search
for them around the camp. But she does not come back.

Yet even now that summer is past, the old man and
the boy remember her.

They still lie under the stars, listening, listening as
they always have for the night's first faraway coyote song.

Ay-eee.

And then they wait for other voices to come from the
moonlit hills, from the deep canyons.

Ay-eee. Ay-eee.

Could one of the voices be that one?

"When she comes back again, that coyote . . . I'll give
her something for supper. A melon, if we have it."

Antonio says. "You saw how skinny she was."

"A melon for your enemy?" the grandfather asks,
surprised.

"Maybe Coyote is not my enemy now," Antonio says very softly.

And then after awhile, it seems to him that the coyote voices have changed. He hears in them now a sound he must never have noticed before.

It is a song coyotes sing only to the moon. You hear it only when the moon is yellow and low.

The boy knows suddenly what the song is about. He knows.

It is about being alive. It is about this rocky land, these windy hills where Coyote runs.

So Antonio says, "Someday I will be one of those people who can tell you what things Coyote is saying."

And the coyote song rises to the moon.

Ay-eee. Ay-eee.

Understanding What You've Read

1. Look at the details on page 364 that describe the grandfather. What does the grandfather say that shows he knows and understands the coyote?

2. What does the author say about Antonio on page 371 to let you know how Antonio feels when the puppy is missing? What does Antonio do and say (on the same page) to show how he feels?

3. Why do you think that the coyote took the puppy? What does Antonio say on page 380 to show that he has changed his mind about the coyote?

Writing

1. Write your own description of a coyote.

2. Write a few sentences or a short story about a person or an animal. Tell what the character is like. Tell what the person says or does to show how the person feels. Tell what the animal does to show how it feels.

Janey, who is blind, is in a cave with her brother, Tim, and their friend, Perdita. They had been chasing a thief. But the thief had escaped, taking the only light with him. Perdita and Tim can see until they reach the mouth of the tunnel that leads out of the cave to the sea. After that, they are lost, and only a special kind of magic can save them.

A Kind of Magic

by NINA BAWDEN

Tim and Perdita led Janey to the mouth of the tunnel. Once there, Janey put her hand on the wall. Tim put his hand on her shoulder, and Perdita clutched the back of Tim's jacket. They began to walk down the rocky stairs. For the first few yards, while the light lasted, Janey's pace seemed slow to them. Then, as soon as the last blue glimmer vanished and they were in the dark, it seemed terrifyingly fast. They stumbled, panic-stricken.

"Go slower, Janey," Tim begged.

"I'm going slow," she said. "Why don't you walk properly, instead of bumping about all over the place?"

"I don't know how," Tim said humbly. It was true. Walking in the pitch dark was different—and frightening: You lifted your foot and it was like stepping off a cliff into black, empty air.

Janey stood still. "Feel," she said, after a pause. "Feel with your feet. That's what I do."

She moved on again. The two behind her began to learn. Keeping one hand on the wall, they slid their feet forwards, feeling with their toes and the balls of their feet. Their progress became steadier and their panic ebbed a little.

"That's better," Janey said. "You're doing fine—just fine."

She spoke in the bright, encouraging voice her mother sometimes used to her, when she was trying to do something that was hard for a blind girl to do.

Once she stopped. "I'm listening," she explained. Tim and Perdita tried to listen, too. They strained their ears, but they heard nothing. It was horrible standing still and waiting in that cold, silent darkness. Tim remembered the ravine they had passed over. That terrible drop! Janey had not seen it. She couldn't know how dangerous it was.

He whispered hoarsely, "Janey—there's a sort of hole in the rock, with water a long way down."

"I know," she said, quite calmly. "Wait a minute." She stamped with her feet. "It's soon—can't you hear? The ground's sort of hollow."

She was right. They couldn't hear—or feel—the hollowness, but a few steps later they heard the water. Miles below them, miles and miles. . . . Tim stood still, suddenly, and Perdita bumped into him.

"Come on," Janey said. "It's all right close to the wall." She led on and they followed, fearful but trusting her. They had to trust her. They went on, slowly shuffling. The water sounded loud on their right. They were crossing the ravine. Tim tried so hard to see into the darkness that his eyeballs burned.

"Past it now," Janey said.

One more step, then another. Was it his imagination, or was Janey's progress less certain now? She

seemed to be stopping more often. She had stopped now, and they all stood still waiting.

Perdita said, "Go on, Janey." Her voice was impatient, not frightened. That was because she believed in magic, Tim thought. He had some idea, anyway, of how Janey could find her way. Perdita had none. It was a kind of magic to her.

Suddenly Janey shouted. "Aaaaaaah. . . ."

Tim almost screamed with fright. He tried to speak in an ordinary voice. "What on earth did you do that for?"

"This is one of the places where we shouted on the way in," Janey said. "I think I can tell where we are, by the echo."

They began to shout. Their cries rang back at them from the unseen walls. Then they stood silent and listened to the echoes die away.

"Once more," Janey said. They shouted again. And listened.

Janey gave a little sigh. She left the wall and walked slowly, her hands spread out. She bumped into rock. She gave a little cry. Then her shoulder moved as she began to feel the rock. *"There was a little crack. My fingers went in it. Only it was the other hand because I was going the other way. And there was a bit jutting out lower down. I banged my knee on it and it bled a little and stuck up my sock, so it must have been a bit sharp. . . ."*

Tim held his breath. Then Janey gave a low, triumphant giggle. "I'm *right*," she said. "This is the right place. In a minute, we'll be able to hear the sea."

And they did. But before they heard the sea, they saw the light. At first it was just a faint paling of the darkness ahead. Then the darkness seemed to form round to make a shape. It was the mouth of the tunnel that led into the main cave and out to the beach and the sea. . . .

Janey seemed to be moving very slowly now. "Hurry," Tim urged. Then he ran past her, toward the light.

Perdita followed him. They reached the main cave, tumbling over each other like puppies. The light was gray because the day was darkening with a curtain of rain. But it was *light.* Light—after that terrible darkness. Perdita and Tim shouted with joy. They shouted so loud that for a little Janey could not make herself heard.

"Tim . . . Tim . . ."

He heard her at last. She had come out of the tunnel and was standing in the cave, her hands out in front of her. "I can't see anymore, there aren't any more walls," she said.

The other two fell silent. They looked at each other and then down at their feet. Neither of them spoke.

"What's the matter?" Janey smiled broadly and wrapped her arms across her chest, hugging herself with delight: "I found the way out, didn't I? You'd never have found it yourselves. . . ."

Tim ran to her, put his arms round her and hugged her. "You were wonderful," he said. "A heroine, Janey. You saved our lives."

"Oh, it wasn't very hard," Janey said modestly. "Can we go home now? I'm so hungry."

Understanding What You've Read

1. Find a sentence on page 385 that tells how Tim felt about being lost in the dark.
2. Why was Janey so calm? Look at the details on page 385.
3. What was one way in which Janey used her sense of touch to find her way through the cave? What was one way in which she used her sense of hearing to find her way?
4. What did Janey mean when she said, on page 390, "I can't see anymore, there aren't any more walls"?
5. On page 390, what did Janey say and do to show she was happy and proud of herself? What did Tim say and do to show that he was happy and proud of Janey?

Writing

1. Write a sentence or paragraph describing one of the characters in the story.
2. Write a paragraph or story about two characters who are lost in the woods. Use details that tell about the characters by describing what they look like, how they feel, and what they say.

To Catch a Bird

by JAY WILLIAMS

Chris loved to have pets. He liked to watch all sorts of animals, and to catch them and tame them. He had a toad named Harold, a snake named Streak, and two mice named Pickle and Peekle. He also had some beetles, a jar full of polliwogs, and a lizard. None of these had any names yet.

One day, Chris was lying on his stomach in the field
out behind his house. He was watching some ants, trying
to decide whether they would make good pets. He heard
a flutter of wings and looked up. On a nearby fence post a
bird had perched.

Chris liked to watch birds. He liked the way robins
walked about like solemn fat men with their hands
behind their backs. He liked to watch the way chicka-
dees swung upside down on tiny branches. He liked the
way nuthatches walked headfirst down a tree trunk.

He had never seen a bird like this one before. It was
about the size of a robin. But it had a fierce little head

with round bright eyes and a sharp hooked beak. It sat on the post with its brown wings neatly folded, turning its head and staring all around. It cocked its head and looked at Chris. It gave a fierce little cry: *Killee-killee!* It snapped its wings and flew high into the air. It flew far above the treetops. Chris saw it swoop down into the woods.

He waited for a long time, and after a while the bird came back. It sat on the post and looked about.

Chris wondered what it would feel like to be a bird like that.

You would grip things with your sharp claws. You would fly high above all the other birds. You would dive out of the air like someone diving into a pool.

This bird wasn't like other birds. There was something fast and free and proud about it. When Chris looked at it, he felt as light as wings.

He told his mother and father about the bird.

"Oh, that must be a sparrow hawk," said his mother. "It is called that because it is the smallest of the hawks. It's real name is kestrel."

Chris put his elbows on the table and his chin on his hands. "I like that bird," he said. "I wish I could catch it."

"Oh, Chris," said his father. "I don't think a kestrel would be happy in a cage."

"I wouldn't put it in a cage," said Chris. "I just want to have it."

"Why?" asked his mother.

"To look at whenever I wanted to. It would make me feel good to look at it."

"Well," said his father, "you can look at it outside any
time you want to, can't you?"

Chris went to the window. From the house he could
see into the garden. He could see into the field next to the
garden.

"The kestrel isn't there now," he said. "There would
be lots of times when I would want to see it and it
wouldn't be there."

The next day he went out to the field again, and there was the kestrel. It sat on the fence post. Chris began to think of ways to catch it.

He tried the way he had caught his toad, Harold. He crept very close to the post, and then ran out to grab the bird in his hands. But the kestrel was gone, high in the air. It didn't come back for a long time. When it came back, it sat on a high tree branch.

Chris got some clothesline and made a lasso. He stood under the tree and threw up his lasso. The lasso got tangled in the branches. The kestrel flew off, laughing *Killee!*

"Oh, how I wish I could catch that bird," said Chris. "But I don't see how I can."

Then he forgot about the kestrel for a while, because Uncle George came for a visit.

Uncle George was an artist. He painted pictures for people to hang on their walls and look at. He drew pictures for books, too. He didn't look like an artist, Chris thought. He was a large, fat, cheerful sort of uncle, something like a robin. When he drew a picture he would put his head to one side to look at it as if it were a nice worm.

There was lots to do with Uncle George. There were games to play, and walks to take, and stories to hear. The days went quickly.

One day, Uncle George said, "Come out into the garden, Chris. I want to do a portrait of you."

"How will you do that?" asked Chris. "And what's a portrait?"

"A portrait is a picture of how somebody looks to an artist," said Uncle George. "Come with me."

He made Chris sit under a tree. He took a pad of paper and began to draw with soft, colored chalks called pastels. He looked at Chris and looked at the paper. He put his head to one side the way a bird does, and hummed to himself.

He winked. "I am going to catch you, my friend Chris," he said. "I'm going to put you right here on this paper."

"How can you do that?" Chris asked in surprise.

"These are magic chalks," said Uncle George. "They do whatever I tell them to do. I look at you, and I draw the way you look to me. Some hair. A-ha! Two eyes. A freckle and another freckle. A nose, round and freckled. A grin. And there you are."

Chris peered over his uncle's shoulder. "Why, it does look like me," he said.

Uncle George seemed very pleased. "Not bad," he said. "I certainly caught you, didn't I? I tell you, these chalks are pretty magical."

"And is that a portrait?"

"That's right."

"What will you do with it, Uncle George?" Chris asked.

"I'll take it along with me wherever I go. Then, when I feel like seeing you, I'll pull it out and look at it. There you will be, freckles and all," said Uncle George. "When I look at your grin, I will feel happy."

The next morning, when Chris woke up and looked out of his bedroom window, there was the kestrel. It was sitting on the fence post at the edge of the field. The bird bent over and pecked at its toes. It stretched out one long wing and then the other. It shook its wings and sat still.

Chris went into his uncle's bedroom. Uncle George was sound asleep, rolled up under the blankets. Chris took the pad of paper and some magic pastel chalks.

He went out into the garden and down to the field. He walked as softly as he could toward the kestrel. He walked the way he had when he had caught his two mice. When he was as close as he could get, he sat down in the grass. He began to draw.

He did what Uncle George had done. He looked at the bird and then he looked at what he was drawing. He drew the fierce little head with its black cap. He drew the round bright eyes. He drew the reddish-brown wings and the brown spots on its front.

The kestrel sat up straight for Chris. It watched Chris, but it didn't move. When Chris was finished, he jumped to his feet. The bird jumped up, too, into the air. It cried *Killee!* and flew away.

Chris ran to his uncle's bedroom. "Wake up, Uncle George!" he shouted.

Uncle George rolled over. He yawned. "Where's the fire?" he said.

"Look!" said Chris. "I caught a bird."

Uncle George sat up. "What? A bird in my bed? Where is it?"

Chris showed him the picture. "Did I catch him?" he said.

Uncle George put his head to one side. He looked at the picture of the kestrel. "My, my," he said, "you certainly did."

Chris's mother and father came in. "What's all this about birds?" said his father.

Chris showed them the picture.

"It looks like a bird," said his father.

"It looks just like a kestrel," said his mother.

She found a picture frame and put the picture in it. She hung it on the wall next to Chris's bed.

And then, whenever he wanted to, Chris looked at it. He would look at it when the ground was covered with snow. He would look at it when the rain came down and kept him in. He would look at it when he was sick and had to stay in bed. When he looked at it, he remembered the fierce little head and the round bright eyes.

He always loved Harold and Streak and Pickle and Peekle. He loved the beetles and polliwogs and lizards that he caught many times and let go again. But when he looked at the picture of the bird he had caught, he felt free and proud, and as light as wings.

Understanding What You've Read

1. On page 392, find a sentence that tells something about the kind of person Chris is.
2. What did Uncle George mean when he told Chris that the chalks were magical?
3. Find a sentence on page 400 that tells how Chris felt when he finally "caught" the bird.

Writing

1. You can "catch" an animal with words. Write three sentences that tell what the animal looks like. Write three sentences that tell some things the animal does.
2. Write a paragraph or a story that tells how Chris caught his pet snake Streak. Describe both Chris and Streak in your story.

More Stories Drawn from Life

The Day the Hurricane Happened by Lonzo Anderson. Scribner, 1974. A family in the Virgin Islands must protect themselves and their farm from the fierce winds of a hurricane.

Ox-Cart Man by Donald Hall. Illustrated by Barbara Cooney. Viking Press, 1979. A lyrical telling of the seasons' changes in the life of a man and his family in eighteenth-century New England.

Something Queer at the Ball Park: A Mystery by Elizabeth Levy. Delacorte, 1975. Jill is the star player on her baseball team. When her lucky bat vanishes, her friend Gwen tries to find the reason for the mysterious disappearance.

Wingman by Manus Pinkwater. Dodd, Mead, 1974. His imagination and his talent as an artist help Donald Chen through some difficult times.

Three Stalks of Corn by Leo Politi. Scribner, 1976. A young Mexican-American girl learns about the importance of corn and many other things as well from her grandmother.

A Taste of Blackberries by Doris Buchanan Smith. T. Y. Crowell, 1973. A boy is shocked when his best friend dies unexpectedly from a bee sting.

Ferris Wheel by Mary Stolz. Harper & Row, 1977. A new friend, Consuela, helps Polly appreciate her own good qualities in this story set in Vermont.

Part 7
Enjoying the World

Recognizing Fact and Opinion

It is important to know what is a fact and what is an opinion.

When we know something can be proved, we say it is a **fact.** The following sentence states a fact.

A planetarium is a room or building that can show stars and other bodies on a domed ceiling.

We know this can be proved. We can look in an encyclopedia, a magazine, a book, or another source. We can read about it in a library.

Does the following sentence state a fact?

A planetarium is a nice place to visit.

How is the second sentence different from the first one?
The second sentence cannot be proved. It states an **opinion.**
An opinion is what someone thinks, or feels, or believes.

Every day we read both facts and opinions. We can learn
from both kinds of writing. Facts give us information we
need. Knowing the opinions of other people helps us to think
about things and form our own opinions. But it is important
to see the difference between facts and opinions.

Facts and opinions may both be given in the same selection. They may even be given in the same paragraph. Sometimes writers help us see the difference by using such words
as "The fact is," "In my opinion," "Some people believe," "It
seems to me," or "I think." More often, though, facts and
opinions are given without such clues. Then it is our job to
notice whether a statement is a fact or an opinion.

How can you tell that the first sentence below gives an
opinion and the second sentence gives a fact?

Cartoons are fun to watch.
To make a TV cartoon, many drawings are needed.

The word *fun* tells how someone feels. Since people feel
differently about cartoons, it would be impossible to prove
that the first sentence is true for everyone. The second sentence can be proved to be true. You can look in a book about

making cartoons. Or you might look up *cartoons* in an encyclopedia.

Now read the following paragraph. Notice that the writer gives both facts and opinions. Which sentences give facts? Which sentences give opinions?

Building and flying paper airplanes is enjoyable for young people and grown-ups, too. Several years ago, the magazine *Scientific American* held a paper airplane contest. They received almost 12,000 entries. It seems as if almost everyone likes to make and fly paper airplanes.

The first sentence gives an opinion. The word *enjoyable* tells how the writer feels. It would be impossible to prove that everyone feels the same way. The next two sentences are facts. You can prove them to be true. You can look in the magazine itself. You can write to the magazine company. The last sentence gives an opinion. The clue is the words, "It seems as if." The writer uses these words to help you know that what follows is an opinion.

Remember to read carefully for facts and opinions. They are both important. If the writer gives no clue, look for words that tell how someone feels. Look for words such as:

fun	better
enjoyable	easier
beautiful	interesting

Try This

1. Read the sentences. Tell whether each is fact or opinion.

   a. You can see dinosaur bones in some museums.
   b. Some people keep snakes as pets.
   c. It is easy to learn ballet.
   d. The moon is closer to the Earth than any star or planet.
   e. Pencils are better than pens.
   f. The people in California are the friendliest in the world.

2. Read the following paragraph. Each sentence is numbered. Tell whether each is a fact or an opinion.

   (1) Yellowstone Park is the oldest and largest national park. (2) It is probably one of the most popular. (3) It is easy to see why it is so popular. (4) There are geysers, hot springs, and waterfalls. (5) There is also Yellowstone Lake. (6) It is beautiful. (7) Many animals can be found there, especially bears. (8) The bears are the best sight of all.

3. Make up three sentences that state facts and three sentences that give opinions.

VOCABULARY STUDY

Homophones

Do you remember what homophones are? They are "words that sound alike but are spelled differently and have different meanings." Now here's the challenge: Can you tell what each homophone in boldface means? Use clues in the sentences to help you. Are you ready? Good! Then it's time to meet the twins, Stan and Fran!

The case of the missing marbles will be a hard one to crack. No one was **seen** at the **scene** of the crime.

The place where this happened was the marble factory on the mountain, wasn't it?

Yes.

I think we should take a **peek** at the **peak.**

Why should we take a quick look at the mountaintop? Why can't we take our time and look it over carefully?

Because the person who took the marbles might notice us if we look around for too long.

You may be right. But let's think this through first. Now, who would want to **steal** marbles made of **steel?** Oh, wait a minute. There's the phone. Will you answer it?

Sure. Hello? You did? It has? That's wonderful! Good-by.

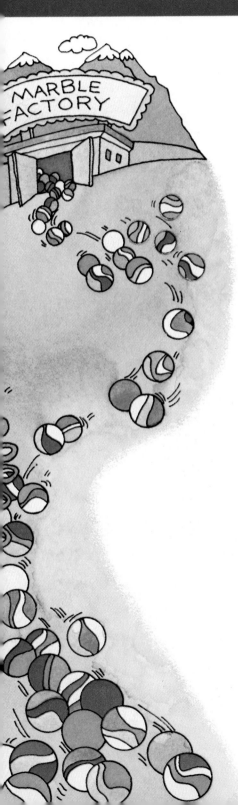

What happened?

No one took those metal marbles without permission. They rolled out of the factory when the door was open. The marbles were found at the bottom of the mountain.

Too bad. I would like to have seen the scene of the crime.

But since there was no crime, there was no scene! However, we could take a peek at the peak. We could also look at the steel marbles that no one ever did steal!

Word Play

1. Match each homophone from Column 1 with its meaning in Column 2.

1	2
seen	the place where an event happens
peak	a quick or secret look
steel	to take without permission or right
scene	the top of a mountain
peek	a strong metal
steal	noticed

2. Think of a homophone for each word below:
   one   not   heel   through

3. Write your own mystery story, using the homophones you thought of for number 2.

409

As you read, decide which statements are facts and which are opinions.

How can drawings on paper come to life?

Find out when you read about . . .

CARTOON MAGIC

by Seymour Reit

If you watch TV cartoons, you may know Tom the cat and Jerry the mouse. These characters may be your old friends. You may also know Mickey Mouse, Donald Duck, and Popeye the Sailor. Almost everyone knows Casper the Ghost, Bugs Bunny, and the Flintstones, too. These people and animals all seem very much alive. Sometimes it's hard to believe that they're only drawings on paper. They're tiny "actors" in a certain kind of movie called an *animated* cartoon.

What makes these drawings come to life? How can Bugs Bunny do all his tricks? How can Popeye gobble his spinach, or Casper fly so smoothly through the air?

Making cartoons isn't easy. It takes a lot of time, a lot of work, and a lot of people.

Have you ever looked at a strip of movie film? On it, you will see many tiny photos. In each photo, the figures have moved a little bit. When the film is run quickly through a projector, these figures seem to "come alive."

A cartoon works the same way. But instead of photos, drawings are used. A great many of

them are needed. There are twenty-four little pictures, or "frames," to every *second* of action. This means that, in a two-minute Tom and Jerry scene, over 2,880 separate drawings will be used!

How are so many drawings made? And how are they all put together? Let's see how the "magic" happens step by step.

Every cartoon begins with an idea. Writers talk over this idea. Their job is to think up an exciting *plot*.

When the story is ready, it is not written down. It is sketched out! Many drawings are made. They show the major parts of the story. All the drawings are tacked up on a big cork wall, called a *storyboard*.

When the story is finished, the *animators* take over. These people have an important job. They plan all the drawings to show the final action.

Does an animator do all this work alone? No. There are many other trained artists helping. They all work together. Each drawing is carefully numbered.

You may wonder how all these artists can get their cartoons to look alike. They do it with drawings called *model charts*. These charts show each character in many different ways. Each may be running, jumping, laughing, or crying. A trained artist has no trouble copying the poses shown on these charts.

After the pencil drawings are ready, they go to *inkers*. These people trace each drawing on a clear plastic sheet. Each sheet is given a number.

Next the clear sheets go to *painters*. These people paint the colors. They use paints that stick to the shiny plastic surfaces.

Now the "scenery" is prepared. On TV and in the movies, people build "sets." In cartoons, the sets are flat paintings, called *backgrounds*.

Can you see now why all the drawings were traced on clear sheets? Yes, it saves time and work. It means that one background can be used for many scenes. The clear sheets are simply placed over the same background, one after the other.

MAKING CARTOONS

1   A storyboard shows the order of events.
2   A model chart shows each character in many poses.
3   An animator draws each character. For every new action or movement, a new drawing is necessary.
4   An inker traces the drawing on a clear plastic sheet, or cel. The white gloves protect the surface from smudges.
5   The yellow sheet is a written record of every cel in the cartoon. The inker follows it closely.
6   The cels are painted on the backs.
7   The finished cels are placed over a painted background. The same background can be used for many different scenes.
8   The camera operator photographs each cel.

Sounds and voices are put on tapes. The tapes and cartoon are viewed on a moviola to see that the sound track and pictures work together.

Next the camera operator comes in. This person takes a picture of each drawing, one by one. The background lies flat on the table. The camera is mounted high above it, pointing down.

The operator places each clear sheet on the background and then snaps the camera. This is done frame after frame. To be a camera operator, you need a lot of patience!

Now there's one important step left — adding the *sound track*. Actors with scripts watch the film on a screen. They "dub in" the voices of the different characters.

One person may take many voices.

Sound effects come next. These are all the bumps, barks, crashes, squeaks, and whistles that you will hear. Finally, someone adds music. The cartoon is finished at last!

Making a cartoon is costly, but today there are many shortcuts. To save time, some studios use paper cutouts. They may also use small figures with movable parts.

Shortcuts or not, cartoons are fun. In the movies or on TV, our favorite friends entertain us. Mickey fights with Minnie. Tom

414

chases Jerry. Olive Oyl flashes her eyes at Popeye. Casper flies up into the air. Bugs Bunny chews on carrots.

We know these friends are only drawings. Yet on the screen, they seem to be real—just as real as life. That is the magic!

Understanding What You've Read

1. What is an animated cartoon?
2. How do several artists get their cartoons to look alike?
3. Where do the voices of the cartoon characters come from?

Applying the Skills Lesson

1. The following sentences are from the selection you just read. Tell whether each sentence is a fact or an opinion.

   a. Every cartoon begins with an idea.
   b. Shortcuts or not, cartoons are fun.
   c. After the pencil drawings are ready, they go to *inkers*.
   d. In the movies or on TV, our favorite friends entertain us.

2. The following paragraph is from the selection you just read. Which sentence gives a fact? Which sentences give opinions?

   We know these friends are only drawings. Yet on the screen they seem real—just as real as life. That is the magic!

Find out why April 17 was so special when you read part of a diary from . . .

April: Specimen A

April 17   *by* Barbara Brenner

I'll begin by telling the reason for this diary. Something special happened today. I was taking my dog Shalom for his afternoon walk. We went down to that old farm field. We were enjoying all the signs of spring. Suddenly Shalom's nose smelled something. He high-tailed it over to a log. Then he began poking and digging around it. I didn't see anything. But I figured something had to be there. So I picked up one end of the log. Under it, coiled tightly in a ring, was a garter snake.

I reached down and picked it up. It hardly moved. It stayed in my hand, still groggy from its long winter sleep. I turned it over and over. White stripes ran along its tan body. There were two small, yellow dots on its head. It was a great-looking snake. I decided to take it home.

With Shalom at my heels, I headed for the house. On the way, my plan began to take shape. I decided that I'd start a study of snakes. I'd keep a diary of my findings. The garter snake would be my first specimen. I named it Specimen *A*.

So here I am in my bedroom. In front of me on the desk is our old fish tank. In it is Specimen *A*. Dad helped me set it up in here. He even helped me fix a light bulb to keep Specimen *A* warm on these chilly spring nights. "Snakes are cold-blooded," Dad said. "All reptiles are."

I never really understood before about that cold-blooded business. I always pictured some sort of refrigerator making their blood cold. It really means they don't have a heating system inside them the way we do. If it gets cold outside, their body temperature drops. If it's warm outside, they get warm, too. The only thing a snake can do to make itself cooler is to move out of the heat. If it gets too cold, a snake might go down under the ground to sleep, I guess. So that's what cold-blooded is about.

Well, tomorrow I begin my study of snakes.

April 18

Today Dad and I went to the bookstore. We bought *A Field Guide to Reptiles and Amphibians*. It's written by Roger Conant. "No snake collector should be without it," the person in the bookstore said. It tells about every snake, lizard, frog, toad, and turtle in the eastern part of the United States and Canada. It has pictures of them, too. (If you live out West, get the *Field Guide to Western Reptiles and Amphibians*.)

April 19

Today my brother Timmy caught a spring peeper, a kind of frog. He says it's for my reptile collection. I tried to explain to him that a frog is not a reptile. And we are collecting only reptiles. But Timmy has already named the frog Specimen *B*. He put it in a big pickle jar. He punched holes in the lid for air. Then he gave the frog a branch to climb on. I guess we'll have to keep it.

April 20

After school today I told Timmy something about frogs. He can't read real books yet. I told him there are frogs all over the world. They live wherever it's warm. Some of them live close to the water. Others live in it. Most frogs come to the water to mate and lay their eggs.

Frogs are amphibians. The word *amphibian* is Greek. The real meaning of this word is "living a double life." The frogs' double life is that they don't hatch right out into frogs. They spend time being tadpoles first. Then they become frogs.

My book says spring peepers eat live insects. So we spent the whole afternoon catching live insects for Specimen *B*. It took us about two hours to catch ten garbage flies and a few early mosquitoes. Then we went to put them into the jar. But something went wrong. Now there are ten garbage flies and a few mosquitoes flying around the house.

April 21

Today Timmy and I caught some more frog food. We turned the porch light on as soon as it got dark. Soon moths came flying toward the light. We just picked them off the screen door. We saved them in a can. If I do say so myself, that was a brilliant idea of mine. This time we got them into the frog jar without any accidents.

419

Meanwhile, the garter snake seems to be doing well. I haven't done anything about getting food for it. But snakes can go without food for a long time. I'll get it something tomorrow.

April 22

A tragedy has happened. This morning I looked for the spring peeper. It was nowhere to be found. I asked Timmy about it. He said he had taken it out of the jar. He wanted to put it in the tank with the garter snake. He thought the frog looked lonesome! It never dawned on me to tell Timmy about garter snakes and frogs. But now he knows. There is no question about it. Specimen *A* has eaten Specimen *B*.

May 2

It's about two weeks since the garter snake came to live on my desk. The tank seems to suit it well. There's a dish of water big enough for the snake to drink from or climb into. There's also a branch to climb on or rub against. I put a good tight-fitting wire screen on top of the tank, so the snake can't get out. At first there was nothing on the bottom of the tank. Now I've covered it with cut-up newspaper.

I've learned what this snake likes to eat. It likes frogs and toads. It likes raw fish, too. Dad and I went fishing the other night. We gave the snake the insides of the fish after we cleaned them. Specimen *A* loved them.

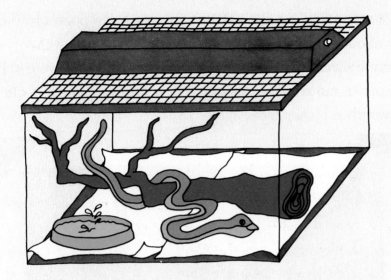

This snake is very gentle when it's handled properly. It doesn't like to be held upside down. It tries to bite me if I hold it by the tail. I try to hold it so that most of its body rests on my hand or arm. Then it moves around on me in a very relaxed way.

Conclusions: A garter snake is a perfect pet. It's clean. It's easy to feed. And it doesn't make any noise. It doesn't have to be walked, either!

May 3

"What's so special about snakes?" A kid asked me that today in school. I was so surprised that anyone would ask such a question. I really had to think for a minute. Before I was able to answer, he went away. I hope I see him tomorrow, though. I've thought of some good answers. First I'll tell him that there are about 6,000 species of reptiles. And that includes 2,700 kinds of snakes.

I wonder if he knows that snakes have been around for about a million years. Their ancestors were the early lizards. They go back maybe 250 million years. It seems to me that anything with a family tree that old is worth a closer look.

May 4

Today I was thinking about my two pets. I love Shalom, my dog. I wouldn't trade him for any other animal. But a snake *is* unusual. I think that's what I like about Specimen *A*.

Dogs can't walk without legs. They can't eat something twice their size. They can't take care of themselves from the minute they are born. Dogs can't shed their skins every few months. But snakes do all those things.

Snakes may not be the smartest animals around. But people don't choose their pets only by how smart they are. If they did, everyone would keep a chimpanzee. And look how many people have tropical fish!

Snakes have *charisma* [kə·riz′mə]. I looked up this word in the dictionary. It means "having a power to attract people." That's just what snakes have. For me, anyway.

Understanding What You've Read

1. Why did the writer decide to keep a diary?
2. What was the writer's plan for the garter snake?
3. What does cold-blooded mean?
4. Name three reasons why the writer likes snakes.

Applying the Skills Lesson

1. The following sentences are from the selection you just read. Tell whether each sentence gives a fact or an opinion.

   a. Snakes are cold-blooded.
   b. Frogs are amphibians.
   c. Snakes have *charisma*.

2. Read the paragraph at the top of page 422. Tell which sentences give facts. Tell which sentence gives an opinion.

Recognizing Fact and Opinion

Most of what you read in textbooks is factual. Textbook writers do not often state their opinions. When they do, they are usually careful to support them with facts.

As you read the following selections, refer to the side-notes. They will help you think about what the writers are telling you.

Recognizing Fact and Opinion in Science

The Water We Drink

The first sentence is an opinion. Are the other sentences facts? How can they be proved?

Here is a strange sight to most of us. This man is a water carrier. He sells drinking water. In his country, Morocco, water is so scarce that it is sold, cup by cup, to thirsty travelers.

When you are thirsty, you can go to a faucet or a well and drink as much as you want. You probably drink over six glasses of water a day, besides the water that you eat. You have enough water to bathe in. In most parts of our country, there is also enough water to grow healthy crops with.

Most of the sentences in this paragraph are opinions. The writer "thinks" you can do these things. The last sentence is different. It is a fact.

Without water, you could not live. Without water, all plants and animals would soon die.

Are these facts or opinions? Can they be proved?

How do we get the water we need? Will we always be able to get enough water?

—*Concepts in Science:* Orange
Harcourt Brace Jovanovich

Building Skills

Tell whether the following sentences are facts or opinions. They are *not* sentences from the selection you just read. These sentences are *statements about the selection.*

1. In one part, this selection talks about a water carrier from Morocco.
2. This selection is interesting.
3. This selection tells how important water is to people, plants, and animals.
4. This selection should have told more about Morocco.

Recognizing Fact and Opinion in Social Studies

The writer mixes facts and opinions in this paragraph. The second sentence is an opinion. The clue is the words "There seems to be."

This last sentence is an opinion, but the writer gives facts in the next paragraph to support that opinion.

Can all the sentences in this paragraph be proved to be true?

People live in many different kinds of groups. There seems to be something about people that makes them want to come together. In doing so, they form groups—for all kinds of reasons. Very few people really want to live alone.

The Ashanti in Ghana and the Pitjantjatjara people of Australia are people who live in groups. The village of Ramipur in India and the city of Denver are other kinds of groups. People join clubs, unions, and churches. At the same time, most people are part of a very large group—a country.

Nearly everyone, no matter where he or she lives, is a member of a country. There are also groups of countries, such as the United Nations. Finally, there is the largest group of all —the human family. When we say the human family, we mean all men, women, and children everywhere in the world. We are all neighbors in the world. We may be members of many smaller groups. But we *all* belong to

the human family. We all live on the
same earth.

—People and Ideas
Silver Burdett

Building Skills

1. Read the last sentence of the first paragraph again. How
   can you tell this sentence is an opinion?
2. Read the last sentence of the second paragraph again. How
   can you tell this sentence gives a fact?

Drawing Conclusions

Study the picture story above. What happened to the first sand castle the girl made?

You see the sand castle is very near the water. You see a big wave is coming toward the shore. You see that the castle is gone. You can reason that the wave washed away the castle even though you don't see it happening in one of the pictures.

428

In other words, you **draw the conclusion** that the wave washed away the castle. When you draw a conclusion, you decide something based upon what has already happened or on what you already know.

Sometimes writers want you to understand things they don't actually say in their writing. They expect you to draw a conclusion.

Read the following sentences. What conclusion can you draw that is not stated in the sentences?

The dark, heavy clouds burst, and thunder roared in the sky. We got very wet as we hurried home.

Without saying so, the writer is telling you that it was raining. The writer does tell you that *the clouds burst, the thunder roared,* and *we got wet.* You know that these are signs of a certain kind of weather. Knowing this should help you draw the conclusion that it was raining. Did the writer actually say that?

Here is another sentence in which the writer does not state a meaning directly.

As he spoke, his voice grew louder, his face turned red, and he pounded his hand on the table.

Which conclusion can you draw?

1. The man was angry.
2. The man was happy.
3. The man liked pounding tables.

Without actually saying so, the writer has told you that the man was angry. You know what the man did. You also know that people who behave in that way are usually angry.

In much of your reading you may need to draw conclusions. Remember to look for the facts that are stated. Then use your own knowledge and powers of reasoning to decide what the writer wants you to conclude.

Try This

Read the following sentences. Below each sentence are some conclusions. Choose the one you think is right.

1. People were bundled in coats, gloves, and hats pulled down over their ears.

   a. It was winter.
   b. It was summer.
   c. It was hot.

2. Hilda took ballet lessons and practiced every day for years until she became a good ballerina.

   a. Hilda worked hard to become a good ballerina.
   b. Hilda didn't care about ballet.
   c. It didn't take long for Hilda to become a good ballerina.

3. The magician ended his act with a deep bow, and the audience went wild, cheering and clapping loudly.

   a. The people didn't like the magic show.
   b. The people wanted to go out to eat.
   c. The people enjoyed the magic show.

Greek and Latin Word Parts

"Look at that big, round fish," said Jetsam. "Why, it looks like my cousin Leo, only bigger."

"That's no fish, Jetsam," said Flotsam. "That's a **bathysphere.** It's a kind of round submarine that is used to study deep-sea life, like us. In fact, *bathysphere* comes from the Greek language. *Bathy* means 'deep,' and *sphere* means 'ball.' "

"But it's the same shape as my cousin Leo," said Jetsam.

"This thing is made of steel," explained Flotsam. "It has windows all around it so the people inside can see fish like us in the water. Hey, let's look through the windows."

"Oh, wow!" cried Jetsam. "There *are* people inside. What are they using?"

"That's a **microscope,**" Flotsam explained again. "People use it to view or look at things that are very, very small. *Microscope* comes from Greek, too. *Micro* means 'small,' and *scope* means 'to see.'"

"Oh, they see us," said Jetsam. "What are they trying to do?"

"I think they're trying to **attract** us to another window. Did you know that *attract* comes from Latin? *At* comes from a word part that means 'to,' and *tract* means 'draw' or 'pull.'"

"Very interesting," said Jetsam. "I know now that this is a bathysphere. But it still looks a lot like my cousin Leo. I wonder if the people who built this thing know my cousin Leo. . . ."

Word Play

Find the meaning that Flotsam gave for each word part below.

at   micro   bathy   scope   sphere   tract

The Muppets Are Here!

by Dina Brown Anastasio

As you read, look for ideas that the writer may not have stated directly. What conclusions can you draw from the facts that are given?

What happens when Kermit, Ernie, Cookie Monster, Fozzie Bear, and the rest of the gang get together? You know . . .

The First Muppets

More than twenty years ago, a very special frog was born. He wasn't really a frog. His body was made of cloth. His mouth was made of felt. As a matter of fact, in the *very* beginning, he didn't even look like a frog. He just looked like a funny little green thing with eyes and a mouth. This thing didn't have a name either. It took a year of ideas and changes to turn that funny little thing into a frog. But when that year was over, something wonderful had been added to the world—Kermit the Frog.

Kermit the Frog is one of Jim Henson's family of TV puppets, called Muppets. Kermit wasn't the first Muppet. Jim had made a few before him. That was back in Jim's early days in TV. But Kermit was the first Muppet that is still well known today.

The Muppet family has such "Sesame Street" characters as Bert and Ernie, Cookie Monster, Big Bird, and Grover. Fozzie Bear, Miss Piggy, and Rowlf the Dog also come to life on Jim's own "Muppet Show."

The family has a large number of other Muppets as well. They are used when a certain part of a TV show calls for them. The Muppet family has grown so fast that Jim works with a large group of helpers.

Where Muppets Come From

Bringing a Muppet to life begins with an idea. An idea for a Muppet may come about in many different ways. Often, a Muppet begins in the same way that a character in a story does. One moment you're wondering what to write about. The next moment the character is inside your head, taking shape.

Some Muppets came about because they were needed. Fozzie Bear, from the "Muppet Show," is one example.

When Jim Henson and his people were planning the "Muppet Show," they decided to make it a take-off on the old vaudeville shows. In the early part of the 1900's, these shows were very popular. Actors, dancers, and comics performed live on a stage. Every show had a comic that was nice, lovable, and *not* very funny. The "Muppet Show," Jim decided, would have this, too. There would be a nice, lovable comic who wasn't very funny. Jim and his people then decided on an animal that would fill this need. A bear, they thought, would be just right. That was the beginning of Fozzie Bear, "house comic."

The personalities of the "Sesame Street" Muppets began in a different way. That's because the idea behind the show was to teach children. The first question asked by the Children's Television Workshop* was, "What is the best way to teach?" So the designers always had to think in terms of teaching. What animals do children like best? What is the best way to help children understand themselves? Should

we have puppets that act like children? How do children act? These were the kinds of questions that were asked.

The idea of using a bird came up long before the show began. Once this had been decided upon, Jim began to search for someone to play Big Bird.

Big Bird's words most often come from the writers. But the way he walks, the way he talks, and the way he *is* all come from the person inside.

Not every Muppet has a person inside. Most of the Muppets are worked by people's hands. So a Muppet must be made to fit well on a hand. Later, a puppeteer will move the puppet. This is done by placing one hand in the head, putting the thumb in the lower jaw.

A puppet must also be made so that its face can be moved to show many feelings. Most of the Muppets' feelings are expressed through their eyes and their mouths.

"It is important that the

Fozzie Bear (right) gives Kermit the Frog some friendly advice. Fozzie Bear came to life on the "Muppet Show."

puppets move with ease," says Jim. "The Muppets, like people, find themselves in many situations. So they must be able to react in many ways."

How Muppets Are Made

Many Muppets are made of a plastic foam which allows them to move and stretch with ease. This is then covered with cloth. One kind of cloth, a fake fur, is used for Muppets like Cookie Monster or Grover.

When brushed up, the fake fur has a fuzzy look.

Real fur and feathers are also used when building the puppets. The eyes are made from many different things. They may be plastic balls or the round parts of spoons.

"We try not to use mechanical parts," says Jim. "We don't want people to spend time worrying about how a puppet works. It's what a puppet says and does that is important."

437

Personalities of Muppets

As a Muppet passes from the designers to the builders and on to the writers, its personality grows. Each of these people adds something to the puppet. Most of the words that a Muppet speaks are written by a group of people. But it is the hand and the voice of the puppeteer that give the Muppet its life.

"The relationship between a puppet and a puppeteer," says Jim, "is an odd one." It is not unusual to find a very quiet puppeteer with a noisy, big-mouthed puppet on his or her hand. Puppeteers often allow

Muppets and other members of the Sesame Street cast gather on the set.

their puppets to say things that they themselves would never have the nerve to say.

It was easy to decide on Fozzie Bear's puppeteer, Frank Oz. Frank likes to be funny himself. He brings Fozzie to life. When Fozzie makes a joke, it is Frank who makes us laugh. Frank is also the voice behind many other funny Muppets—Cookie Monster, Grover, Miss Piggy, Animal, and Bert.

Jim Henson's favorite Muppet is Kermit. Jim made Kermit back in 1956. He has been Kermit's voice ever since. Over the years, the little frog has become more and more like Jim.

"He is a part of me," Jim says. "I can speak through him."

How Muppets Work

Some of the Muppets are worked by one person, and some by two. Kermit and Bert need only one person to work them. Ernie needs two people to bring him to life. Jim usually

Miss Piggy.

works Ernie's head and one of his hands. Another person works Ernie's other hand.

There are times on the "Muppet Show" when one puppeteer will work two puppets at once, one with each hand. At times like these, the stage can become quite crowded.

Puppeteers depend on small TV sets. The sets help them to see what their puppets are doing. Several of these sets are placed on the stage.

The man who stands inside of Big Bird's 2.5-meter-high body wears a tiny TV set strapped to his chest. By watching this set, he can see

Jim Henson with two of his Muppet friends: Kermit the Frog (on his shoulder) and Ernie.

everything that is taking place on the stage.

A few years ago, someone asked Jim Henson what he wanted to be when he "grew up." He thought for a few minutes. Then he spoke.

"Well, if I must grow up, I guess I'd like to be a frog."

"Any particular frog?" he was asked.

The man behind the Muppets laughed. "What do you think?" he said.

Understanding What You've Read

1. What are Muppets?
2. How did Kermit the Frog become a Muppet?
3. Why was it easy to decide on Fozzie Bear's puppeteer, Frank Oz?
4. Who gives a Muppet its personality?

Applying the Skills Lesson

Which of the following conclusions can you draw about the Muppets based on the information given in the selection? (There is more than one conclusion you can draw.)

1. It takes many people working together to make a Muppet.
2. Ernie is not the only Muppet that needs two people to work him.
3. The person who stands inside Big Bird is 2.5 meters tall.
4. Each Muppet is at least twenty years old.

The authors give many facts about different museums. Use the facts and your knowledge to help you draw conclusions about the information.

There is a place where, if you turn right, you can take a trip into the past. If you turn left, you can take a trip into the future. What kind of place is that?

A Very Special Place

by Herbert *and* Marjorie Katz

What kind of place will let you explore an old attic filled with things from the past? What kind of place will let you work a big, modern computer? What kind of place will let you wander through a cave or study the stars?

A children's museum is that kind of place. Not every one of them offers all of these things. Yet each of them has good things in store for its visitors. The halls are smaller than those in other museums. You can take part in many of the exhibits. You don't just look at them. You can take trips into the past and the future, as well as the present.

Where are these museums? They are all over the United States. In fact, they are all over the world. There may even be a children's museum near you. Here are just a few of them.

Left, Grandmother's Attic at the Boston Children's Museum. Below right and bottom, exhibits from the Children's Museum of Indianapolis.

The Children's Museum of Indianapolis

This museum has the world's largest children's museum building. There are many different kinds of exhibits. You can see the mummy of Princess Wenuhotep [wen·u·hō′tep], of Egypt. You can visit a cabin that was built to look like a real cabin lived in around 1829. You can view a huge, wood-burning locomotive built in 1868. It once powered freight and passenger cars throughout southern Indiana. You may even see "how to" shows. These shows may have spinning, weaving, candle-dipping, and soap-making.

Two popular exhibits at this museum are quite different from each other. One is a *working* carousel from around 1900. The other is a simulated Indiana limestone cave.

The carousel has colorful, hand-carved wooden animals. This merry-go-round was made and operated in Indianapolis. You can ride the same horse, or giraffe, or lion that some child rode at the turn of the century!

The cave exhibit is for exploring. There are about thirty-six meters of cold, damp passageways, with underground streams. Huge icicle-shaped "limestone" stalactites [stə·lak′tīts] hang from the roof of the cave. Stalagmites [stə·lag′mīts], which look like upside-down stalactites, point up from the floor of the cave.

Caves or cavelike places seem to be favorites in many parts of the country. In a museum in Connecticut, there was a dark, cavelike place with six small windows. There you could pretend to be inside a *bathysphere* [bath′ə·sfir] that was rising from the very bottom of the ocean. (A bathysphere is a round, steel structure with windows. It is used in deep water for studying the sea.) You could see ocean life all around you in paintings. Different kinds of lights made the paintings almost come to life. Unfortunately, this exhibit is no longer being shown.

The Boston Children's Museum

You'll have to go to this place to explore an old attic. This exhibit is called *Grandmother's Attic.* In it you will find all sorts of things. There's an old trunk filled with the kind of clothes your grandparents wore. You can dress up in these clothes. You'll also find the kinds of washing machines and sewing machines that your grandparents might have used.

Playing games with a computer at the Boston Children's Museum.

A very modern exhibit that you can enjoy and work in is the computer exhibit. The computers are programmed to do many things. You can punch in your name and age and play tic tac toe. You can even ask questions about the rocket power needed to land on the moon—and get the answers! And the computers are covered with a kind of clear plastic so that you can see what is going on inside as they are working.

The Fort Worth Museum of Science and History

Before 1968, this museum was called the Fort Worth Children's Museum. It had grown so large that in 1968 its name was changed. The museum still offered many of the same things for children it always had. However, more was added for the whole family to enjoy.

If you want to go back into the past, you can go to the Rocks and Fossils room. You can see two dinosaurs, antrodemus (also

The dinosaurs antrodemus and camptosaurus on display in the Rocks and Fossils room at the Fort Worth Museum of Science and History.

called allosaurus) and camptosaurus, attacking each other. Their bones were put together by hand. It was a long, hard job. Some people said that it was not very different from putting together a huge puzzle.

In another room you can see what brain surgery was like 5,000 years ago. Figures show what the operation looked like. There is no glass around this exhibit. Only a railing keeps you from joining the group of people. You can almost feel like you're present at that operation—5,000 years ago!

Other rooms show scenes with figures, bowls, dolls, and masks. These things tell about people long ago from Mexico and Africa.

You can get away from the past and come back to the

Looking at the stars in the Noble Planetarium at the Fort Worth Museum of Science and History.

present by going into another part of the museum. In this part you can see live animals and hear their sounds. You can pat a lively raccoon or fox. You can run your hand along a friendly snake. This room seems to be a favorite of many children.

What if you're tired of the everyday world? Go to yet another part of the museum. Go to the Noble Planetarium for another kind of trip. A planetarium is a place where you can learn about the Earth and other planets, the stars, and the moon.

When you go into the Noble Planetarium, you will sit down for your trip. A voice will tell you to sit back in your seat and enjoy yourself. Then the lights in the domed room begin to dim. As if by magic, the clouds roll away from the center of the sky. Little lights begin to appear in the black sky above. You are looking up at many thousands of twinkling stars.

There are many more exhibits in each of the museums talked about. You can visit them yourself. There are hundreds of children's museums around the country. No two are exactly alike. But all of them have one thing in common. Beyond their doors lies a special world created with *you* in mind.

Understanding What You've Read

1. What makes a children's museum different from other museums?
2. What children's museum will let you explore a cold, damp cave?
3. In what children's museum can you work with computers?
4. Which of the exhibits talked about in the selection would you like to see? Why?

Applying the Skills Lesson

Which of the following conclusions about children's museums can you draw based on information given in the selection? (There is more than one conclusion you can draw.)

1. Children's museums give people a chance to discover and explore things.
2. Children's museums are no fun at all.
3. The authors hope that their readers will visit children's museums.
4. Adults do not enjoy children's museums.

Drawing Conclusions

Sometimes textbook writers will ask questions. They may want you to draw conclusions from the facts they are giving you. The selections that follow will give you practice in drawing conclusions from sets of facts. The sidenotes will help you understand the facts.

Drawing Conclusions in Social Studies

What Kind of Ocean?

These questions are not asking you to draw conclusions. They are preparing you to think about what is coming.

Have you ever been on the bottom of an ocean? Talked with the creatures that lived there? Played with them?

"How could I do that?" you say. "That's silly!" Is it? Here's a problem to solve. Read the clues.

The writer means that *it may not be so silly* to do some of the things talked about in the first paragraph. Does the writer actually say this?

1. It is an ocean you cannot see.
2. Millions and millions of creatures live in this ocean. They come in hundreds of shapes and sizes. All of these ocean creatures are part of the natural system.

All of the facts or clues listed will help you answer the questions at the end. The questions ask you to draw conclusions based on these facts.

3. Since the day the ocean creatures were born, they have swallowed quarts and quarts and quarts of their ocean. It helps them meet one of their basic needs.

450

4. The ocean creatures usually travel along the bottom of their ocean.

5. The creatures of this ocean are in your classroom right now.

What is this ocean? Who lives in it?

— Planet Earth
Houghton Mifflin

Clue 5 is an important clue. It limits who or what the creatures can be.

The questions ask you to draw conclusions based on the facts. What conclusions can you draw?

Building Skills

1. Read clue 2 again. Which conclusion can you draw about the creatures?

   a. They are ugly.
   b. They all have something in common.

2. Read clue 3 again. Which conclusion can you draw about the creatures this time?

   a. They drink too much.
   b. The creatures have more than one basic need.

451

Drawing Conclusions in Language Arts

Different Alphabets

Mexico

Russia

France

Israel

- **You can use information from this picture to help you draw conclusions.**
- **A word joined by a line to a picture is a *label*. It helps you understand the picture. Find the labels.**

Look at the newspapers in the picture above.

To answer these questions you must use facts from the picture. What else in the picture do you need to know?

What country does each newspaper come from?

What language do you think the people in each country speak?

Are all the newspapers written with the same alphabet?

Use the alphabets in the right-hand margin to help you draw conclusions.

The alphabet that you use when you write English is called the **Roman alphabet.** Many other languages are also written with the Roman alphabet. But many languages have alphabets of their own.

Look at the newspapers in the picture again. Which two newspapers are written with the Roman alphabet? Which two newspapers are written with other alphabets?

— *Exploring English*
Laidlaw Brothers

Which sentences in this paragraph ask you to draw conclusions?

Building Skills

1. In the selection you just read, find the five questions that are asking you to draw conclusions.

2. Using the picture of different alphabets, which of the following conclusions can you draw? (You can draw more than one conclusion.)

   a. Greek is harder to learn than Russian.
   b. Not every alphabet has twenty-six letters.
   c. The letter *T* stands for the same sound in Greek and Russian.
   d. The Greek and Russian alphabets use some of the same symbols that are in the Roman alphabet.

Roman

A	J	S
B	K	T
C	L	U
D	M	V
E	N	W
F	O	X
G	P	Y
H	Q	Z
I	R	

Greek

A	I	P
B	K	Σ
Γ	Λ	T
Δ	M	Υ
E	N	Φ
Z	Ξ	X
H	O	Ψ
Θ	Π	Ω

Russian

А	М	Ч
Б	Н	Ш
В	О	Щ
Г	П	Ъ
Д	Р	Ы
Е	С	Ь
Ж	Т	Э
З	У	Ю
И Й	Ф	Я
К	Х	
Л	Ц	

453

Understanding Cause-and-Effect Relationships

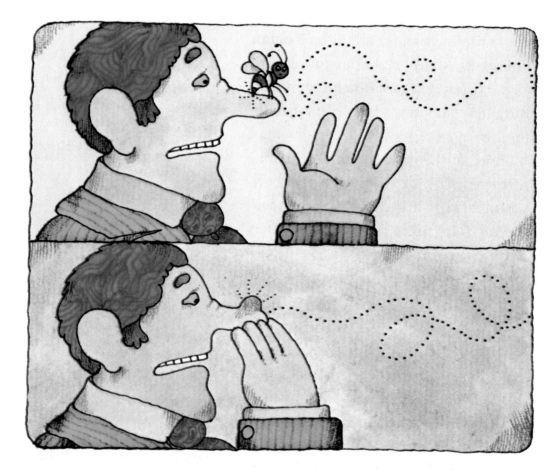

Look at the pictures above. What has happened? You can see that the man has a big bump on his nose. Why did this happen? A bee stung him. The two ideas shown are related in a certain way. It is called a **cause-and-effect relationship.** The bee stinging the man is the *cause.* The bump on the man's nose is the *effect,* or result.

You will come across many cause-and-effect relationships in your reading. Writers will tell you *what happened* and *why it happened*.

Sometimes a cause and an effect are told in one sentence.

The fog moved in all around the people, so they could not see the path.

Other times a cause and an effect are told in separate sentences.

The fog moved in all around the people. That is why they could not see the path.

In each of the examples above, what is the cause? *The fog moving in* is the cause. What is the effect? *The people could not see the path* is the effect.

Sometimes writers tell an effect before they tell the cause.

Carmen broke her leg because she slipped on a waxed floor.

In the sentence above, the effect is *Carmen broke her leg*. What caused this? *She slipped on a waxed floor*.

Now look at the sentence above again. Which word or group of words connects the two ideas in it? The word *because* connects the two ideas. In the earlier examples in this lesson, the words *so* and *that is why* were used to connect the ideas. You can use word clues like these to help you understand cause-and-effect relationships.

Here are other words that may help you.

and so	then	as a result
so that	for this reason	

These words are usually a clue that a cause-and-effect relationship is being described.

Try This

Read the following sentences. Which part of each sentence tells the cause? Which part tells the effect?

1. His boots lay outside of his sleeping bag all night. As a result, they froze.
2. Maria missed the bus to school, and so she was late to class.
3. Louis did not get much sleep during the night; as a result, he was tired in the morning.
4. The fish were healthy because Nancy took good care of her fish tank.
5. Kim became a powerful batter because she practiced every day for a year.

VOCABULARY STUDY

Getting Meaning from Context Clues

The Fleeceville News
_10¢_   _10¢_

EXTRA
Sheep Lost!

Fleeceville, July 12.—Ms. Bo Peep, popular nursery rhyme star, has lost her sheep. The police have been informed. Ms. Bo Peep said that she felt it was a real **tragedy.**

"It's a sad and unhappy thing to lose anything that you love," explained Ms. Bo Peep.

It has been twenty-four hours since Ms. Bo Peep has seen her sheep. It may take some time to find them. But Ms. Bo Peep says she has a great deal of **patience.** "I can wait a long time without complaining," Ms. Bo Peep explained. "Still, I hope I don't have to wait _too_ long."

Many people feel Ms. Bo Peep has a lot of **charisma.** Perhaps her ability to attract and win the loyal affection of others will be all the help she needs to get her lost sheep back.

Recent photo of lost sheep.

Word Play

1. Give a definition for the words _tragedy, patience,_ and _charisma,_ using the context clues above.

2. Define the word _antrodemus,_ using the context clues given here: The antrodemus was large and ate meat. It lived in North America and was also called _allosaurus._

Look for connecting words to help you recognize cause-and-effect relationships.

How does one magician make his magic happen? He understands how to use . . .

The Secrets of Alkazar

by Allan Zola Kronzek

When I was young, nothing excited me more than going to a magic store. Everywhere I looked, there was something I wanted to buy. There were bright feather flowers to be pulled from "empty" tubes. There were boxes for making rabbits appear. There was even a bowl full of fire that a living dove came out of! I longed to own these wonderful things from the magic store. But I didn't have money for a single one. I talked about this to Alkazar. He was a master magician. He had accepted me as a pupil.

"Don't be so sad," Alkazar told me. "Magic comes from you —not from a store. Oh, magic shops sell a lot of things you want to own. But that comes later, when your shows are earning money. Right now, there are dozens of magic tricks that you can make yourself."

To prove his point, Alkazar taught me a great illusion. I only needed a coin, a napkin, a drinking glass, and the art of *misdirection*.

In all of magic there is no skill more important than skill in misdirection. Misdirection is the art of making people see what *you* want them to see. At the same time, you're secretly doing something you don't want them to see. To do this, you must not only be a magician, but a very good actor as well.

The key to misdirection lies in learning to direct people's attention. So Alkazar gave me a set of rules to follow in doing nearly any magic. He has allowed me to pass these rules along to you.

Rule 1. People will look at what moves. They will also look at what makes noise. What doesn't move and doesn't make noise won't attract attention.

Rule 2. People will look where you look. If you look at your foot, they will look at your foot. When there is something you don't want them to see, don't look at it. If you don't want them to look at the ceiling, don't look at the ceiling. Look at your foot.

Rule 3. People will treat as important what you treat as important. In magic, you nearly always treat something important as if it were unimportant. Likewise, you treat something unimportant as if it were important.

Of course, the reading of these rules will do you no good unless you put them into practice. The following trick, called "Passing Through," is a good place to start. Misdirection is built right into it. It is one of Alkazar's favorite tricks.

While seated at a dinner table with friends, Alkazar says that he is going to perform a miracle. He is going to cause a coin to pass *through* the table. He borrows a quarter. He places it on the table a foot or so in front of him. Next, he covers a glass with a napkin. Then he places the glass on top of the coin.

All eyes are on him. Alkazar says his magic words. He orders the coin to pass through the table. Everyone watches quietly. Alkazar then places his empty left hand under the table to receive the coin. With his right hand, he lifts the glass to show that the quarter has vanished. But much to the great Alkazar's surprise, the coin is still there! The magic has seemed to fail.

But wait! Alkazar suddenly notices that the coin is lying heads up instead of tails up. No wonder the magic didn't work! He turns the quarter over and covers it with the glass and napkin. Again he says some magic words. But again the magic fails.

By this time the audience is beginning to wonder if Alkazar is really a magician. Indeed he is! And now he proves it.

"There is a very powerful spell that I don't often use because it can be very dangerous," Alkazar explains. "But this is no time to be careful."

Once again he covers the coin. "Atoms and molecules," he repeats. "By the power that is mine, I order you to make way. *Oomash kabasi zid!*" Without warning, Alkazar slams his right hand down upon the napkin. The napkin is smashed flat against the table! The coin is still there, *but the glass has vanished*. Just then, *it is brought up from under the table*. An impossible show of one solid passing through another seems to have taken place! As for the quarter, Alkazar returns it to its owner with a smile. "Sometimes the powers of magic surprise even me," says Alkazar.

What makes the trick so wonderful in the hands of Alkazar is not only its secret. It is also the way in which misdirection and surprise are used to throw everyone off guard. Here's how the trick is done.

When you cover the glass, squeeze the napkin around the top and sides. The shape of the glass should be clear. Make certain that the napkin hides the whole glass. The bottom of the glass, where the napkin spreads out onto the table, should be well hidden.

Now, the first time you pick up the glass and napkin to show that the coin is there, lean forward a bit. Make it seem that you want to get a closer look at the coin. At the same time, bring the hand with the glass to the edge of the table. Loosen your grip and secretly let the glass drop into your lap. If you are using misdirection well, no one will notice. You have made everyone think you are doing a coin trick. So their attention is on the quarter. That's where *your* attention should be, too. Remember Rule 3. What you look at, they will look at.

461

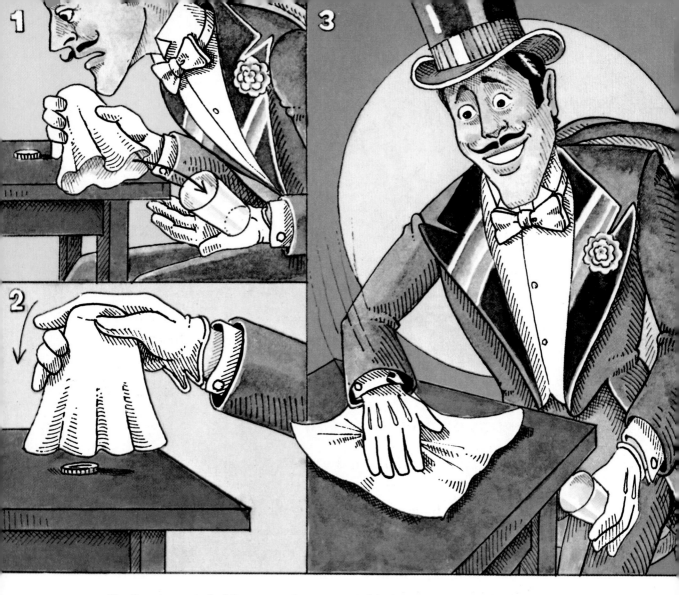

So far, so good. Now you have in your hand a napkin that you have kept in the form of the glass. Magicians often call such an empty form a *shell*. Place the shell over the coin and go on as explained above. (Alkazar turns the coin over as an added bit of misdirection. Perhaps you can think up your own misdirection for this part of the trick.)

The second time you peek at the coin, don't move the glass more than a few inches away from the coin. People will never remember that you moved it farther away the first time. When you are ready to finish the trick, your empty left hand picks up the glass from your lap. Your left hand should move under the table as your right hand slams down on the napkin. Bring the glass up for all to see.

Here are five tips about this trick from Alkazar's Notebook.

- Just as you must make the coin seem important to the trick, you must make the glass seem unimportant.

- Always handle the shell as if it really holds the glass.

- Learn what kinds of napkins will hold a shape. Large paper napkins are ideal. Newspaper is good, too.

- Add or take away from the trick whatever makes it work best for you. Many magicians "steal" the glass on the second peek. It's a matter of choice.

- Don't do a trick. Do magic.

Understanding What You've Read

1. Who is Alkazar? Who is the writer of this selection?
2. What is misdirection?
3. Why does Alkazar pretend that his trick has failed?

Applying the Skills Lesson

The following sentences are from the selection you just read. Which group of words tells the cause? Which group of words tells the effect?

1. You have made everyone think you are doing a coin trick. So their attention is on the quarter.
2. Without warning, Alkazar slams his right hand down upon the napkin. The napkin is smashed flat against the table!

When people ask her what she does, the writer of this selection can proudly answer . . .

I Am a Dancer

by Hilda Morales

Dancing is the thing that I love to do the most. My name is Hilda Morales. I dance with the American Ballet Theater, one of the best dance companies in the world.

I was born in New York City, but I grew up in Puerto Rico. I always wanted to be a dancer. When I was nine, my mother took me to my first ballet class. I liked it so much that I went on studying. I knew then that I wanted to become a ballerina. It became my dream.

The word *ballet* is French. It comes from an Italian word that means "to dance." A ballet is like a play in which graceful moves take the place of words. By using only five basic steps, the dancers can show a whole story. They can show feelings by the way they move in time to the music.

The dance form called ballet began in the 1500's in France. This is why French words are used for the steps in ballet. This dance form became very popular. Soon it spread all over Europe. In time, Italy, Russia, Denmark, and England each had a great ballet company.

Have you ever seen a ballet? If you have, it may seem to you that it is easy for the dancers to move as they do. But it really isn't easy. To look graceful and natural, the dancers have to work very hard. They have to work every day for many years. Their feet and legs must be strong. The dancers must learn to control each movement. In fact, the dancers have to keep their bodies in shape in the same way athletes do.

Dancers go to class every day. They exercise to teach their bodies how to move with the music. They learn all the different steps that they will do on stage. They also have to learn to act. Ballet *is* more than just dance.

Much of my time is spent in rehearsals. There I learn the different parts I will dance. At times, my teacher may stop the music and ask me to repeat a step. I don't mind. The more that I prepare, the better I will dance.

Dancers also have to know how to put on make-up and what colors to use. If they didn't use make-up, people sitting far from the stage would not be able to see the feelings they try to show on their faces. That is why make-up is so important.

Sometimes, before dancers go on stage, they get a little nervous. So they help each other with costumes and make-up. But what's really important is that they try to do their best. The next day, it's back to class. As a great ballerina used to say, "Talent is work, work, work."

Understanding What You've Read

1. What is a ballet?
2. Name three things dancers must learn to do.
3. Why doesn't Hilda Morales mind repeating the steps she is learning?

Applying the Skills Lesson

The following sentences are about the selection you just read. Which group of words tells the cause? Which group of words tells the effect?

1. The dance form called ballet began in the 1500's in France; therefore, French words are used for the steps in ballet.
2. Dancers work very hard every day for many years. As a result, their feet and legs become strong.
3. The more that dancers rehearse and prepare, the better they dance.

Understanding Cause-and-Effect Relationships

Seeing how ideas are related can help you understand sentences in your textbooks. In the following selections, you will find several cause-and-effect relationships. Use the side-notes to help you understand these relationships.

Understanding Cause-and-Effect Relationships in Science

There are two ideas told here. What happens to the water when food is added?

A jar of clear pond water seems to have no life in it. Then you add food to the water, and life appears. Now you can see tiny specks of animals moving about. How does this happen?

When egg yolk (or rice) is added to the water, you can see a change take place in the yolk from day to day. We say the yolk decays. The change takes place because tiny living things in the water are feeding on the yolk. These living things are very tiny plants called bacteria.

The effect is told first here. Why does the yolk decay?

To your eye, the pond water may seem clear. Bacteria are so small that they can be seen only with a strong microscope. Here are some bacteria in

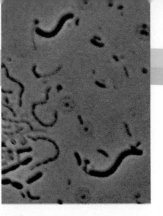

pond water, as seen under the micro-scope. Bacteria are so small that about 100,000 of them might fit into the period at the end of this sentence.

As the bacteria feed on the egg yolk, the yolk decays. When the bacteria feed well, they can make more of themselves. One splits into two. Two bacteria become four. Four bacteria become eight. Eight become sixteen, and so on.

The word *as* is some-times a clue that a cause and an effect are being stated. What is the cause? What is the effect?

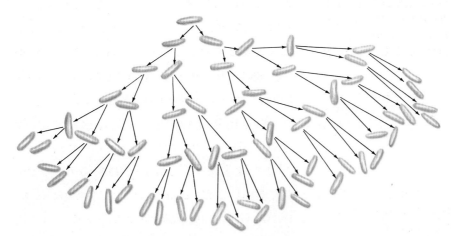

In a few days the clear water in the jar becomes cloudy, because of the millions upon millions of bacteria liv-ing in the water.

Which is told first—the cause or the effect? What is the connecting word?

—*Concepts in Science:* Orange
Harcourt Brace Jovanovich

Building Skills

1. The following sentence is from the selection you just read. The same two ideas are expressed in *two* sentences in another part of the selection. Find the two sentences.

   As the bacteria feed on the egg yolk, the yolk decays.

2. Read the last sentence in the selection again. What is the cause-and-effect relationship?

Understanding Cause-and-Effect Relationships in Social Studies

A cause and effect are told here. What causes the Earth to look blue?

Earth is often called the Blue Planet because that's the way it looks from space. It looks blue because so much of the surface is covered with water.

Venus also looks blue from space. Because it is always covered by clouds, it is a mystery planet. Might Venus have water and air like Earth's?

Because of its clouds, scientists could not learn much about Venus until recently. Some writers studied what had been learned and imagined what Venus might be like. Here's how one writer described the planet:

What word gives you a clue that a cause-and-effect relationship is being stated? Which is told first—the cause or the effect?

"It was a long, lonely valley with a copper-colored floor and gentle slopes clothed in a kind of many-colored forest. It was an island, with hills and valleys which changed places every minute because it was floating on the ocean. There were strange trees with tube-like trunks of gray and purple, and leaves of orange, silver, and blue."

The effect is told first here. Why did the hills and valleys change places every minute?

—Planet Earth
Houghton Mifflin

Building Skills

1. Read the first sentence of the selection again. What word in the sentence connects the cause and the effect? Which is told first—the cause or the effect?
2. Read the second paragraph of the selection again. Find the sentence that states a cause-and-effect relationship. What is the cause? What is the effect?

471

Predicting Outcomes

Look at the picture story above. Can you tell what will happen next? If so, then you are **predicting an outcome.**

When you predict an outcome, you think about what is happening or has already happened. Then you use your powers of reasoning to figure out what is likely to happen next.

Did you predict that the balloon in the picture story on page 472 will probably burst? Look at what is happening in the pictures. You see the balloon keeps getting larger. Now think of what you know about blowing up balloons. You may have done it yourself or have seen a machine like the one in the pictures do it. By using the clues in the pictures and your knowledge, you can tell that the balloon will probably burst.

Writers sometimes ask you to predict an outcome after they tell about some events. Read the paragraph below.

Dorothy and Otis were skating at the rink. They went slowly at first, but then they started skating faster and faster. All of a sudden they both started to slip and lose their balance. No one was nearby to help them. What will happen next?

Did you predict that Dorothy and Otis would fall down? This is a likely outcome because they *started to slip and lose their balance* and *no one was nearby to help them*. The same thing may have happened to you. But even if it never had, you could still guess what will happen next.

Read the paragraph below.

A chameleon is a reptile that changes color. Under its skin are cells that have yellow, black, and red coloring matter. Light is one thing that affects the chameleon's color. Hot sunlight will make the chameleon turn dark, almost black. Darkness makes the chameleon turn to a cream color with yellow spots. Kim put a chameleon into a dark closet.

What will happen to the chameleon?

a. It will turn dark, almost black.

b. It will turn green.

c. It will turn a cream color, with yellow spots.

You know from the clues in the paragraph that *darkness makes the chameleon turn to a cream color with yellow spots.* So you can predict that the chameleon will turn a cream color with yellow spots.

Try This

Read each paragraph. Then read the sentences below each paragraph. Each sentence states a different outcome. Choose the sentence that states the most likely outcome.

1. Early in the evening Lynn began to sneeze. Her head began to ache and her eyes began to water. She started to run a fever. With each new sneeze, her nose felt more stuffy.

   How will Lynn feel in the morning?
   a. She will have a head cold.
   b. She will feel fine.
   c. She will have a stiff leg.

2. In order to have a fire, you need something that will burn and you need oxygen. Air has oxygen that will keep a fire burning. Julius lit a candle and watched it burn. Then he covered it completely with a glass jar. He waited to see what would happen.

What will happen to the burning candle?
a. It will go on burning as it would without the glass jar.
b. It will die out when all the oxygen is used up.
c. It will burn even more brightly.

Suffixes

"Can I help you?" asked Detective Izzy A. Clod.

"We understand that you solve missing-word cases," said the suffixes *-able* and *-or.* "Well, we need that kind of help."

"No problem," said Clod. "There are plenty of words that each of you can be added to. You, *-or,* mean *a person or thing that,* as in **projector** or **operator.** (The *e* is dropped from *operate* before you're added.) And you, *-able,* mean *able to* or *capable of being,* as in **movable** or **lovable.** (The *e* is dropped from *move* and *love* before you're added.)"

"Thanks for the words, Detective Clod," said the two suffixes. "Now how about giving us some sentences?"

"Sure," said Clod, as he pulled four sentences out of a drawer. "I have four sentences right here."

1. My teacher used an overhead **projector** to show us the pictures of the clowns.
2. Since my teacher worked the projector, she was the **operator.**
3. She was able to turn the projector because it had **movable** parts.
4. She turned the projector so that we could see the pictures of the **lovable** clowns.

"Thanks, Detective Clod," said the suffixes. "Once more you proved you're a great detective."

"It's all in a day's work," said Clod. "Next case."

Word Play

1. Use the meanings of the suffixes to help you explain what the word in boldface means in each sentence on pages 476–477.
2. Add the suffix *-or* or *-able* to the words below.
    wash   invent   use   investigate
3. Pretend that you are Detective Clod. Think of a sentence for each of the words you have made in number 2.

As you read, look for some questions that ask you to predict an outcome.

One way to learn a lot and to enjoy our world is to . . .

GO FLY A PAPER AIRPLANE

by Seymour Simon

Have you ever flown a paper airplane? Sometimes it turns and loops through the air. Then it comes to rest, soft as a feather. Other times a paper airplane climbs straight up, flips over, and dives headfirst into the ground.

What keeps a paper airplane in the air? How can you make a paper airplane go on a long flight? How can you make it loop or turn? Does wind help a paper airplane to stay up?

What can you learn about real airplanes from paper airplanes? Let's discover some of the answers.

Gravity and Air

Take two sheets of the same-sized paper. Crush one of the papers into a ball. Hold the crushed paper and the flat paper high above your head. Drop them both at the same time. The force of *gravity* pulls them both downward. Which paper falls to the ground first? What seems to keep the flat sheet from falling quickly?

We live with air all around us. Air is real even though you can't see it. The air pushes back against the flat paper and slows its fall. The paper ball has a smaller surface pushing against the air, so it falls faster.

Lift and Thrust

The spread-out wings of a paper airplane keep it from falling quickly down to the ground. We say the wings give a plane *lift*. But you want a paper airplane to do more than just fall slowly through the air. You want it to move forward.

You can make a paper airplane move forward by throwing it. Usually, the harder you throw a paper airplane, the farther it will fly. The forward movement of an airplane is called *thrust*. What do you think will happen if an airplane stops moving forward through the air?

You can learn something about thrust if you run with a kite in the air. The air pushes against the underside of the moving kite and lifts it up. What will happen if you walk slowly rather than run?

Thrust works to make an airplane move forward. At the same time, lift works to make a plane go up, and gravity tries to make it fall down. These forces are always working on paper airplanes just as they work on real airplanes.

Making a Paper Airplane

Let's make a paper airplane and see how these forces work in flight. Use a sheet of 8½-by-11-inch paper.

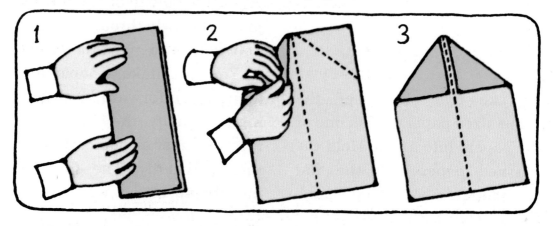

Fold the paper in half lengthwise. Rub your thumbnail along the fold to make it sharp. Open the paper and fold down one corner toward the center. Fold down the other corner in the same way. (See drawings 1, 2, and 3 above.)

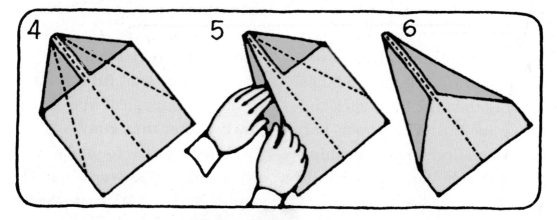

Now fold one side again toward the center along the dotted line. Look at drawings 4, 5, and 6 to see how to do it. Fold the other side along the other dotted line. Make sure the folds are sharply creased.

Turn the paper over. Fold over one side along the left-hand dotted line. Look at drawings 7 and 8 to help you. Open the paper. Fold the other side over along the right-hand dotted line as shown in drawing 9. From the bottom, your airplane should look like the one in drawing 10.

Use a piece of tape to hold the body of the airplane together and to give the wings a little upward tilt.

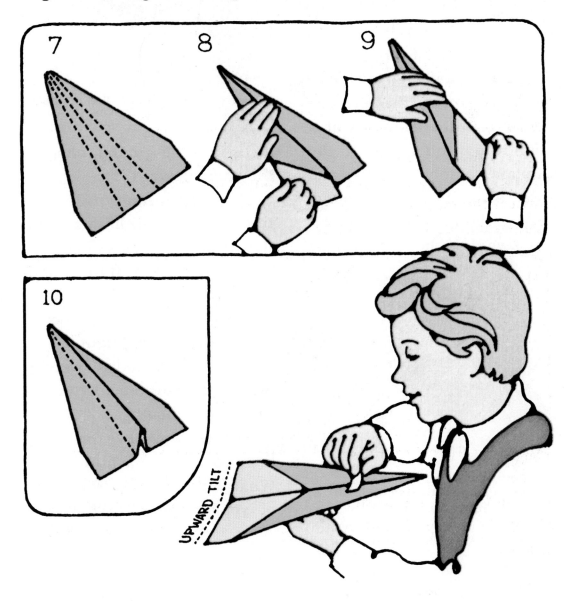

Flying Your Paper Airplane

Launch your airplane in a big room or out-of-doors. Make sure that there is nothing it can hit and knock over. Hold the body of the airplane between your thumb and finger a few inches back from its nose. Raise your hand high over your head and throw the airplane gently forward. Throw it at a slightly upward angle. If the airplane climbs steeply and then dives into the ground, change the angle of thrust a bit downward. If the airplane just

Entry by David Segal, Philadelphia, Pennsylvania.

dives into the ground, change the angle upward.

What will happen if you throw the airplane harder? Will the plane fly longer or higher?

If your airplane flutters and slips from side to side, try putting a paper clip on the body. The clip will add weight to the airplane. The added weight makes the airplane fly more easily and smoothly.

Suppose you move the clip a *little* forward or a little back. What will happen to the flight of your airplane? What will

Entry by Andrew Kimball and Mark B. Wanzenberg, Larchmont, N.Y.

happen if you move the clip all the way forward or all the way back?

What will happen if you just drop your airplane from a height? Will it fall directly or glide down for a landing?

Weight, Balance, and Wind

The position of the clip changes the point at which the airplane's weight is balanced. This point is called the *center of gravity*. To find the center of gravity, place one finger under the front of the airplane and another finger under the back of the airplane. Move your fingers slowly in toward the center. The airplane's center of gravity is where it balances on one finger.

Adding a paper clip not only changes the airplane's balance point, but also adds to its weight. Try flying the airplane with two paper clips in the same position. Does it stay up

Entry at left by Lewis G. Lowe, San Francisco, California.

Entry below by John Craig and George Peck, New York, N.Y.

in the air as long as it does with one clip? What do you think would happen if you added ten paper clips? Can you see why real airplanes are made of lightweight materials?

If you fly your airplane out-of-doors on a slightly windy day, it may toss about wildly. Try putting on some paper clips to add weight. The added weight may make the airplane's flight steadier.

Throw the airplane into the wind. Then try throwing it with the wind. Compare the two flights. In which direction does the flight last longer? Real airplanes try to take off and land into the wind. Can you explain why?

Building and flying paper airplanes is fun for young people and grown-ups, too. Several years ago, the well-known magazine *Scientific American* held a paper-airplane contest. They received almost 12,000 entries. Many entries were from professors and scientists. Entries were sent in from 28 countries. It seems as if almost everyone likes to make and fly paper airplanes.

Understanding What You've Read

1. What keeps a paper airplane in the air?
2. What is the *center of gravity* on a paper airplane?
3. What can you learn about real airplanes from paper airplanes?

Applying the Skills Lesson

1. Read the first full paragraph in the right-hand column on page 479. The paragraph begins, "You can make. . . ." What outcome would you predict if an airplane stopped moving forward through the air?

   a. The airplane would still stay in the air.
   b. The airplane would begin to fall down.

2. Read the second full paragraph in the right-hand column on page 479. Suppose you wanted to fly a kite. What would happen if you walked slowly rather than ran with the kite?

3. Read the last paragraph in the right-hand column on page 483 that ends on page 484. The paragraph begins, "Adding a paper clip. . . ." What outcome would you predict if you added ten paper clips to the airplane?

   a. The airplane would stay up in the air longer.
   b. The airplane would fall more quickly.

Reading about hot-air ballooning can help you predict what may happen to this exciting sport.

Would you like to go up in the air in a beautiful balloon? Read about a sport that takes people . . .

Flying High

by Hal Schell

Hot-air ballooning has become a popular sport. However, the hot-air balloon has been around for a long time. Back in 1783, two Frenchmen, the Montgolfier [Mont·gol′fē·ā′] brothers, astounded the citizens of Versailles [vər·sī′] by sending a rooster, a sheep, and a duck aloft in a hot-air balloon. Two months later in Paris, two men went up in a hot-air balloon. This was the world's first balloon flight with people. The men drifted over the streets of Paris for twenty-five thrilling minutes.

The hot air that made the balloon rise was supplied by a fire of straw and wool in the basket. These early flights were dangerous. The balloon envelope was made of cloth lined with paper. Pilots had to be careful it didn't catch fire. Also, the material was easily punctured.

As balloon envelopes were improved, the gas balloon was developed. It used lighter-than-air gas much like that used in today's gas stoves. These were considered better than hot-air balloons. They could stay aloft longer, carry heavier loads, and fly lower and farther.

The balloon was never thought to be a very trustworthy form of transportation, though. It is not like flying an airplane. A pilot cannot steer a balloon. The balloon goes wherever the wind chooses to take it. The pilot can go up higher by heating the air in a hot-air balloon or by letting go of some ballast on a gas-filled balloon. He or she can go down by letting the air cool in the hot-air balloon or by letting some of the gas escape through a valve on the gas balloon.

The wind sometimes blows in different directions at different heights. So the pilot may take the balloon higher or lower to find a wind that is blowing in the direction he or she wants to go. At times when there is no wind, the balloon is like a becalmed sailing ship and hardly moves at all.

There are now thousands of hot-air balloons in the United States, and the number is growing fast. Most of these are used for sport. They're used for the pure fun of lazily drifting with the wind high above the ground. Quite a number are also used for advertising purposes. They carry a company's name or "logo" on the side of the envelope for all to see. Some fly above shopping centers or new markets to draw attention to a grand opening or a sale. These are fastened to the Earth by a long tether line so they won't go flying off.

These balloons are wonderful to look at. Many are as high as an eight-story building and draw a great deal of attention. This is just what the advertisers want them to do.

Two recent improvements made hot-air ballooning more practical. First was the use of lightweight but strong, nylon material for the envelope. Because nylon is light, the balloon can be made to rise without great amounts of hot air. Because nylon is tough, the balloon may be flown time after time. Nylon will tear if it hits something sharp. But it can be patched.

The second improvement that made hot-air ballooning more practical was the development of special gas burners. These burners made it possible to feed a great deal of heat per hour into a balloon. This fuel is generally safe. It is held in tanks that share the balloon's basket with pilot and passengers.

In flight, the pilot turns the burners on for a blast of heat, then drifts for many minutes on the heat supplied. All is quiet and peaceful because he or she is drifting with the wind. When the pilot notes the fuel supply is getting low, it's time to look for a nice flat spot to land in.

The best hours for ballooning are usually just after the crack of dawn and in the late afternoon when the winds are light. A balloon is hard to handle on the ground if winds are over five miles an hour.

Ballooning contests are held in many parts of the country. Seeing dozens of balloons inflated at one time is a magnificent sight. When they take to the air, the sky seems to be alive with balloons.

It is certain that the sport has nowhere to go but up. If you have not already seen a hot-air balloon, you probably will see one someday soon. Just keep your eye on the sky.

Understanding What You've Read

1. Why were the early hot-air balloon flights dangerous?
2. How is flying a hot-air balloon different from flying an airplane?
3. How can a pilot make a hot-air balloon rise?
4. What two things happened that made hot-air ballooning practical?

Applying the Skills Lesson

1. Read again the first full paragraph in the left-hand column on page 488. The paragraph begins, "The wind sometimes blows. . . ." Suppose the wind carries a balloon in an easterly direction and the pilot wants to go toward the west. What will happen next?

   a. The pilot will not do anything and just let the balloon drift further east.
   b. The pilot will take the balloon higher or lower to find a wind that is blowing toward the west.

2. What do you think may happen to the sport of hot-air ballooning? Choose the most likely outcome from the sentences below.

   a. People will forget about hot-air ballooning.
   b. People will stop flying hot-air balloons until they can steer them.
   c. Hot-air ballooning will become even more popular.

Predicting Outcomes

Good readers think ahead as they read. They use facts from their reading plus what they already know. They ask themselves, "What will happen next?"

Sometimes in textbooks you will read questions that ask you to predict outcomes. In the following selections, you will read such questions.

Predicting Outcomes in Science

Whenever you do a science experiment, you most likely think ahead to the outcome. You try to prove your prediction. Think about how you could prove the outcome of the following experiments. Use the sidenotes to help you.

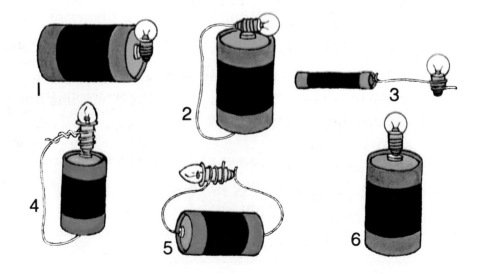

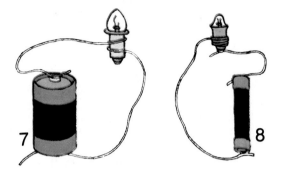

Bulbs and Cells

You often need to look at illustrations in textbooks in order to answer a question.

Here are eight different ways to connect cells ▮▮▮ and bulbs 💡💡. Some are connected by wires ⌇⌇.

Not all of these bulbs will light, but four will. Can you predict which four?

The first sentence gives you a fact that you need in order to make your prediction. What are you supposed to predict?

Some Things to Try

1. Check your predictions. See if you can make a bulb light by —
   - just touching it to a cell.
   - connecting it to the cell with one piece of wire.
   - connecting it to the cell with two pieces of wire.

   Were your predictions right?

If you have used cells and bulbs in the past, you may be able to predict the outcome. If not, you would have to do these things in order to know what will happen.

2. Will string or thread work in place of wire? How about rubber bands?

—*Elementary School Science*
Addison-Wesley

493

Building Skills

Read the first two paragraphs of the selection again. In order to correctly predict which four connections will light, which of the following sentences must be true? (There is more than one answer.)

1. You must know something about cells and bulbs and the way they work.
2. You must know a great deal of math.
3. You must look at the pictures carefully.
4. You must try each connection yourself.

Predicting Outcomes in Health

There are no sidenotes for this selection. Read it carefully. As you read, study the pictures also. Then answer the questions that follow.

How Can You Avoid Burns?

Julie is boiling water for hot chocolate. What might happen now?

Alan is helping to make breakfast. How is he picking up the pan?

Which way is better? Why? Alan has a rule: Stop and think before you act. Why is this a good rule?

People can get burned in other ways, too. If Bruce stays in the sun too long, what might happen? How will he feel?

Laura goes to the lake every summer. She knows what the sun can do. Where does she rest? How does this help protect her? What else could Laura do to protect herself?

— *You Learn and Change:* Orange
Harcourt Brace Jovanovich

Building Skills

1. Below are some outcomes for Julie from the selection you just read. Look again at the picture. What will happen next? (There is more than one answer.)

   a. She will forget about the boiling water and will walk away.

   b. She will get a potholder.

   c. She will touch the pot and burn herself.

2. Below are some outcomes for Bruce from the selection you just read. Look again at the picture. What will happen next? (There is more than one answer.)

   a. He will fall asleep and the tide will come in. A big wave will carry him to Ireland.

   b. He will cover himself up before he gets a bad sunburn.

   c. He will get a bad sunburn that will hurt for days.

Books About Enjoying the World

Let's Start a Puppet Theatre by Benny E. Andersen. Van Nos. Reinhold, 1975. You'll find information about everything you need to start a puppet theater.

Balloons: From Paperbags to Skyhooks by Peter Burchard. Macmillan, 1960. The author introduces ballooning, using many drawings and photographs.

The Young Ballet Dancer by Liliana Cosi. Stein & Day, 1979. This book tells how young dancers study and train to perform in famous ballets.

Frozen Snakes and Dinosaur Bones: Exploring a Natural History Museum by Margery Facklam. Harcourt Brace Jovanovich, 1976. This book provides an interesting look at the way collections are gathered and exhibits are prepared, and at the people who do the work.

The Great American Book of Sidewalk, Stoop, Dirt, Curb, and Alley Games by Fred Ferretti. Workman, 1975. The rules and equipment are explained for over sixty old games that are still played today, such as hopscotch.

Mr. Mysterious's Secrets of Magic by Sid Fleischman. Little, 1975. The author, a former magician, gives directions for magic tricks.

Making Pictures Move by Harry Helfman. Morrow, 1969. Nine projects you can do to make pictures move are explained. There is information on magic wheels, pocket combs, animated cartoons, and so forth.

Part 8

Author Study

The Story of
Laura
Ingalls Wilder
and Her
Little House Books

UNDERSTANDING AND APPRECIATING LITERATURE

Setting

The man in the pictures is Lance Rex, the famous explorer. These pictures are from Lance's adventure scrapbook. Each picture has a different **setting.** The setting tells you *where* and *when* the picture was taken.

In the first picture, Lance is exploring the desert at night. You can tell where Lance is because of details like the cactuses and sand. What other details tell you where Lance is? Which details tell you *when* Lance was in the desert? The dark sky is one detail that tells you it is night.

Now look at the second picture. Where is Lance? He is in the middle of the jungle. How do you know? The trees and animals tell you he is in the jungle. When was the picture taken? What details tell you that it is daytime? The settings of Lance's pictures tell you where and when his adventures took place.

Understanding Setting

A story has a setting, too. The setting is where and when the story takes place. One way an author tells you the setting of a story is with details. Sometimes an author tells you exactly where and when the story happens. Read the following paragraph.

> Lance reached the Amazon River in the late afternoon. It was a hot July day, the hottest so far in 1981.

What is the setting of the story? The author has told you it is the Amazon River in July 1981.

Authors don't always tell you the exact place and date. An author may only *suggest* where and when the story takes place. Then you have to pay even closer attention to the details. Read the next paragraph. Look closely for details that suggest where and when this adventure takes place.

> The sun was low in the west. Lance was still far from the cabin. Ice crystals stung Lance's cheeks. Snow and ice beat against his goggles. Lance shivered and pulled the parka further down over his face.

What is the setting of the story? Where is Lance? How do you know that he is outdoors in a snowstorm? The author tells you that Lance is far away from his cabin and that snow and ice beat against his goggles.

When does this story take place? The snow and ice tell you it is winter. How does the author suggest the time of day? The sun is low in the west, suggesting that it is sunset or late afternoon. The setting is outdoors on a late, winter afternoon. The author used details to tell you the setting, but you had to read carefully for those details.

In nearly every story, the setting and the plot are closely tied together. Where and when a story takes place has a lot to do with what happens in the story. Imagine a story about a family traveling across North America in the early 1800's. The setting would be North America in the early 1800's. If the setting were changed to today, this story would be very different. The 1800's family might have made the trip by wagon train, or simply on horseback. The trip might have taken many months. Today's family could fly across the country in five hours.

The 1800's family would have had to blaze its own trails. There were hardly any maps and even fewer roads in those days. The trip across country was very dangerous. Travelers often ran into rattlesnakes and herds of buffalo. What kinds of problems do you think today's family might have traveling across the country?

As you can see, the setting is very important to the story. Remember to look for the details that tell you where and when a story takes place. Knowing the setting will help you understand the story.

Try This

1. What two things does the setting of the story tell you?
2. Read the paragraph below.

> The old wooden door creaked on rusty hinges. Lance peeked into the musty room. Moonlight streamed through the window onto the faded couch. Only the scratching of mice beneath the furniture broke the thick silence.

What is the setting in the paragraph above?
What details tell you where and when the story takes place?

Writing

Lance's grandmother Abigail was also a famous explorer. Study the picture below from Abigail's scrapbook. Then write a sentence or paragraph that describes the setting of Abigail's adventure. Use details.

As you read the Little House stories, look for when and where each story takes place. Notice how Laura Ingalls Wilder uses details to make the settings come alive.

The Story of Laura Ingalls Wilder
and Her *Little House* Books

When Laura Ingalls Wilder wrote the *Little House* books, she wrote about things that really happened. The main character is called Laura. This Laura is also the author of the books.

The stories you will read here all come from the *Little House* books. Laura led an exciting life during an interesting period in history. Before and after the stories you will find out more about Laura and the things she did.

Wilder Memorial

WILDER HOMESTEAD AND BIRTHPLACE OF ROSE WILDER LANE

On the low hill immediately west of this spot stood the homestead claim shanty of Almanzo and Laura Ingalls Wilder. Mrs. Wilder (1867-1957) is known all over the world as the author of the "Little House" books, a series of auto-biographical accounts of pioneering by the Ingalls and Wilder families. Six of her books have their settings in the De Smet area. *The First Four Years* tells of farm life at this location from 1885-1889.

A shanty on the hilltop was the birthplace of the Wilders' only surviving child Rose Wilder Lane (1886-1968). Mrs. Lane became a well-known novelist, journalist and political essayist. Two of her 1930's novels, *Free Land* and *Let The Hurricane Roar* describe South Dakota pioneering. She also wrote biographies, translated books and served as a foreign correspondent. Her last reporting assignment took her to Viet Nam in 1965, when at 78 Rose Wilder Lane was America's oldest war correspondent. Although her career included travels around the world, Mrs. Lane stated that the entire pattern of her life was formed by the immense prairie skies, the acres of waving grain and the struggling saplings of her Dakota childhood.

One and one half miles north of this spot is another quarter section of land which was the tree claim of Laura and Almanzo Wilder. Some of the original tree plantings still survive. Here the Wilders also lived during their early married life, experiencing a fire which destroyed their home, the death of an infant son and other natural disasters which were a part of the daily lives of the courageous South Dakota pioneers. "No one," Mrs. Wilder wrote, "who has not pioneered can understand the fascination and the terror of it."

ERECTED 1974 BY THE LAURA INGALLS WILDER MEMORIAL SOCIETY, THE DE SMET CHAMBER OF COMMERCE, THE SOUTH DAKOTA DEPARTMENT OF TRANSPORTATION AND THE SOUTH DAKOTA STATE HISTORICAL SOCIETY.

502

The Story of
the *Little House* Books

One day in 1930 a white-haired farm woman sat down to write. She used a pencil and wrote on large, old-fashioned school tablets. She wrote on both sides of the page so that she wouldn't waste paper. She and her husband ran a large chicken and dairy farm. Often she had to stop writing to do housework and take care of the chickens and cows.

Who was this busy writer? Her name was Laura Ingalls Wilder. She lived in the Ozark Mountains at Rocky Ridge Farm, near the town of Mansfield, Missouri. She was sixty-three, and she had lived on the same land for more than thirty years. She and her husband had cleared the land and built their own house there.

What was she writing? In the past, she had written mainly for farm magazines and newspapers. Now she had something quite different in mind. She tells us herself what it was: "I had heard my father tell many stories of my very early childhood, and I decided to write them down, for I wanted them preserved."[1]

The book she wrote to tell these stories was called *Little House in the Big Woods*. It was written especially for children, and it was published in 1932.

Since then, thousands of children all over the world have read what Laura's pa told her: stories about when she was a little girl in the big woods of Wisconsin. Besides Pa and Laura, some of the other characters in the book are Ma, Laura's sisters, Mary and Carrie—and Jack, the bulldog.

Here is one story from *Little House in the Big Woods*.

[1] Mrs. Wilder said this to a newspaper reporter for the Springfield, Missouri, *News and Leader* on May 22, 1949.

Winter Days and Winter Nights

by LAURA INGALLS WILDER

All alone in the wild Big Woods, and the snow, and the cold, the little log house was warm and snug and cozy. Pa and Ma and Mary and Laura and Baby Carrie were comfortable and happy there, especially at night.

Then the fire was shining on the hearth, the cold and the dark and the wild beasts were all shut out, and Jack the brindle bulldog and Black Susan the cat lay blinking at the flames in the fireplace.

Ma sat in her rocking chair, sewing by the light of the lamp on the table. The lamp was bright and shiny. There was salt in the bottom of its glass bowl with the kerosene, to keep the kerosene from exploding, and there were bits of red flannel among the salt to make it pretty. It was pretty.

Laura loved to look at the lamp, with its glass chimney so clean and sparkling, its yellow flame burning so steadily, and its bowl of clear kerosene colored red by the bits of flannel. She loved to look at the fire in the fireplace, flickering and changing all the time, burning yellow and red and sometimes green above the logs, and hovering blue over the golden and ruby coals.

And then, Pa told stories.

When Laura and Mary begged him for a story, he would take them on his knees and tickle their faces with his long whiskers until they laughed aloud. His eyes were blue and merry.

One night Pa looked at Black Susan, stretching herself before the fire and running her claws out and in, and he said:

"Do you know that a panther is a cat; a great, big, wild cat?"

"No," said Laura.

"Well, it is," said Pa. "Just imagine Black Susan bigger than Jack, and fiercer than Jack when he growls. Then she would be just like a panther."

He settled Laura and Mary more comfortably on his knees and he said, "I'll tell you about Grandpa and the panther."

"Your Grandpa?" Laura asked.

"No, Laura, your Grandpa. My father."

"Oh," Laura said, and she wriggled closer against Pa's arm. She knew her Grandpa. He lived far away in the Big Woods, in a big log house. Pa began:

The Story of Grandpa and the Panther

"Your Grandpa went to town one day and was late starting home. It was dark when he came riding his horse through the Big Woods, so dark that he could hardly see the road, and when he heard a panther scream he was frightened, for he had no gun."

"How does a panther scream?" Laura asked.

"Like a woman," said Pa. "Like this." Then he screamed so that Laura and Mary shivered with terror.

Ma jumped in her chair, and said, "Mercy, Charles!"

But Laura and Mary loved to be scared like that.

"The horse, with Grandpa on him, ran fast, for it was frightened, too. But it could not get away from the panther. The panther followed through the dark woods. It was a hungry panther, and it came as fast as the horse could run. It screamed now on this side of the road, now on the other side, and it was always close behind.

"Grandpa leaned forward in the saddle and urged the horse to run faster. The horse was running as fast as it could possibly run, and still the panther screamed close behind.

"Then Grandpa caught a glimpse of it, as it leaped from treetop to treetop, almost overhead.

"It was a huge, black panther, leaping through the air like Black Susan leaping on a mouse. It was many, many times bigger than Black Susan. It was so big that if it leaped on Grandpa it could kill him with its enormous, slashing claws and its long sharp teeth.

"Grandpa, on his horse, was running away from it just as a mouse runs from a cat.

"The panther did not scream any more. Grandpa did not see it any more. But he knew that it was coming, leaping after him in the dark woods behind him. The horse ran with all its might.

"At last the horse ran up to Grandpa's house. Grandpa saw the panther springing. Grandpa jumped off the horse, against the door. He burst through the door and slammed it behind him. The panther landed on the horse's back, just where Grandpa had been.

"The horse screamed terribly, and ran. He was running away into the Big Woods, with the panther riding on his back and ripping his back with its claws. But Grandpa grabbed his gun from the wall and got to the window, just in time to shoot the panther dead.

"Grandpa said he would never again go into the Big Woods without his gun."

When Pa told this story, Laura and Mary shivered and snuggled closer to him. They were safe and snug on his knees, with his strong arms around them.

They liked to be there, before the warm fire, with Black Susan purring on the hearth and good dog Jack stretched out beside her. When they heard a wolf howl, Jack's head lifted and the hairs rose stiff along his back. But Laura and Mary listened to that lonely sound in the dark and the cold of the Big Woods, and they were not afraid.

They were cozy and comfortable in their little house made of logs, with the snow drifting around it and the wind crying because it could not get in by the fire.

Understanding What You've Read

1. Who are the characters in "Winter Days and Winter Nights"?
2. On page 505, the author compares the setting of the world outside with the setting inside the log cabin.

   a. Find the details that describe the setting outside.
   b. Find the details that describe the setting inside.

3. What is the setting of "The Story of Grandpa and the Panther"? Who are the characters in this story?
4. Tell the plot of "The Story of Grandpa and the Panther." Be sure that you tell about the problem Grandpa had, what happened next, and how he solved the problem.
5. Do you think Grandpa was a brave man? How do you know this? Find details in "The Story of Grandpa and the Panther" that tell you what kind of character Grandpa is.
6. Why do you think Grandpa said, on page 511, that "he would never again go into the Big Woods without his gun"?
7. Why do you think Laura and Mary enjoyed hearing Pa tell stories?

Writing

1. Write a sentence or paragraph that describes the setting of your neighborhood on a winter day.
2. The first paragraph on page 507 describes some things

that Laura loved to look at. Write a sentence or paragraph about something you enjoy looking at. Explain why you enjoy it.

3. Write several sentences or paragraphs describing how you think Grandpa felt as he was riding through the Big Woods. Include details about the setting in your description.

4. Write your own story about people living in the Big Woods. Before you start writing, decide on the following:

    a. the setting of the story, including the details that you will use to tell the reader where and when the story takes place

    b. the characters who will be in the story, and how you, as the author, will describe them for your readers

    c. the plot of the story, including the problem, the action or important events, and the solution

More About the *Little House* Books

One book was all Mrs. Wilder planned to write. But children wrote to her asking for more stories. Next came *Farmer Boy*, a book about her husband's boyhood.

Children wanted to know still more about Laura and her family. So Mrs. Wilder wrote a book to tell what happened after Ma and Pa left Wisconsin. It was called *Little House on the Prairie*. It tells about the trip to Indian territory by covered wagon.

Pa and Ma Ingalls

There Pa built their house and dug a well. Soon the family was feeling settled. But there were some problems between some of the Native Americans and some of the settlers. So the U. S. government told all settlers to move out of Indian territory.

Ma, Pa, Mary, Laura, and Baby Carrie packed everything into the covered wagon again. This time they moved to Minnesota. They stayed there for three years. So Mrs. Wilder wrote still another book, *On the Banks of Plum Creek*. It tells about the fine new house with real glass windows and the wheat crop that was eaten up by grasshoppers. In this book, Laura is grown-up enough to help Ma and Pa.

Keeping House

by LAURA INGALLS WILDER

Now in the daytimes Pa was driving the wagon up
and down Plum Creek, and bringing load after load of
logs to the pile by the door. He cut down old plum trees
and old willows and cottonwoods, leaving the little ones
to grow. He hauled them and stacked them, and chopped
and split them into stove wood, till he had a big woodpile.

With his short-handled ax in his belt, his traps on his
arm, and his gun against his shoulder, he walked far up

Plum Creek, setting traps for muskrat and mink and otter and fox.

One evening at supper Pa said he had found a beaver meadow. But he did not set traps there because so few beavers were left. He had seen a fox and shot at it, but missed.

"I am all out of practice hunting," he said. "It's a fine place we have here, but there isn't much game. Makes a fellow think of places out West where—"

"Where there are no schools for the children, Charles," said Ma.

"You're right, Caroline. You usually are," Pa said. "Listen to that wind. We'll have a storm tomorrow."

But the next day was mild as spring. The air was soft and warm and the sun shone brightly. In the middle of the morning Pa came to the house.

"Let's have an early dinner and take a walk to town this afternoon," he said to Ma. "This is too nice a day for you to stay indoors. Time enough for that when winter really comes."

"But the children," said Ma. "We can't take Carrie and walk so far."

"Shucks!" Pa laughed at her. "Mary and Laura are great girls now. They can take care of Carrie for one afternoon."

"Of course we can, Ma," said Mary; and Laura said, "Of course we can!"

They watched Pa and Ma starting gaily away. Ma was so pretty in her brown and red Christmas shawl, with her brown knit hood tied under her chin, and she stepped so quickly and looked up at Pa so merrily that Laura thought she was like a bird.

Then Laura swept the floor while Mary cleared the table. Mary washed the dishes and Laura wiped them and put them in the cupboard. They put the red-checked cloth on the table. Now the whole long afternoon was before them and they could do as they pleased.

First, they decided to play school. Mary said she must be Teacher, because she was older and besides she knew more. Laura knew that was true. So Mary was Teacher and she liked it, but Laura was soon tired of that play.

"I know," Laura said. "Let's both teach Carrie her letters."

They sat Carrie on a bench and held the book before her, and both did their best. But Carrie did not like it. She would not learn the letters, so they had to stop that.

"Well," said Laura, "let's play keeping house."

"We *are* keeping house," said Mary. "What is the use of playing it?"

The house was empty and still with Ma gone. Ma was so quiet and gentle that she never made any noise, but now the whole house was listening for her.

Laura went outdoors for a while by herself, but she came back. The afternoon grew longer and longer. There was nothing at all to do. Even Jack walked up and down restlessly.

He asked to go out, but when Laura opened the door he would not go. He lay down and got up, and walked around and around the room. He came to Laura and looked at her earnestly.

"What is it, Jack?" Laura asked him. He stared hard at her, but she could not understand, and he almost howled.

"Don't, Jack!" Laura told him, quickly. "You scare me."

"Is it something outdoors?" Mary wondered. Laura ran out, but on the doorstep Jack took hold of her dress and pulled her back. Outdoors was bitter cold. Laura shut the door.

"Look," she said. "The sunshine's dark. Are the grasshoppers coming back?"

"Not in the wintertime, goosie," said Mary. "Maybe it's rain."

"Goosie yourself!" Laura said back. "It doesn't rain in the wintertime."

"Well, snow, then! What's the difference?" Mary was angry and so was Laura. They would have gone on quarreling, but suddenly there was no sunshine. They ran to look through the bedroom window.

A dark cloud with a fleecy white underside was rolling fast from the north-west.

Mary and Laura looked out the front window. Surely it was time for Pa and Ma to come, but they were nowhere in sight.

"Maybe it's a blizzard," said Mary.

"Like Pa told us about," said Laura.

They looked at each other through the gray air. They were thinking of those children who froze stark stiff.

"The woodbox is empty," said Laura.

Mary grabbed her. "You can't!" said Mary. "Ma told us to stay in the house if it stormed." Laura jerked away and Mary said, "Besides, Jack won't let you."

"We've got to bring in wood before the storm gets here," Laura told her. "Hurry!"

They could hear a strange sound in the wind, like a far-away screaming. They put on their shawls and pinned them under their chins with their large shawl-pins. They put on their mittens.

Laura was ready first. She told Jack, "We've got to bring in wood, Jack." He seemed to understand. He went out with her and stayed close at her heels. The wind was colder than icicles. Laura ran to the woodpile, piled up a big armful of wood, and ran back, with Jack behind her. She could not open the door while she held the wood. Mary opened it for her.

Then they did not know what to do. The cloud was coming swiftly, and they must both bring in wood before the storm got there. They could not open the door when their arms were full of wood. They could not leave the door open and let the cold come in.

"I tan open the door," said Carrie.

"You can't," Mary said.

"I tan, too!" said Carrie, and she reached up both hands and turned the door knob. She could do it! Carrie was big enough to open the door.

Laura and Mary hurried fast, bringing in wood. Carrie opened the door when they came to it, and shut it behind

them. Mary could carry larger armfuls, but Laura was quicker.

They filled the woodbox before it began to snow. The snow came suddenly with a whirling blast, and it was small hard grains like sand. It stung Laura's face where it struck. When Carrie opened the door, it swirled into the house in a white cloud.

Laura and Mary forgot that Ma had told them to stay in the house when it stormed. They forgot everything but bringing in wood. They ran frantically back and forth, bringing each time all the wood they could stagger under.

They piled wood around the woodbox and around the stove. They piled it against the wall. They made the piles higher and bigger.

Bang! they banged the door. They ran to the woodpile. Clop-clop-clop they stacked the wood on their arms. They ran to the door. Bump! it went open, and bang! they back-bumped it shut, and thumpity-thud-thump! they flung down the wood and ran back outdoors to the woodpile, and panting back again.

They could hardly see the woodpile in the swirling whiteness. Snow was driven all in among the wood. They could hardly see the house, and Jack was a dark blob hurrying beside them. The hard snow scoured their faces. Laura's arms ached and her chest panted and all the time she thought, "Oh, where is Pa? Where is Ma?" and she felt "Hurry! Hurry!" and she heard the wind screeching.

The woodpile was gone. Mary took a few sticks and Laura took a few sticks and there were no more. They ran to the door together, and Laura opened it and Jack bounded in. Carrie was at the front window, clapping her hands and squealing. Laura dropped her sticks of wood and turned just in time to see Pa and Ma burst, running, out of the whirling whiteness of snow.

Pa was holding Ma's hand and pulling to help her run. They burst into the house and slammed the door and stood panting, covered with snow. No one said anything while Pa and Ma looked at Laura and Mary, who stood all snowy in shawls and mittens.

At last Mary said in a small voice, "We did go out in the storm, Ma. We forgot."

Laura's head bowed down and she said, "We didn't want to burn up the furniture, Pa, and freeze stark stiff."

"Well, I'll be darned!" said Pa. "If they didn't move the whole woodpile in. All the wood I cut to last a couple of weeks."

There, piled up in the house, was the whole woodpile. Melted snow was leaking out of it and spreading in puddles. A wet path went to the door, where snow lay unmelted.

Then Pa's great laugh rang out, and Ma's gentle smile shone warm on Mary and Laura. They knew they were forgiven for disobeying because they had been wise to bring in wood, though perhaps not quite so much wood.

Sometime soon they would be old enough not to make any mistakes, and then they could always decide what to do. They would not have to obey Pa and Ma any more.

They bustled to take off Ma's shawl and hood and brush the snow from them and hang them up to dry. Pa hurried to the stable to do the chores before the storm grew worse. Then while Ma rested, they stacked the wood neatly as she told them, and they swept and mopped the floor.

The house was neat and cozy again. The teakettle hummed, the fire shone brightly from the draughts above the stove hearth. Snow swished against the windows.

Pa came in. "Here is the little milk I could get here with. The wind blew it up out of the pail. Caroline, this is a terrible storm. I couldn't see an inch, and the wind comes from all directions at once. I thought I was on the path, but I couldn't see the house, and — well, I just barely bumped against the corner. Another foot to the left and I never would have got in."

"*Charles!*" Ma said.

"Nothing to be scared about now," said Pa. "But if we hadn't run all the way from town and beat this storm here—" Then his eyes twinkled, he rumpled Mary's hair and pulled Laura's ear. "I'm glad all this wood is in the house, too," he said.

Understanding What You've Read

1. When does "Keeping House" take place? What details help you know what time of year it is?
2. Why do you think Ma and Pa couldn't take Carrie into town with them?
3. Find some details on page 525 that tell you how Laura felt during the storm. How do you think it might feel to be caught in a blizzard?
4. Were Ma and Pa angry with Mary and Laura for disobeying them and going out during the storm? Why do you think Ma and Pa acted this way?
5. Look at your answer to question 1. How is the setting of "Keeping House" the same as the setting of "Winter Days and Winter Nights"? How is it different?

Historical marker at Laura's childhood home

'ON THE BANKS OF PLUM CREEK'

A DUGOUT ALONG PLUM CREEK SOUTHEAST OF THIS POINT WAS THE CHILDHOOD HOME OF LAURA INGALLS WILDER, WHO WROTE "ON THE BANKS OF PLUM CREEK" WIDELY KNOWN AS A CHILDREN'S STORY THE BOOK TELLS ACTUAL INCIDENTS OF PIONEER LIFE HERE AND IN WALNUT GROVE, INCLUDING BLIZZARDS AND A GRASSHOPPER PLAGUE IN THE 1870'S LAURA'S PARENTS WERE AMONG THE EARLY SETTLERS OF NORTH HERO TOWNSHIP
REDWOOD COUNTY CENTENNIAL COMMITTEE 1862-1962

Writing

1. Write one or more sentences that would describe one of the following settings to a person who had lived in another time period:

   a. a kitchen   b. a classroom   c. a playground

2. Pretend that you are Ma or Pa. Write one or more paragraphs that tell what happened when you walked home in the blizzard. Be sure to include details about the setting.

3. Write your own story with one of the following settings:

   a. in a cabin during a big storm
   b. in a boat during a big storm
   c. in an airplane during a big storm

   Before you begin writing, choose the characters for your story and decide on the plot, or what will happen in your story.

Footbridge over Plum Creek

More About the *Little House* Books

Because the family had very bad luck at the end of *Plum Creek*, Mrs. Wilder wrote a book that told how things got better. *By the Shores of Silver Lake* describes how the family moved from Minnesota to South Dakota.

Mary was now blind from scarlet fever. Jack, the bulldog, had died, and Ma was unhappy about not being settled. During the next year the family lived in the claim shanty. Then they lived in a house. Finally they lived in the store building Pa built in the new town of De Smet, South Dakota.

At last, though, the family was settled again in the country. Pa owned some homestead land. They lived on the land in the summer and in town in the winter.

The winter of 1880–81 was so fierce that

Laura's home by the shores of Silver Lake

Mrs. Wilder wrote *The Long Winter* to tell about it. One blizzard followed another quickly. Soon the train could no longer get through with supplies. Many families would have starved if not for a young man named Almanzo Wilder. He went out on the prairie between blizzards to buy wheat. He was able to get some from a settler who was keeping it to plant in the spring.

Almanzo Wilder had brought his Morgan horses all the way from New York State. Now he settled on the prairies in the very town where Laura, now fifteen, was living.

One day Almanzo asked Laura to ride in his buggy behind the beautiful horses. Mrs. Wilder wrote about that in *These Happy Golden Years*. She tells about the years she spent as a teacher. Then she tells how she married Almanzo and went to live in a new home that he had built with his own hands.

Carrie, Mary, Laura
when they lived
in the Little Town
on the Prairie

Cottonwoods Pa planted on the homestead

Little Gray Home in the West

by LAURA INGALLS WILDER

They drove over the road they had traveled so many
times, across the neck of Big Slough, around the corner
by Pearson's livery barn, up Main Street and across the
railroad tracks, then out on the road toward the new
house on Almanzo's tree claim.

It was a silent drive until almost the end, when for the first time that day Laura saw the horses. She exclaimed, "Why, you are driving Prince and Lady!"

"Prince and Lady started this," Almanzo said. "So I thought they'd like to bring us home. And here we are."

The tracks of his wagon and buggy wheels had made a perfect half-circle drive curving into the grove of little sapling trees before the house. There the house sat, and it was neatly finished with siding and smoothly painted a soft gray. Its front door was comfortably in the middle, and two windows gave the whole house a smiling look. On the doorstep lay a large, brown shepherd dog, that rose and politely wagged to Laura as the buggy stopped.

"Hello, Shep!" Almanzo said. He helped Laura down and unlocked the door. "Go in while I put up the horses," he told her.

Just inside the door she stood and looked. This was the large room. Its walls were neatly plastered a soft white. At its far end stood a drop-leaf table, covered with Ma's red-checked tablecloth. A chair sat primly at either end of it. Beside it was a closed door.

In the center of the long wall at Laura's left, a large window let in the southern sunshine. Companionably placed at either side of it, two rocking chairs faced each other. Beside the one nearest Laura stood a small, round table, and above it a hanging lamp was suspended from the ceiling. Someone could sit there in the evening and read a paper, while in the other chair someone could knit.

The window beside the front door let still more sunny light into that pleasant room.

Two closed doors were in the other long wall. Laura opened the one nearest her, and saw the bedroom. Her Dove-in-the-Window quilt was spread upon the wide bed, and her two feather pillows stood plumply at the head of it. At its foot, across the whole length of the partition, was a wide shelf higher than Laura's head, and from its edge a prettily flowered calico curtain hung to the floor. It made a perfect clothes closet. Against the wall under the front window stood Laura's trunk.

537

She had seen all this quickly. Now she took off her poke bonnet and laid it on the shelf. She opened her trunk and took out a calico dress and apron. Taking off her black cashmere, she hung it carefully in the curtain closet, then slipped into the blue calico dress and tied on the crisply ruffled, pink apron. She went into the front room as Almanzo came into it through the door by the drop-leaf table.

"All ready for work, I see!" he said gaily, as he set Ma's basket on the chair near him. "Guess I'd better get ready for my work, too." He turned at the bedroom door to say, "Your Ma told me to open your bundle and spread things around."

"I'm glad you did," Laura told him.

She looked through the door by the table. There was the lean-to. Almanzo's bachelor cook-stove was set up there, and pots and frying pans hung on the walls. There was a window, and a back door that looked out at the stable beyond some little trees.

Laura returned to the front room. She took up Ma's basket, and opened the last door. She knew it must be the pantry door, but she stood in surprise and then in delight, looking at that pantry. All one wall was covered with shelves and drawers, and a broad shelf was under a large window at the pantry's far end.

She took Ma's basket to that shelf, and opened it. There was a loaf of Ma's good bread, a ball of butter, and what had been left of the wedding cake. She left it all on the shelf while she investigated the pantry.

One whole long wall was shelved from the ceiling

halfway down. The upper shelves were empty, but on the lowest was a glass lamp, Almanzo's bachelor dishes, and two pans of milk, with empty pans near. At the end, where this shelf was above the window shelf in the corner, stood a row of cans of spices.

Beneath this shelf were many drawers of different sizes. Directly below the spices, and above the window shelf, were two rather narrow drawers. Laura found that one was almost full of white sugar, the other of brown sugar. How handy!

Next, a deep drawer was full of flour, and smaller ones held graham flour and corn meal. You could stand at the window shelf and mix up anything, without stirring a step. Outside the window was the great, blue sky, and the leafy little trees.

Another deep drawer was filled with towels and tea towels. Another held two tablecloths and some napkins. A shallow one held knives and forks and spoons.

Beneath all these drawers there was space for a tall, stoneware churn and dasher, and empty space for other things as they should come.

In a wide drawer of the bottom row was only a crust of bread and half a pie. Here Laura put Ma's loaf of bread and the wedding cake. She cut a piece from the ball of butter, put it on a small plate, and placed it beside the bread. Then she pushed the drawer shut.

By the iron ring fastened in the pantry floor, she knew there was a trap door. She straightened the ring up, and pulled. The trap door rose, and rested against the pantry wall opposite the shelves. There, beneath where it had been, the cellar stairs went down.

Carefully covering the ball of butter, Laura carried it down the stairs into the cool, dark cellar, and set it on a hanging shelf that swung from the ceiling. She heard steps overhead, and as she came up the cellar stairs she heard Almanzo calling her name.

"I thought you were lost in this big house!" he said.

"I was putting the butter down cellar so it would keep cool," said Laura.

"Like your pantry?" he asked her, and she thought how many hours he must have worked, to put up all those shelves and to make and fit those many drawers.

"Yes," she said.

"Then let's go look at Lady's big little colt. I want you to see the horses in their stalls, and the place I have fixed for your cow. She's picketed out to grass now, just out of reach of the young trees." Almanzo led the way through the lean-to and outdoors.

They explored the long stable and the yard beyond it. Almanzo showed her the new haystacks on the north, to shelter the yard and stable when the winter winds came. Laura petted the horses and the colt and Shep, as he followed close at their heels. They looked at the little maples and box elders and willows and cottonwoods.

Quickly, the afternoon was gone. It was time for chores and supper.

"Don't build a fire," Almanzo told her. "Set out that bread and butter your mother gave us; I'll milk Fawn, and we'll have bread and new milk for supper."

"And cake," Laura reminded him.

When they had eaten supper and washed the few dishes, they sat on the front doorstep as evening came. They heard Prince blow out his breath, whoof! as he lay down on his bed of clean hay in the stable. They saw the dim bulk of Fawn on the grass, where she lay chewing her cud and resting. Shep lay at her feet; already he was half Laura's dog.

Laura's heart was full of happiness. She knew she need never be homesick for the old home. It was so near that she could go to it whenever she wished, while she and Almanzo made the new home in their own little house.

All this was theirs; their own horses, their own cow, their own claim. The many leaves of their little trees rustled softly in the gentle breeze.

Twilight faded as the little stars went out and the moon rose and floated upward. Its silvery light flooded the sky and the prairie. The winds that had blown whispering over the grasses all the summer day now lay sleeping, and quietness brooded over the moon-drenched land.

"It is a wonderful night," Almanzo said.

"It is a beautiful world," Laura answered, and in memory she heard the voice of Pa's fiddle and the echo of a song:

Golden years are passing by,
These happy, golden years.

Understanding What You've Read

1. Who is the new character from the *Little House* books? Find the sentence on page 541 that tells you what Laura thinks of him.
2. At what time of year does this story take place? What details on page 542 help you know this?
3. Find at least five details that describe the setting inside the house.
4. How is the house in this story like the house Laura lived in in "Winter Days and Winter Nights" and "Keeping House"? How is it different? Find details in the stories to help you answer this question.
5. Why do you think Laura was delighted with the pantry? Find details on pages 538–540 to help you answer this question.
6. On page 543 Laura says, "It is a beautiful world." Why do you think she feels this way?

Laura's lap desk

Writing

1. Laura's pantry is described with many details. Think of a very small room, such as a tool room or closet, and write a sentence or paragraph describing it. Include as many details as you can.

2. Write a sentence or paragraph that tells how the setting in "Little Gray Home in the West" is different from the setting in "Keeping House."

3. Write a letter to a friend. Tell your friend some of the things you liked in the *Little House* stories you have read.

Laura Ingalls Wilder's writing desk in her home in Mansfield, Missouri

Laura and Almanzo
the winter they
were married

What Happened Then?

Mrs. Wilder wrote *These Happy Golden Years* in 1943. That was eleven years after she wrote her first book. She thought that the *Little House* books were finally finished. Mrs. Wilder was then seventy-six years old. Her husband, Almanzo, was eighty-six. They had been married for fifty-seven years.

Almost everyone who finished reading the *Little House* books wanted to know what happened after Laura and Almanzo were married. In 1971 they found out. In that year a book came out that started just where *These Happy Golden Years* stopped. This book is called *The First Four Years.* It tells about Laura and Almanzo's life in the "little gray home in the West" during the first four years of their marriage.

Mrs. Wilder wrote this book around 1950. But it didn't come out until after she died. Why wasn't it published sooner? Did she plan to work on it longer? Did she grow tired of writing before it was just the way she wanted it? We do not know for sure. Mrs. Wilder may have thought that the story was too sad to tell. There were some happy times, such as the birth of Laura and Almanzo's daughter Rose. But there were many hard times during these years.

Crops were bad. Almanzo had been very sick. Worst of all, Laura and Almanzo's second baby, a little boy, died. These things made Laura and Almanzo decide to leave South Dakota. They moved first to Florida because they thought it would be good for Almanzo's health. But they were not happy in such a different place. So they moved back to De Smet, the town where they had lived during the time of *These Happy Golden Years*. They stayed there until they saved enough money to buy a farm in the Ozark Mountains.

Rose Ingalls Wilder at age three

They moved to the farm by covered wagon. It was the same way Laura had moved with Ma and Pa from the big woods to the prairie when she was a little girl. Their first house was a log cabin. Later they built a one-room farmhouse. This house grew over the years into a ten-room farmhouse. The farm became a large chicken and dairy farm.

Their daughter Rose grew up and married. Her name became Rose Wilder Lane. She became a writer, too. One of her best-known books is called *Let the Hurricane Roar*. It is an adult story about pioneer life. Her story takes place in the same country that her mother wrote about in the *Little House* books.

After Mrs. Wilder wrote the *Little House* books, she became famous. Children from the United States and other countries read her books. Many children felt they knew her. They wrote to ask her about herself and the other people they had read about in her books. Mrs. Wilder continued to work around the farm as she always had, and she also made time to answer the letters that came to her from all over the world.

Almanzo died in 1949, when he was ninety-two years old. Laura was ninety years old when she died in 1957.

This sign stands near Pepin, Wisconsin

Mansfield Missouri
Jan. 10th 1950

Dear Miss Wenzel,

Thank you so much for the picture of Pa's fiddle and for your interesting letter, I am glad you saw the museum and the town of De Smet.

At times I long so much for the old places and the old times Especially is this so now when I am so lonely for Almanzo.

Ah Well! "the moving finger writes And having writ moves on,"

Again I thank you for the picture of Pa's dear old fiddle

Yours sincerely

Laura Ingalls Wilder

Mrs. Wilder wrote this letter (which is printed here with the permission of her daughter, Rose Wilder Lane) when she was eighty-three, after she had received a picture of Pa's fiddle taken in the Museum in North Dakota, where the fiddle was kept for several years. It is now in the Laura Ingalls Wilder Home and Museum in Mansfield, Missouri.

Honors for the Author and Her Books

Laura Ingalls Wilder, the farm woman who became a famous writer, won many honors.

The *Little House* books were translated into several languages. Children from Sweden, Holland, and Japan read the books and wrote to her about them.

Children from Oregon, California, and Chicago chose her as their favorite author.

A Laura Ingalls Wilder Award is given every year to a writer of good books for children. Mrs. Wilder herself won the first award in 1954.

After Mrs. Wilder's death, her home became the Laura Ingalls Wilder Home and Museum. Visitors who stop there may see many things from the books, including the original hand-written copies of the *Little House* books.

Probably the greatest honor of all is that children still love the stories that Mrs. Wilder wrote.

Why are these books so popular? One reason is that they are so interesting to read. Mrs. Wilder thought that children liked her books because they were true.

She thought that children today like to read about children in old times. So she told what pioneer life was like for her family: the houses, food, clothes, tools, and furniture they had. She told about the games children played and the work they did. She told how holidays were celebrated. She showed us the many small details that made living then very different from living now. She has saved for us a part of our history that just cannot be found in history books.

Laura Ingalls Wilder's *Little House* Books

Little House in the Big Woods

Farmer Boy

Little House on the Prairie

On the Banks of Plum Creek

By the Shores of Silver Lake

The Long Winter

Little Town on the Prairie

These Happy Golden Years

The First Four Years

Glossary

This glossary is a little dictionary. It contains the difficult words found in this book. The pronunciation, which tells you how to say the word, is given next to each word. That is followed by a word's meaning or meanings. Sometimes, a different form of the word follows the definition. It appears in boldfaced type.

The special symbols used to show the pronunciation are explained in the key that follows.

PRONUNCIATION KEY*

a	add, map	m	move, seem	u	up, done
ā	ace, rate	n	nice, tin	û(r)	urn, term
â(r)	care, air	ng	ring, song	yōo	use, few
ä	palm, father	o	odd, hot	v	vain, eve
b	bat, rub	ō	open, so	w	win, away
ch	check, catch	ô	order, jaw	y	yet, yearn
d	dog, rod	oi	oil, boy	z	zest, muse
e	end, pet	ou	out, now	zh	vision, pleasure
ē	even, tree	ōo	pool, food	ə	the schwa,
f	fit, half	ŏo	took, full		an unstressed
g	go, log	p	pit, stop		vowel representing
h	hope, hate	r	run, poor		the sound spelled
i	it, give	s	see, pass		a in above
ī	ice, write	sh	sure, rush		e in sicken
j	joy, ledge	t	talk, sit		i in possible
k	cook, take	th	thin, both		o in melon
l	look, rule	th	this, bathe		u in circus

Foreign: N is used following a nasal sound: French *Jean* [zhäN].
~ indicates the [ny] sound: Spanish *señor* [sä·nyôr'].

In the pronunciations an accent mark (') is used to show which syllable of a word receives the most stress. The word *bandage* [ban'dij], for example, is stressed on the first syllable. Sometimes there is also a lighter accent mark (') that shows where there is a lighter stress, as in the word *combination* [kom'bə·nā'shən].

The following abbreviations are used throughout the glossary: *n.*, noun; *v.*, verb; *adj.*, adjective; *adv.*, adverb; *pl.*, plural; *sing.*, singular.

*The Pronunciation Key and the short form of the key that appears on the following right-hand pages are reprinted from *The HBJ School Dictionary*, copyright © 1977, 1972, 1968 by Harcourt Brace Jovanovich, Inc.

A

ac·cord·ing [ə·kôr′ding] *adj.* Agreeing. —
ac·cord·ing to In agreement with.

ac·ro·bat [ak′rə·bat] *n.* A person skilled
in tumbling and in stunts on a trapeze,
rings, etc.

ac·tiv·i·ty [ak·tiv′ə·tē] *n.* A kind of work,
sport, hobby, etc., that a person gives
time to.

ad·min·is·tra·tion [ad·min′is·trā′shən]
n. A group of people who run a business,
an office, etc.

ad·vis·er [ad·vī′zər] *n.* A person who
gives advice to another person.

aer·i·al [âr′ē·əl] *adj.* Of or in the air.

a·loft [ə·lôft′] *adv.* High up; in or to a
higher place.

am·a·teur [am′ə·chŏŏr] *n.* A person who
takes part in sports, sings, paints, acts
in plays, etc., for fun, not for pay.

am·phib·i·an [am·fib′ē·ən] *n.* A cold-
blooded animal, like a frog or toad,
that spends the first part of its life in
water and the latter part on land.

an·ces·tor [an′ses·tər] *n.* **1** A person from
whom one is descended, generally fur-
ther back than grandparents. **2** An
early kind of animal from which certain
animals have come.

an·gle [ang′gəl] *n.* The figure that is
formed by two lines that meet.

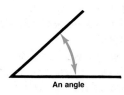
An angle

an·i·mate [an′ə·māt] *v.* To make lively or
to give movement.

An·to·nio [än·tō′nyō] *n.* A Spanish
male's name, the equivalent of the English name *Anthony.*

an·tro·de·mus [an′trə·dē′məs] *n.* A large

dinosaur of North America that
hunted and ate meat. Also called
allosaurus.

a·quar·i·um [ə·kwâr′ē·əm] *n.* **1** A water
tank used for fish and plants. **2** A
building in which fish, etc., are shown.

A·shan·ti [ə·shänt′ē] *n.* A people of western Africa, with the same language,
beliefs, etc. They live in family groups
and obey village leaders.

as·phalt [as′fôlt] *n.* A hard, black material that often covers sidewalks and
roads.

as·tound [ə·stound′] *v.* **as·tound·ed**
To greatly surprise; dumbfound.

as·trol·o·ger [ə·strol′ə·jər] *n.* A person
who studies astrology.

as·trol·o·gy [ə·strol′ə·jē] *n.* The study of
the stars and planets because of their
believed effect on people and the future.

as·tro·naut [as′trə·nôt] *n.* A person who
travels in space.

ath·lete [ath′lēt] *n.* A person with skill in
games or sports that require strength,
speed, or body control.

at·tract [ə·trakt′] *v.* To draw toward.

at·trac·tion [ə·trak′shən] *n.* A power or
thing that draws something nearer,
though not connected with it, as a mag-
net draws iron.

av·a·lanche [av′ə·lanch] *n.* A large
amount of snow, ice, etc., that breaks
loose from a mountain and slides or
falls.

av·e·nue [av′ə·n(y)ōō] *n.* **1** A way of
achieving something. **2** A street, usually a wide one. **3** A road or path with
trees along its sides.

av·er·age [av′rij] *adj.* Usual; ordinary.

a·ware [ə·wâr′] *adj.* Having knowledge.

B

---

bac·te·ri·a [bak·tir′ē·ə] *n., pl.* Tiny one-cell plants that can be seen only through a microscope. Some are helpful to people; others cause disease. — **bac·te·ri·um,** *sing.*

bail [bāl] *v.* **bail·ing** To take water out of something, such as a boat.

bal·ance [bal′əns] **1** *n.* The ability to keep one's body steady without falling. **2** *n.* The amount of money in a bank account. **3** *v.* To keep in a steady position.

bal·last [bal′əst] *n.* Anything heavy, as sand, stone, or water, that is carried in a ship or balloon to steady it.

bal·le·ri·na [bal′ə·rē′nə] *n.* A female ballet dancer.

bare·back rid·er [bâr′bak′ rī′dər] *n.* **1** A circus performer who leaps on the bare back of a moving horse, dances, and does other tricks on it. **2** Any person who rides on the bare back of a horse.

Bar·thol·di, Au·guste [bär·tôl′dē, ō·gōost′] 1834–1904, French sculptor who designed a number of patriotic statues. His best-known work is the Statue of Liberty.

base [bās] **1** *n.* The foundation or bottom of something. **2** *v.* To place on a foundation; serve as support. — **based upon** Clearly suggested by.

ba·sic [bā′sik] *adj.* **1** Forming a base; most important. **2** Important for life.

bath·y·sphere [bath′ə·sfir] *n.* A hollow, round structure that is lowered into the water to study deep-sea life.

be·calmed [bi·kämd′] *adj.* Unable to move because of a lack of wind.

beck·on [bek′ən] *v.* **beck·oned** To signal someone to come close by moving a hand.

be·head [bi·hed′] *v.* To cut off the head.

Ben·gal lights [ben′gəl līts′] *n.* Bright, lasting blue lights, used as fireworks or signals.

blare [blâr] **1** *v.* To sound loudly, as a trumpet. **2** *n.* A loud, brassy sound. **3** *v.* To speak loudly.

blue·ber·ry [blōō′ber′ē] *n.* A berry with purplish-blue color.

boast [bōst] *v.* **boast·ing** To brag.

boost [bōost] **1** *n.* A lift; help; upward push. **2** *v.* To raise by pushing from the back or bottom.

boot [bōot] *v.* **boot·ed** To kick.

breed [brēd] **1** *v.* To produce young. **2** *v.* To raise (plants and animals) for sale; develop a new kind (of plant or animal). **3** *n.* a particular kind or race of animals or plants.

---

add, āce, câre, pälm;   end, ēqual;   it, īce;   odd, ōpen, ôrder;   tŏŏk, pōŏl;   up, bûrn;
ə = a in *above*, e in *sicken*, i in *possible*, o in *melon*, u in *circus*;   yōō = u in *fuse*;   oil;   pout;
check;   ring;   th in *thin*;   th in *this*;   zh in *vision*.

bril·liant [bril′yənt] *adj.* Very bright; clever.

brin·dled [brin′dəld] *adj.* Tawny or grayish with darker streaks or spots: a *brindled horse.*—**brin·dle** *n.*

bris·tle [bris′əl] **1** *v.* To make the bristles or the hair stand up in anger or annoyance. **2** *n.* Any stiff hair, often used for brushes.

broad [brôd] *adj.* **1** Wide. **2** Of great size.

bump·y [bum′pē] *adj.* Rough, uneven.

bur·row [bûr′ō] *n.* A hole or tunnel in the ground made by an animal to live or hide in.

C

cal·i·co [kal′i·kō] **1** *n.* Cotton cloth printed with a figure design. **2** *adj.* Made of calico.

camp·to·sau·rus [kam(p)′tə·sôr′əs] *n.* A dinosaur that walked mostly on its back feet, had a mouth like a duck's bill, and ate plants.

ca·reer [kə·rir′] *n.* A person's life-work or profession.

car·ni·val [kär′nə·vəl] *n.* An amusement show with rides and sideshows.

ca·vies [kā′vēz] *n., pl.* A group of animals including guinea pigs, with short tails and rough hair.—**ca·vy,** *sing.*

cel·e·brate [sel′ə·brāt] *v.* To observe or honor in a special way.

cel·e·bra·tion [sel′ə·brā′shən] *n.* A special observation, as for a birthday.

cen·tu·ry [sen′chə·rē] *n.* A period of one hundred years.

cer·e·mo·ny [ser′ə·mō′nē] *n.* A formal act or series of acts done in a set way: a wedding *ceremony.*—**cer·e·mo·nies,** *pl.*

char·ac·ter [kar′ik·tər] *n.* **1** A person, animal, etc., in a story, play, or movie. **2** All of the feelings, behavior, and habits that make up a person's personality.

char·coal [chär′kōl′] *n.* A black stick of partly burned wood that is used for drawing.

cha·ris·ma [kə·riz′mə] *n.* The ability to attract the affection and loyalty of others.

char·i·ty [char′ə·tē] *n.* The giving of help, often money, to the poor.

chick·a·dee [chik′ə·dē] *n.* A small bird having the top of its head and its throat a darker color than its body.

chil·e [chil′ē] *n.* A hot red pepper.

churn [chûrn] **1** *n.* A container or machine in which milk or cream is beaten to make butter. **2** *v.* To move or stir rapidly.

ciph·er [sī′fər] *n.* A secret kind of written message. Each letter or number or sign stands for a letter in the alphabet.

cir·cu·la·tion [sûr′kyə·lā′shən] *n.* The flow of blood through the body.

cleft [kleft] *n.* A division between two parts; crack or dent.

cloak [klōk] *n.* A loose outer garment, nearly always without sleeves.

clump [klump] *n.* A group of things of the same kind (such as trees) very close together.

clutch [kluch] *v.* **clutched** To grasp and hold firmly.

coach [kōch] *v.* **coach·ing** To train; instruct; direct.

cock·le·shell [kok′əl·shel′] *n.* The shell of a cockle, a small water animal that can be eaten.

code [kōd] *n.* **1** Letters, words, or symbols with a secret meaning used for sending messages. **2** A set of rules: honor *code*.

coil [koil] *v.* **coiled** To make into rings by twisting or winding.

A coiled snake

cold [kōld] **1** *adj.* With no warning or preparation. **2** *adj.* Not involving one's feelings. **3** *adj.* Having little heat or low temperature. **4** *adj.* Chilled. **5** *adj.* Not new or fresh: a *cold* trail. **6** *n.* A mild illness often with sneezing, running nose, etc.

com·bi·na·tion [kom′bə·nā′shən] *n.* Two or more things that are joined together.

com·ic [kom′ik] *n.* A performer who tells funny stories or jokes; comedian.

com·mand [kə·mand′] *v.* To deserve and call for.

com·pañ·er·o [kom′pän·yer′ō] *n. Spanish* Friend, companion.

com·pa·ny [kum′pə·nē] *n.* A group of dancers, actors, or singers who perform together. —**com·pa·nies,** *pl.*

com·pan·ion [kəm·pan′yən] *n.* A person or animal who stays with another person or animal. —**com·pan·ion·a·bly** [kəm·pan′yən·ə·blē] *adv.* In a friendly or nice way.

com·pare [kəm·pâr′] *v.* **com·pared** To study two or more things to see how they are alike and how they are different.

com·pete [kəm·pēt′] *v.* To take part in a contest.

con·nect [kə·nekt′] *v.* To join together; link.

cot·ton·wood [kot′(ə)n·wŏŏd′] *n.* A tree that has seeds covered with bunches of soft, white hair and has soft wood, used for making paper.

Cou·ber·tin, Pi·erre de [kŏŏ′bər·taN′, pē·âr′ də] 1863–1937, Frenchman interested in sports as an aid to peace. He started the modern Olympic Games.

count [kount] *v.* **1** To matter; be important. **2** To add up; find the total of.

cour·age [kûr′ij] *n.* The strength to face danger or pain without fear; bravery.

coy·o·te [kī·ō′tē *or* kī′ōt] *n.* A small prairie wolf.

cram·pon [kram′pən] *n.* Either of a pair of iron pieces that is put on a shoe to aid in walking on ice.

creek [krēk] *n.* A small stream. Same as *crick*.

crew [krŏŏ] *n.* A group of people working together to do a particular job: the *crew* of the ship.

cui·da·do [kwē·dä′dō] *v. Spanish* Look out; be careful.

D

---

dar·ing [dâr′ing] *adj.* Brave.

---

add, āce, câre, pälm;   end, ēqual;   it, īce;   odd, ōpen, ôrder;   tŏŏk, pōōl;   **up,** bûrn;
ə = a in *above,* e in *sicken,* i in *possible,* o in *melon,* u in *circus;*   **yōō** = u in *fuse;*   **oil;**   pout;
     check;   **r**ing;   **th**in;   **th**is;   **zh** in *vision.*

dart [därt] *v.* To move about suddenly and quickly.

dash·er [dash′ər] *n.* A stick like a paddle, used to stir and beat cream in a churn to make butter.

dawn [dôn] *v.* **dawned 1** To begin to be clear in one's mind: I hope the answer will *dawn* on me. **2** To begin to become light in the morning.

de·but [di·byoo′ *or* dā′byoo] *n.* First public appearance.

de·cay [di·kā′] *v.* To break down; rot.

ded·i·cate [ded′ə·kāt] *v.* To set apart for or devote to a special purpose.

ded·i·ca·tion [ded′ə·kā′shən] *n.* The act of dedicating.

dem·on·stra·tion [dem′ən·strā′shən] *n.* A showing of how something works or is done: The teacher gave a *demonstration* on how to ride a horse.

de·part·ment [di·pärt′mənt] *n.* A separate part or division, as of a business, government, school, etc.

de·sert [di·zûrt′] *v.* **de·sert·ed** To leave a person, place, or thing. — **de·sert·ed** *adj.* Empty.

de·sign·er [di·zī′nər] *n.* A person who plans new things, as machines, dresses, puppets, etc. Or a person who makes patterns, models, or sketches for machines, dresses, etc.

de·vel·op [di·vel′əp] *v.* **de·vel·oped** To bring into being. — **de·vel·op·ment** *n.* A bringing into being of something.

di·a·ry [dī′ə·rē] *n.* A written, day-by-day record of what happens and what one thinks about.

dim [dim] *adj.* **dim·mer 1** Not having enough light. **2** Not clearly seen. **3** Not clearly remembered.

di·rect [di·rekt′] *v.* To show the way.

dis·a·gree [dis′ə·grē] *v.* **1** To have a different opinion. **2** To quarrel.

dome [dōm] *n.* A round roof. — **domed,** *adj.*

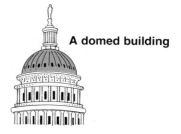

A domed building

do·min·ion [də·min′yən] *n.* A self-governing member of the British Commonwealth of Nations.

Do·min·ion Day [də·min′yən dā′] *n.* A holiday in Canada celebrating July 1, 1867, when Canada was given control of its own government.

dou·bles [dub′əlz] *n.* Two people playing as a team against two other people, as in tennis.

down [doun] *n.* The fine, soft feathers of birds, especially young birds. — **down·y** *adj.* **1** Soft like down. **2** Covered with down.

draft [draft] *n.* A current of air.

draught [draft] Another spelling of *draft*.

drib·ble [drib′əl] *v.* **drib·bling 1** To move a ball with quick, short kicks, as in soccer. **2** To move a ball by bouncing, as in basketball. **3** To fall in drops.

drill [dril] *n.* **1** Practice; an exercise that is done over and over. **2** A tool for making holes.

E

ear·nest·ly [ûr′nist·lē] *adv.* Seriously; sincerely. — **ear·nest,** *adj.*

ebb [eb] *n.* The flowing of the tide back to the ocean.

ed·i·tor [ed'i·tər] *n.* A person in charge of a newspaper or magazine.

Eif·fel, A·lex·an·dre [ī'fəl, ä·lek·sän'drə] 1832–1923, French scientist and builder who built the very tall tower named for him in Paris, France.

em·bar·rass [im·bar'əs] *v.* **em·bar·rassed** To make to feel awkward, shy, and uneasy.

en·light·en [in·līt'ən] *v.* **en·light·en·ing** To give understanding and knowledge to.

e·nor·mous [i·nôr'məs] *adj.* Huge; unusually large.

en·try [en'trē] *n.* A person or thing put in a list, as for a contest. — **en·tries,** *pl.*

e·vent [i·vent'] *n.* **1** A happening, especially an important one. **2** One of the items that make up a sports program.

ex·change [iks·chānj'] *v.* **ex·changed** To trade one thing for another.

ex·hib·it [ig·zib'it] *n.* A public display.

ex·pe·di·tion [ek'spə·dish'ən] *n.* A journey made for a purpose.

ex·pert [ek'spûrt] *n.* A person who knows a great deal about a certain field.

ex·plo·ra·tion [eks'plə·rā'shən] *n.* A careful study of a new or strange area to find out about it.

F

fake [fāk] *adj.* Not real; false.

fa·mil·iar [fə·mil'yər] *adj.* Often seen or heard; well known.

fan·cy [fan'sē] **1** *n.* An imagined idea. **2** *v.* To imagine or picture. **3** *n.* A liking: took a *fancy* to.

fan·ta·sy [fan'tə·sē] *n.* An imaginary story very different from real life.

fea·ture [fē'chər] *n.* An outstanding part of something: The waterfall was the most beautiful *feature* of the scene.

felt [felt] *n.* A soft kind of cloth made of matted wool, fur, or hair.

fetch [fech] *v.* To go for, get, and bring back: to *fetch* a package.

fi·nan·cial [fi·nan'shəl *or* fī·nan'shəl] *adj.* Having to do with money.

fire·crack·er [fīr'krak'ər] *n.* A paper cylinder with an explosive inside, usually used as a noisemaker on the Fourth of July.

fish·er·folk [fish'ər·fōk] *n., pl.* People whose work is catching fish.

flag·ship [flag'ship'] *n.* The ship that carries the fleet commander and the flag.

flail [flāl] **1** *v.* To beat or hit with a flail. **2** *n.* A tool for beating off or threshing the heads of ripened grains.

flan·nel [flan'əl] **1** *n.* A very soft cotton or wool fabric with a nap. **2** *adj.* Made of flannel.

flap [flap] *n.* A piece of cloth, fastened at one edge, used to cover the opening of a tent or a pocket.

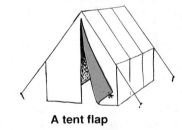

A tent flap

flash [flash] **1** *n.* A very short time; an instant. **2** *n.* A sudden blaze of light or fire. **3** *v.* To move or appear suddenly or quickly: They watched the train *flash* by. **4** *v.* To show suddenly: I saw the officer *flash* a badge.

---

add, āce, câre, pälm;   end, ēqual;   it, īce;   odd, ōpen, ôrder;   to͞ok, po͞ol;   up, bûrn;
ə = a in *above*, e in *sicken*, i in *possible*, o in *melon*, u in *circus;*   yo͞o = u in *fuse;*   oil;   pout;
check;   ring;   thin;   this;   zh in *vision.*

flit [flit] *v.* To move or fly rapidly.

flut·ter [flut′ər] *v.* To shake rapidly or wave back and forth unevenly.

force [fôrs] **1** *n.* Something that changes the state of motion or rest in a body. **2** *n.* Power; strength: the *force* of the waves. **3** *n.* A group of people organized to do certain work: a police *force*. **4** *v.* To break open, as a door or lock. **5** *v.* To make someone do something: She tried to *force* me to tell the truth.

For·est Hills [fôr′ist hilz′] *n.* A part of New York City on Long Island where the U.S. Open tennis tournament was played each year through 1977.

for·ward [fôr′wərd] *n.* A player in the front line of a team, or one who leads a play made by a team.

fos·sil [fos′əl] *n.* The imprinted remains of a plant or animal of an earlier age, hardened and left in rock or earth.

frag·ile [fraj′əl] *adj.* Easily broken; delicate.

frame·work [frām′wûrk′] *n.* A strong structure around which something is built, as a building or ship.

freight [frāt] *n.* Goods shipped by train, plane, boat, or ship.

furl [fûrl] *v.* To roll up and fasten: to *furl* a sail.

fu·ture [fyōō′chər] *n.* **1** The time yet to come. **2** Chance for success: a job with a *future*.

G

gas [gas] *n.* A substance that is not solid or liquid. **—gas·es,** *pl.*

Ga·ston [gä·stōN′] *n.* A French male's name.

gath·er·ing [gath′ər·ing] *n.* A meeting or assembly.

ga·zette [gə·zet′] *n.* A newspaper; used mostly in the names of newspapers.

gear [gir] *n.* Tools or equipment needed to do something.

gen·er·al [jen′ər·əl] **1** *adj.* As a whole; usual. **2** *n.* Any of several military ranks higher than a colonel.

gen·er·ate [jen′ər·āt] *v.* **gen·er·at·ed** To produce or cause to be.

gen·er·ous [jen′ər·əs] *adj.* Quick to give or share; unselfish.

ge·og·ra·pher [jē·og′rə·fər] *n.* A person who studies the Earth's surface, including climate, soil, land use, etc.

ges·ture [jes′chər] *n.* A movement of the body that expresses an idea or feeling.

Gha·na [gä′nə] *n.* A country in western Africa and a member of the British Commonwealth.

glide [glīd] *v.* To move downward smoothly and without power.

glim·mer [glim′ər] **1** *v.* To shine with a faint, unsteady light. **2** *n.* A faint, unsteady light.

glimpse [glimps] **1** *v.* To look for an instant. **2** *n.* A quick look or view.

goal [gōl] *n.* **1** Aim or purpose. **2** A place where a score can be made in certain sports. **3** A score made in these sports.

goal·ie [gō′lē] *n.* The player who guards the goal; the goalkeeper.

gong [gông] *n.* A round metal plate that makes a ringing sound when struck.

gos·pel [gos′pəl] *n.* **1** A religious folk song. **2** Something thought to be true.

grace·ful [grās′fəl] *adj.* Having beauty or delicacy in movement or manners.

grad·u·ate school [graj′ōō·it skōōl′] *n.* A school that offers advanced study to students who have finished college.

grad·u·a·tion [graj′ōō·ā′shən] *n.* The ceremony performed when a student finishes a course of study, as at a school or college.

graph [graf] *n.* A chart that uses dots, curves, or bars to show how one set of numbers changes in relation to another.

grav·i·ty [grav′ə·tē] *n.* The force that pulls objects toward the center of the Earth.

graze [grāz] *v.* To feed on growing grass.

green·house [grēn′hous′] *n.* A heated building with glass sides and roof, used for growing plants that need warmth.

greens [grēnz] *n., pl.* The leaves and stems of certain plants used as food, such as spinach.

grog·gy [grog′ē] *adj.* Feeling very sleepy; not completely awake.

guide [gīd] **1** *n.* A dog or person that leads a person or group. **2** *v.* To show the way; lead.

gym·nast [jim′nast] *n.* A person skilled in gymnastics.

gym·nas·tics [jim·nas′tiks] *n., sing.* Exercises that develop muscular strength and body control.

H

hall [hôl] *n.* A large building or room.

har·ness [här′nis] *n.* Leather straps, bands, etc., used to hitch an animal to a cart, a plow, etc.

harsh [härsh] *adj.* **1** Rough. **2** Unpleasant or unkind.

heap [hēp] *n.* A pile or mound.

hearth [härth] *n.* **1** The floor of a fireplace, furnace, etc. **2** The fireside; home.

heav·en·ly [hev′ən·lē] *adj.* Located in the sky.

heel [hēl] **1** *n.* The rounded back part of a person's foot, below the ankle. **2** *v.* To follow closely.

height [hīt] *n.* **1** High place or region. **2** The distance upward from the bottom to the top: the *height* of a tree.

hel·i·cop·ter [hel′ə·kop′tər] *n.* An aircraft that is lifted and propelled by large rotors and is able to fly in any direction.

helms·man [helmz′mən] *n.* The person who steers a ship.

her·mit [hûr′mit] *n.* A person who lives alone, away from other people.

High·ness [hī′nis] *n.* A title used in speaking to or of a ruler.

high·tail [hī′tāl′] *v.* **high-tail it** To run quickly; rush.

hit [hit] *v.* To deal a blow to; strike. — **hit on** Find after searching; think of.

---

add, āce, câre, pälm;   end, ēqual;   it, īce;   odd, ōpen, ôrder;   tŏŏk, pōōl;   up, bûrn;
ə = a in *above*, e in *sicken*, i in *possible*, o in *melon*, u in *circus*;   yōō = u in *fuse*;   oil;   pout;
check;   ring;   thin;   this;   zh in *vision*.

hitch [hich] **1** *n.* Something in the way; a block. **2** *v.* To fasten or tie: to *hitch* a rope to a post.

hos·pice [hos′pis] *n.* A rest house for travelers.

host [hōst] *n.* **1** A living plant or animal on or in which another animal lives. **2** A person who entertains guests.

house com·ic [hous′ kom′ik] *n.* A person who tells funny jokes and stories and who performs regularly at a certain club or theater.

hump [hump] *n.* A large round lump: a *hump* of snow; or the *hump* on the back of a camel.

formed to do something for a special purpose. Schools, banks, and hospitals are institutions.

in·tel·li·gence [in·tel′ə·jəns] *n.* The ability to understand and learn.

in·vent [in·vent′] *v.* To think out or bring into being for the first time.

in·ves·ti·gate [in·ves′tə·gāt] *v.* To look into thoroughly to find facts or details.

in·volve [in·volv′] *v.* **in·volv·ing** To include (someone or something) as a necessary part.

ire [īr] *n.* Wrath; anger.

is·sue [ish′o͞o] *n.* A copy, as of a magazine: the May *issue*.

I

il·lu·sion [i·lo͞o′zhən] *n.* A false appearance; a trick done to make something appear to be real or true that is not real or true.

im·ag·i·nar·y [i·maj′ə·ner′ē] *adj.* Not real; existing only in the mind.

im·i·tate [im′ə·tāt] *v.* To copy another's actions, speech, or other behavior.

in·dus·tri·al·ism [in·dus′trē·ə·liz′əm] *n.* An economic and social system of manufacturing and business.

in·flate [in·flāt] *v.* **in·flat·ed** To swell or blow up, as with air or gas.

in·flu·ence [in′flo͞o·əns] *v.* **in·flu·enced** To cause changes or differences in something or someone without using direct force.

in·her·it [in·her′it] *v.* **in·her·it·ed** **1** To receive traits from parents, grandparents, etc.: She did *inherit* her dad's red hair. **2** To receive money or property left by someone who has died.

in·ner [in′ər] *adj.* Having to do with what is inside.

in·sti·tu·tion [in′sti·to͞o′shən] *n.* A group

J

jag·ged [jag′id] *adj.* Having sharp edges.

Jean [zhäN] *n.* A French male's name, the equivalent of the English *John*.

jel·ly·fish [jel′ē·fish′] *n.* A sea animal with an umbrellalike body, looking much like a blob of jelly.

joint [joint] *n.* A place in the body where two or more bones join, usually in a way that allows motion.

jug·gler [jug′lər] *n.* A person who can keep a number of balls, plates, or other objects in the air at the same time by cleverly tossing and catching them.

jut [jut] *v.* **jut·ting** To extend outward; to project.

K

Kat·man·du [kät′män·dōō′] *n.* The capital city of Nepal, a small country between India and Tibet.

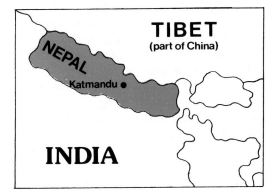

keen [kēn] *adj.* **1** Sharp or sensitive: *keen* eyesight. **2** Able to cut easily; very sharp: a *keen* knife.

ker·o·sene [ker′ə·sēn] *n.* A thin oil burned in lamps and stoves.

kes·trel [kes′trəl] *n.* A small falcon known for its ability to stay over one spot on the ground by gliding against the wind.

key [kē] *n.* **1** Something that controls or is important to something else. **2** Anything that explains or solves something. **3** A small metal instrument used for locking or unlocking a door.

kil·o·gram [kil′ə·gram *or* kē′lə·gram] *n.* In the metric system, a weight equal to 1,000 grams or about 2.2 pounds.

kind [kīnd] **1** *adj.* Willing to help; gentle. **2** *n.* Sort; type.

Kin·sha·sa [kēn·shä′sä] *n.* Capital city of the African country Zaire.

knead [nēd] *v.* **knead·ed** To press, squeeze, bend, and pull with the hands.

knight [nīt] *n.* **1** A person who is given the honorary title "Sir" in recognition of service to the country. **2** In the Middle Ages, a person with the rank and duties of a mounted officer.

L

La·bou·laye, Ed·ouard de [lä·bōō·lä′, ā′dwär′ də] 1811–1883, French writer, jurist, and politician.

launch [lônch] *v.* **launched** **1** To release or send into the air. **2** To hurl; throw with force. **3** To move or push (a boat) into the water.

lead·ing [lē′ding] *adj.* Most important; main.

league [lēg] *n.* A group of sports teams that compete with each other.

lean [lēn] **1** *v.* To rest on for support: I can *lean* on her shoulder. **2** *v.* To bend or slant from an upright position. **3** *v.* To rely or depend on for help, comfort, advice, etc. **4** *adj.* Thin.

lean-to [lēn′tōō′] *n.* A low building placed against one wall of a taller building, from which its roof slopes out and down.

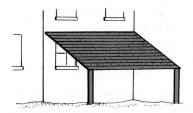

lib·er·al arts [lib′ər·əl ärts′] *n.* A group of college courses, such as language, history, and literature, giving a broad education instead of training for a certain type of work.

---

add, āce, câre, pälm;   end, ēqual;   it, īce;   odd, ōpen, ôrder;   tŏŏk, pōōl;   up, bûrn;
ə = a in *above*, e in *sicken*, i in *possible*, o in *melon*, u in *circus*;   yōō = u in *fuse;*   oil;   pout;
check;   ring;   thin;   this;   zh in *vision.*

life-forms [līf′fôrmz′] *n., pl.* Living things.

like·wise [līk′wīz′] *adv.* In the same way.

lime·stone [līm′stōn′] *n.* A kind of rock that is made up mostly of calcium carbonate.

line [līn] *n.* **1** A route along which trains, buses, ships, or airplanes go back and forth. **2** A company carrying passengers or freight along a certain route.

live [līv] *adj.* **1** Actually being performed as it is being broadcast on TV or radio. **2** Having life; alive.

liv·er·y barn [liv′ər·ē bärn′] *n.* A place where horses can be rented; a livery stable.

lo·cal [lō′kəl] *adj.* Having to do with a neighborhood or small area.

log·o [lôg′ō] *n.* A distinct company trademark, or signature. It is short for **log·o·type.**

long [lông] *v.* **longed** To want very much.

look·out [lŏŏk′out′] *n.* A person or animal that watches and listens for enemies, dangers, or interesting happenings.

lov·a·ble [luv′ə·bəl] *adj.* Capable of being loved.

ly·ing [lī′ing] Present participle of *lie:* The dog is *lying* on the rug.

M

mag·nif·i·cent [mag·nif′ə·sənt] *adj.* Making a wonderful appearance or show of beauty, size, etc.

main·land [mān′land] *n.* The main part of a continent or country; not an island.

ma·jor [mā′jər] **1** *n.* The main subject or field of study that a student chooses. **2** *adj.* Having great importance or value: a *major* dancer.

man·u·al [man′yŏŏ·əl] **1** *adj.* Done with the hands. **2** *n.* A small reference book.

man·za·ni·ta [man′zə·nē′tə] *n.* A bush or small tree that grows in the western U.S.

ma·rine [mə·rēn′] *adj.* Having to do with the sea.

match [mach] **1** *n.* Contest. **2** *n.* A small, thin piece of wood or cardboard tipped with a substance that catches fire when rubbed against a rough surface. **3** *v.* To be like: Your scarf does not *match* your coat. — **match·es,** *pl.*

meth·od [meth′əd] *n.* A plan of action; way of doing something.

mi·cro·scope [mī′krə·skōp′] *n.* An instrument that makes very small objects look larger.

mir·a·cle [mir′ə·kəl] *n.* A wonderful event that cannot be rationally explained.

mod·ern [mod′ərn] *adj.* Having to do with the present time.

mois·ture [mois′chər] *n.* Very small drops of water or other liquid causing dampness in the air.

monk [mungk] *n.* A man belonging to a religious group that usually lives apart from others in a place called a monastery.

mon·u·ment [mon′yə·mənt] *n.* A statue or plaque built in memory of a person or happening.

moon rov·er [mŏŏn′ rō′vər] *n.* A vehicle that moves along the moon's surface.

Morse code [môrs′ kōd′] *n.* Groups of dots and dashes, or short and long sounds, used to stand for letters and numbers.

mor·tar [môr′tər] *n.* A soft mixture that hardens to hold stone or brick in place.

mo·tion [mō′shən] **1** *n.* Any change in position or location. **2** *v.* A movement of some part of the body. **3** *v.* To signal someone with the hands or head.—**mo·tioned.**

mot·to [mot′ō] *n.* A word or short saying that tells a rule or way of acting.

mount [mount] *v.* **mount·ed 1** To grow in number. **2** To fasten in place for use.

mov·a·ble [mōo′və·bəl] *adj.* Able to be moved.

movement [mōov′mənt] *n.* The act of moving; a motion.

mu·sic [myōo′zik] *n.* The art of combining sounds, as of the human voice or an instrument, into organized patterns of expression.

musk·rat [musk′rat] *n.* A water animal that has glossy brown fur and looks like a rat.

mut·ter [mut′ər] *v.* **mut·ter·ing 1** *v.* To speak in a low tone with half-closed lips. **2** *n.* a low, unclear phrase.

N

na·tion [nā′shən] *n.* **1** A tribe or federation: the Iroquois *nation.* **2** A group of people who live under one government. They usually have a common way of life and speak the same language.

na·tion·al [nash′ə·nəl] *adj.* Of or having to do with a nation as a whole.

nat·u·ral [nach′ər·əl] *adj.* **1** Made by nature; not artificial. **2** Not forced or stiff-looking.

nec·tar [nek′tər] *n.* A sweet juice found in flowers, used by bees to make honey.

Nep·tune [nep′t(y)ōon] The god of the sea, in Roman mythology.

nerve [nûrv] *n.* Courage; bravery.

ner·vous [nûr′vəs] *adj.* Excited or scared; upset; anxious.

nip [nip] *v.* To bite or pinch.

note [nōt] **1** *n.* In music, a symbol that shows the pitch and length of a sound. **2** *n.* A short, written message. **3** *v.* To write down a few words.

nut·hatch [nut′ hach′] *n.* A small, short-tailed bird that eats nuts and insects.

nuz·zle [nuz′əl] *v.* To shove or rub with the nose, or as if with the nose.

O

ob·ser·va·to·ry [əb·zûr′və·tôr′ē] *n.* A place with instruments used to study stars, weather conditions, etc.

off·shore [ôf′shôr′] *adj.* Moving or located in water away from the land.

off·spring [ôf′spring′] *n.* A descendant from another; young: We saw the elephant's *offspring* at the zoo.—**off·spring** or **off·springs,** *pl.*

on be·half of [bi·haf′] *prep.* For.

op·er·a·tor [op′ə·rā′tər] *n.* A person who runs something, such as a machine.

or·gan·i·za·tion [ôr′gən·ə·zā′shən] *n.* A number of people, clubs, companies, etc., joined together for some special work or purpose.

o·rig·i·nal [ə·rij′ə·nəl] **1** *n.* The first form of anything. **2** *adj.* Belonging to the beginning of something; earliest; first.

out·er [ou′tər] *adj.* Having to do with what is outside.

ox·y·gen [ok′sə·jin] *n.* A gas, found in the air, that has no color, odor, or taste. People, animals, and plants cannot live without this gas.

---

add, āce, câre, pälm; end, ēqual; it, īce; odd, ōpen, ôrder; tŏŏk, pōol; **up**, bûrn;
ə = a in *above*, e in *sicken*, i in *possible*, o in *melon*, u in *circus;* yōo = u in *fuse;* oil; pout;
check; **r**ing; **th**in; **th**is; **zh** in *vision.*

P

pace [pās] **1** *n.* A step in walking. **2** *v.* To walk with slow or regulated steps.

palm [päm] *n.* **1** The inside surface of the hand between the wrist and the base of the fingers. **2** Any of a group of tropical evergreen trees or shrubs. **3** A leaf of a palm tree.

pan·to·mime [pan′tə·mīm′] *n.* Acting out what one has seen or done, or what one feels, etc., without words.

par·tic·u·lar [pər·tik′yə·lər] *adj.* Having to do with one person, animal, or thing.

par·ti·tion [pär·tish′ən] *n.* A wall that separates one room or space from another.

pa·tience [pā′shəns] *n.* **1** The ability to do the same thing over and over without complaining. **2** The ability to wait without complaining.

pa·tient [pā′shənt] **1** *adj.* Able to wait for someone or something without complaining. **2** *adj.* Calm, understanding. **3** *n.* A person being treated for an illness.

peak [pēk] *n.* The top of a mountain.

peek [pēk] *v.* To look at secretly or quickly.

Per·di·ta [per·dē′tə] *n.* A female's name.

per·son·al·i·ties [pûr′sə·nal′i·tēz] *n., pl.* Those feelings, looks, behavior, etc., that make people or animals themselves and different from others. — **per·son·al·i·ty**, *sing.*

pho·to·graph [fō′tə·graf] *n.* A picture made with a camera.

pho·tog·ra·phy [fə·tog′rə·fē] *n.* The art or business of taking photographs.

pick·et [pik′it] **1** *n.* A pointed stick or post, as in a fence. **2** *v.* To tie to a picket, as a horse. — **pick·et·ed.**

piñ·on [pin′yən] *n. Spanish* Any of several low-growing nut-pine trees.

piñ·on·er·o [pin′yən·er′ō] *n. Spanish* A small blue bird found in the American Southwest; like a blue jay.

pin·wheel [pin′(h)wēl′] *n.* A firework that spins around and throws off sparks.

pitch [pich] **1** *v.* To fall forward. **2** *v.* To set up: to *pitch* a tent. **3** *v.* To throw or toss, as a ball. **4** *v.* To help; join in. **5** *n.* The high or low level of a sound.

Pi·tjan·tja·tja·ra [pi·tyän′tyä·tyä′rä] *n.* An ancient people still living in Australia. They share the same beliefs and manner of life but live mostly in scattered groups.

plat·form [plat′fôrm] *n.* A raised flat surface or floor.

plot [plot] *n.* **1** The plan of events in a story, movie, or play. **2** A small piece of ground.

point·er [poin′tər] *n.* **1** A useful bit of information. **2** A thin rod used to point out things on maps, charts, etc.

poke bon·net [pōk bon′it] *n.* A woman's or child's hat that has a projecting brim at the front and is tied under the chin.

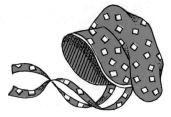

pol·li·wog [pol′ē·wog] *n.* A young frog or toad that lives in water and has a tail and gills; a tadpole.

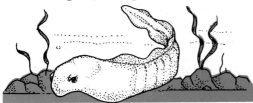

pol·lu·tion [pə·lōō′shən] *n.* The dirt, smoke, gases, and so forth, that get into air, water, etc., making them dirty and often not fit for use.

pop [pop] *n.* Short for **pop·u·lar**: current *popular* music.

pop·u·la·tion [pop′yə·lā′shən] *n.* The total number of people in a country, city, or other area.

por·trait [pôr′trit *or* pôr′trāt] *n.* A painting, drawing, or photograph of a person or animal, showing the face.

pose [pōz] *n.* A position of the body and face, as for a photograph.

po·si·tion [pə·zish′ən] *n.* The place where something or someone is.

pos·ses·sive [pə·zes′iv] *adj.* In grammar, showing ownership: *City's* is the possessive form of *city.*

prac·ti·cal [prak′ti·kəl] *adj.* Able to be put to use; useful.

pre·fer [pri·fûr′] *v.* To like better; decide by choice.

pre·serve [pri·zûrv′] *n.* An area where wildlife is protected.

pres·sure [presh′ər] *n.* The act of pressing or the state of being pressed.

prick·ly [prik′lē] *adj.* Having small, sharp points; stinging.

prim·i·tive [prim′ə·tiv] *adj.* **1** Not modern; from an early time. **2** Simple; crude.

Prince Ru·pert [prins′ rōō′pərt] *n.* A port city in Canada near the Alaskan border.

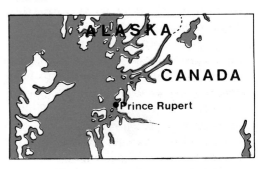

pro·duce [prə·d(y)ōōs′] *v.* **pro·duced 1** To make (a play or movie) ready for the public to see. **2** To manufacture.

prod·uct [prod′əkt] *n.* Something grown, mined, or made.

pro·fes·sion·al [prə·fesh′ən·əl] **1** *n.* A person who takes part in a sport for money. **2** *adj.* Performed by or consisting of professional people.

pro·gram [prō′gram] **1** *n.* A performance, entertainment, or ceremony, especially as scheduled on TV or radio. **2** *v.* To work out a series of instructions or make up a program. **—pro·grammed.**

prog·ress [prog′res] *n.* A move forward; an improvement.

proj·ect [proj′ekt] *n.* A special undertaking or activity.

pro·jec·tor [prō·jek′tər] *n.* A machine that projects pictures onto a screen.

prop·er [prop′ər] *adj.* Correct; fitting.

Pul·it·zer, Jo·seph [pōōl′it·sər *or* pyōō′lit·sər, jō′zef] 1847–1911, owner of a large newspaper in New York. He left money for the Pulitzer Prize, one of a group of yearly prizes given in the U.S. in journalism, music, etc.

---

add, āce, câre, pälm;   end, ēqual;   it, īce;   odd, ōpen, ôrder;   tŏŏk, pōōl;   up, bûrn;
ə = a in *above*, e in *sicken*, i in *possible*, o in *melon*, u in *circus;*   yōō = u in *fuse;*   oil;   pout;
check;   ring;   thin;   this;   zh in *vision.*

pulp [pulp] *n.* The soft part of certain fruits and vegetables, often the part people eat.

punc·ture [pungk′chər] *v.* **punc·tured** To pierce with a sharp point.

pu·pil [pyoo′pəl] *n.* **1** The round opening in the middle of the eye that grows bigger in dim light, smaller in bright light. **2** Student.

pup·pet·eer [pup′i·tir′] *n.* A person who works puppets and makes them move.

Q

quail [kwāl] *n.* Any of several birds related to the partridge.

quilt [kwilt] *n.* A covering for a bed made by stitching together two layers of cloth in patterns or crossing lines.

R

rab·bi [rab′ī] *n.* A person trained to teach Jewish religious law or to be spiritual head of a Jewish community.

rack·et [rak′it] *n.* **1** A loud noise. **2** A light bat used in some games, as badminton or tennis.

ra·dar [rā′där] *n.* An electronic machine that locates moving objects that are far away and measures their speed through the use of radio waves.

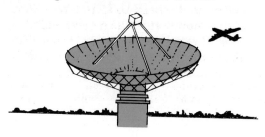

rain·for·est [rān′fôr′ist] *n.* A thick forest, or jungle, that grows in a warm area with much rain all through the year.

rare [râr] *adj.* **1** Not often seen or found; not ordinary. **2** Not completely cooked: *rare* meat.

rat·ing [rā′ting] *n.* A list ranking members of a group according to their abilities or performance.

ra·vine [rə·vēn′] *n.* A long, narrow, deep depression in the earth with very steep sides.

re·act [rē·akt′] *v.* To act in answer to a happening, such as an emergency.

rec·ord [rek′ərd] *n.* **1** A note written for future use. **2** A disc played on a phonograph. **3** Best listed achievement.

rec·re·a·tion [rek′rē·ā′shən] *n.* An amusement, pastime, or hobby.

re·duce [ri·d(y)oos′] *v.* **1** To make smaller in number or size. **2** To decrease weight, as by dieting.

reed [rēd] *n.* A grass that has a hollow stem.

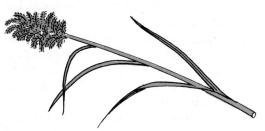

reef [rēf] *n.* A ridge of sand, rocks, or coral at or near the surface of the water.

re·fuse [ri·fyooz′] *v.* To turn down; say that one will not take or agree to something.

re·hears·al [ri·hûr′səl] *n.* A practice session for a performance.

re·lax [ri·laks′] *v.* **re·laxed** To become less nervous or uneasy.

rep·tile [rep′til *or* rep′tīl] *n.* A cold-blooded animal, like a snake or turtle, that crawls on its belly or creeps on very short legs.

res·er·va·tion [rez′ər·vā′shən] *n.* **1** Land selected and held by the government for a special purpose. **2** An agreement by which a seat on a plane, a hotel room, etc., is held in advance for someone.

rev·el [rev′əl] **1** *v.* To have noisy fun. **2** *n.* Loud merrymaking.

ridge [rij] *n.* The long, narrow top of something, as on a wave or mountain.

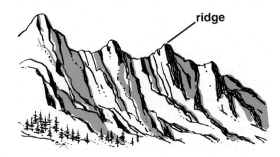

ridge

Rob·in·son Cru·soe [rob′in·sən krōō′sō] The sailor in Daniel Defoe's book of the same title (written in 1719). Left alone on an island by a wreck, he used his skills to make a new life.

Rum·pel·stilts·kin [rum′pəl·stilt′skin] In a fairy tale, the little man who spins straw into gold for a maiden. In return she must give him her first child or guess his name.

run·way [run′wā′] *n.* A hard surface, like a wide road, where airplanes can land and take off.

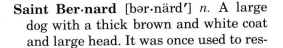

S

Saint Ber·nard [bər·närd′] *n.* A large dog with a thick brown and white coat and large head. It was once used to res-cue people lost in the snow in the Swiss Alps.

salm·on [sam′ən] *n.* An ocean fish that swims up coastal rivers to lay eggs.

sap·ling [sap′ling] *n.* A young tree.

scale [skāl] **1** *n.* Marks used in measuring length, as those showing centimeters on a ruler. **2** *n.* Marks or lines on a chart or map, each space measuring a given number or amount. **3** *n.* In music, a series of tones going up or down in order. **4** *n.* One of the thin, flat plates of horny tissue that forms a pro-tective cover on the bodies of fish and reptiles. — **scaly,** *adj.* **5** *v.* Climb over or to the top of.

scene [sēn] *n.* The place in which an event happens.

scen·er·y [sē′nər·ē] *n.* In theater, the backgrounds on a stage used to repre-sent a place.

schol·ar·ship [skol′ər·ship] *n.* Money given to or won by a student to help pay for his or her education.

sci·en·tist [sī′ən·tist] *n.* A person who is devoted to the study of science.

score·board [skôr′bôrd] *n.* A board for keeping the score of a game.

scour [skour] *v.* **scoured** To clean or brighten by washing and rubbing hard, as with sand or steel wool.

scrub [skrub] *n.* Small trees or shrubs kept from growing, often by bad soil or climate.

sculp·tor [skulp′tər] *n.* An artist who makes figures or shapes out of stone, metal, clay, etc.

sea a·nem·o·ne [sē′ ə·nem′ə·nē′] *n.* A sea animal whose body is like a tube, with a mouth at one end surrounded by "arms," or tentacles. These "arms" look like flowers but can sting and seize food.

---

add, āce, câre, pälm;   end, ēqual;   it, īce;   odd, ōpen, ôrder;   tŏok, pōol;   up, bûrn;
ə = a in *above,* e in *sicken,* i in *possible,* o in *melon,* u in *circus;*   yōō = u in *fuse;*   oil;   pout;
check;   ring;   thin;   this;   zh in *vision.*

sea·plane [sē′plān′] *n.* A plane that can take off from or land on water.

se·lect [si·lekt′] **1** *v.* To choose in preference over another. **2** *adj.* Chosen for worth or high quality.

sense [sens] **1** *v.* To become aware of. **2** *n.* An understanding or awareness. **3** *n.* A nerve or group of nerves that send messages to our brain and allow us to see, hear, smell, taste, and touch.

se·quoi·a [si·kwoi′ə] *n.* Either of two kinds of giant evergreen trees that grow in California.

sharp·shoot·er [shärp′shoo̅′tər] *n.* An expert at hitting a target with a gun.

shed [shed] *v.* To get out of or discard: Each year the snakes *shed* their skins.

sheet [shēt] *n.* **1** A large, lightweight piece of cloth. **2** A piece of paper. **3** A piece of metal.

short·cut [shôrt′kut′] *n.* **1** A shorter or quicker way (of saving time). **2** A path between two places that is shorter than the regular route.

shout [shout] *n.* A sudden, loud outcry.

side·line [sīd′līn′] *n.* **1** A second or extra kind of job that is less important than one's regular job. **2** A line that shows the edge of the playing area on one side, as of a football field.

sign [sīn] **1** *n.* A symbol. **2** *n.* A board that has information written on it. **3** *v.* To write one's name or initials on.

sig·nal [sig′nəl] **1** *n.* A sign that is a way of sending a message. **2** *v.* To move or wave something so as to communicate a message without using words.

sign lan·guage [sīn′ lang′gwij] A large set of signs that stand for whole words or ideas, made mostly with the hands and arms and used by deaf people.

sim·plest [sim′pləst] *adj.* Having the smallest number of parts; easiest.

sim·u·lat·ed [sim′yə·lāt·id] *adj.* Made to look real, or appear like; fake.

sin·gles [sing′gəlz] *n.* In tennis, a game in which one person plays against another.

sit·u·a·tion [sich′oo̅·ā′shən] *n.* A condition brought about by a combination of happenings, pleasant or unpleasant.

sketch [skech] *v.* **sketched** To make a quick drawing or drawings.

skir·mish [skûr′mish] *n.* A small, short fight, not as important as a battle.

sledge [slej] *n.* **1** A large, heavy hammer. **2** A vehicle, mounted on sled runners, used to travel over snow and ice.

slip [slip] **1** *v.* To slide or fall. **2** *n.* A woman's undergarment. **3** *n.* A piece of paper or note. **4** *v.* To escape: Can you *slip* past the guard?

slith·er [slith′ər] *v.* **slith·ered** To slide or slip.

slope [slōp] **1** *n.* A piece of ground that slants, as a hillside. **2** *v.* To lie at an angle; slant. — **slop·ing.**

slum·ber [slum′bər] *v.* To sleep.

slung [slung] *v.* Thrown or flung. — past tense of **sling.**

sly [slī] *adj.* Clever in a secret or sneaky way.

smart [smärt] **1** *adj.* Quick in mind; bright; clever. **2** *adj.* Sharp and stinging. **3** *adj.* Fashionable; stylish. **4** *v.* To experience a stinging sensation.

snow·mo·bile [snō′mō·bēl′] *n.* A motor vehicle that moves on circular treads used on snow. Drivers control the skis in front to steer.

so·ci·e·ty [sə·sī′ə·tē] *n.* A group of people living as a community in a set place.

so·lar sys·tem [sō′lər sis′təm] *n.* The sun and all the heavenly bodies that orbit around it.

sol·emn [sol′əm] *adj.* **1** Sacred; religious. **2** Serious; grave; earnest.

sol·id [sol′id] *n.* Something firm with a definite shape that is not easy to bend or change: Wood is a *solid.*

so·lo·ist [sō′lō·ist] *n.* A person who performs alone.

source [sôrs] *n.* A thing, place, or person from which something comes.

spare [spâr] **1** *adj.* Extra: *spare* parts. **2** *v.* To part with; give up: to *spare* food.

spe·cies [spē′shēz] *n.* A group of living things that are much alike and whose members breed with each other.—**spe·cies,** *pl.*

spec·i·men [spes′ə·mən] *n.* One thing or person of a group, taken as a sample.

spir·it [spir′it] *n.* **1** A widely held feeling or tendency. **2** Energy; liveliness.

spot·light [spot′līt′] *n.* A circle of strong light thrown on a stage, ring, etc.

spring [spring] *n.* A sudden, quick leap.

star·fish [stär′fish′] *n.* A small sea animal with a star-shaped body and five or more arms.

steal [stēl] **1** *v.* To take from another without right or permission. **2** *n.* The act of stealing.

steel [stēl] *n.* A strong metal made of iron, carbon, and sometimes other metals.

steep·ly [stēp′lē] *adv.* In a sharply slanting or sloping way.—**steep,** *adj.*

stout [stout] *adj.* Fat or thickset in body.

strain [strān] *v.* **strained** To make a great effort.

struc·ture [struk′chər] *n.* Something that is built, such as a machine or a building.

strug·gle [strug′əl] **1** *n.* A great effort or series of efforts to do something. **2** *n.* A fight or a battle. **3** *v.* To work hard; make a great effort.

stu·di·o [st(y)ōō′dē·ō] *n.* **1** The place where an artist or musician works. **2** A place where films, recordings, etc., are made.

stum·ble [stum′bəl] *v.* **stum·bled** To miss a step in walking or running; trip.

stur·dy [stûr′dē] *adj.* **1** Strong. **2** Firm; not giving in.

suf·fer [suf′ər] *v.* To be harmed; to feel or endure pain.

sug·gest [səg·jest′] *v.* To propose or offer a theory.

suit [sōōt] *v.* To satisfy or please.

sus·pend [sə·spend′] *v.* **sus·pend·ed** To hang.

swerve [swûrv] *v.* To turn or cause to turn aside from a course: I had to *swerve* around the dog.

syc·a·more [sik′ə·môr] *n.* A tree with broad leaves and bark that often flakes or peels off.

---

add, āce, câre, pälm;   end, ēqual;   it, īce;   odd, ōpen, ôrder;   tŏŏk, pōōl;   up, bûrn;
ə = a in *above,* e in *sicken,* i in *possible,* o in *melon,* u in *circus;*   yōō = u in *fuse;*   oil;   pout;
check;   ring;   thin;   this;   zh in *vision.*

syl·la·bar·y [sil′ə·ber′ē] *n.* A list of signs used for writing a language. Each sign is for a whole syllable.

syl·la·ble [sil′ə·bəl] *n.* A word or part of a word said in a single vocal impulse.

sys·tem [sis′təm] *n.* A group of things acting together to form a whole.

T

---

tab·let [tab′lit] *n.* **1** A thin sheet of metal, wood, or stone with words or designs on it. **2** A small, flat disk or square, such as a medicine *tablet.*

tack [tak] *n.* **1** Equipment needed for horses, such as saddles, bridles, and harnesses. **2** A short nail having a sharp point and usually a flat head.

take-off [tāk′ôf′] *n.* A humorous copying of something or someone.

tech·nol·o·gy [tek·nol′ə·jē] *n.* Skills in science used to make things useful for everyday life.

ten·ta·cle [ten′tə·kəl] *n.* One of the slender parts that stick out like arms from certain sea animals. They move, feel, grab food, and sometimes sting.

This octopus has eight tentacles.

teth·er [teth′ər] *n.* A rope or chain used to fasten something so it won't drift or wander away from a place.

thatch [thach] A covering of reeds, straw, etc., used on a roof. — **thatched,** *adj.:* a *thatched* roof.

thrash [thrash] *v.* **thrash·ing 1** To beat. **2.** To make or cause to make violent swinging or twisting movements: The lion should not *thrash* in the net.

threat [thret] *n.* A warning that one intends to hurt or punish another person or thing.

through [thrōō] **1** *adv.* Into one point and out the other. **2** *adv.* Finished; done. **3** *prep.* By way of.

Tib·et [ti·bet′] *n.* A part of China. Before it became part of China, it was one of the small mountain nations between India and China.

tight·rope [tīt′ rōp′] *n.* A rope stretched high above the ground, used by acrobats to perform on.

tilt [tilt] **1** *n.* A slope. **2** *v.* To lean; tip.

torch [tôrch] *n.* A source of light that can be carried by hand.

tor·til·la [tôr·tē′yä] *n.* Mexican bread made of cornmeal and shaped like a pancake.

toss [tôs] *v.* To move up and down and sideways with rapid, jerky motions.

tour·na·ment [tŏŏr′nə·mənt *or* tôr′nə·mənt] *n.* A series of matches in a sport or game involving many players.

trace [trās] **1** *n.* Mark or sign left by some person or animal or past event. **2** *v.* To copy a drawing by placing a clear sheet (of paper, etc.) over it and following the lines exactly.

tra·di·tion [trə·dish′ən] *n.* A set of customs, beliefs, and habits passed down from parents to children.

trag·e·dy [traj′ə·dē] *n.* A terrible and unhappy happening; disaster.

trait [trāt] *n.* A special feature or quality of one's character.

trans·con·ti·nen·tal [trans′kon′tə·nən′təl] *adj.* Stretching or going across a continent from one side to the other.

trea·ties [trē′tēz] *n. pl.* Agreements between two or more nations on peace, land rights, trade, etc. — **trea·ty,** *sing.*

tri·umph [trī′əmf] *n.* A victory.

trust·wor·thy [trust′wûr′thē] *adj.* Worthy of someone's trust; dependable.

tu·a·ta·ra [tōō′ə·tä′rə] *n.* A slow four-footed animal, like a lizard, with a long row of pointed scales down its back. It hunts at night.

tur·ban [tûr′bən] *n.* A head covering made of cloth wrapped about the head.

twin·kle [twing′kəl] *v.* **twin·kling** To shine with sparkling lights.

U

um·pire [um′pīr] *n.* A person who rules on plays in a sports contest.

un·fa·mil·iar [un′fə·mil′yər] *adj.* Not known; strange.

un·hap·py [un·hap′ē] *adj.* Not content; sad.

un·ion [yōōn′yən] *n.* Group of workers formed to protect or improve the condition and attitude of all members.

u·ni·ver·si·ty [yōō′nə·vûr′sə·tē] *n.* An institution of higher learning, usually made up of a college or colleges as well as one or more schools for graduate study, as in law, medicine, etc. — **u·ni·ver·si·ties,** *pl.*

urge [ûrj] *v.* **urged** 1 To drive or force forward. 2 To plead with.

use [yōōz] 1 *v.* To put into action. 2 *v.* To spend or consume: I *used* up my energy. 3 *n.* [yōōs] The act of using: Skills improve through *use.*

V

valve [valv] *n.* A device often used to control the flow of gas or liquid through a pipe.

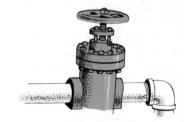

Van·cou·ver [van·kōō′vər] *n.* 1 A port city in southwest British Columbia, in Canada. 2 A large island off the southwest coast of Canada (part of British Columbia).

van·ish [van′ish] *v.* **van·ished** To disappear from sight suddenly.

va·ri·e·ty show [və·rī′ə·tē shō] *n.* A show with music, dancing, and other entertainment.

vast [vast] *adj.* Of great size; enormous.

---

add, āce, câre, pälm;   end, ēqual;   it, īce;   odd, ōpen, ôrder;   tŏŏk, pōōl;   up, bûrn;
ə = a in *above,* e in *sicken,* i in *possible,* o in *melon,* u in *circus;*   yōō = u in *fuse;*   oil;   pout;
check;   ring;   thin;   this;   zh in *vision.*

vau·de·ville [vôd′(ə·)vil] *n.* A type of stage show made up of unconnected acts, such as singers, dancers, jugglers, and trained animals.

vic·to·ry [vik′tər·ē] *n.* The overcoming of something difficult; success.

vocal cords [vō′kəl kôrdz′] *n., pl.* Either of two pairs of folds in the throat that make sound.

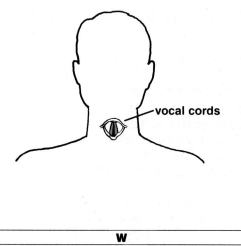

vocal cords

W

wail [wāl] *v.* To cry in pain or sorrow.

wait [wāt] **1** *v.* To remain or stay. **2** *n.* Time spent in waiting. **3** *v.* To serve food as a waiter or waitress.

wash [wôsh] **1** *v.* To clean dirt. **2** *v.* To be worn or carried away: The soil may *wash* away. **3** *n.* A shallow part of a river or bay.

watch [woch] **1** *v.* To look at or for. **2** *n.* A small clock that can be worn on a person.

weight [wāt] *n.* The amount something weighs.

whip [(h)wip] *v.* To move or go very fast.

whir [(h)wûr] **1** *v.* To fly, move, or whirl with a hum or buzz. —**whir·ring**. **2** *n.* Such a sound: the *whir* of the bird's wings.

whirl [(h)wûrl] **1** *v.* To spin rapidly. **2** *n.* A rapid series of events, parties, etc.

won·der [wun′dər] **1** *n.* A person or thing that is amazing or wonderful. **2** *v.* To want to know. **3** *n.* Surprise: It isn't any *wonder* that she became a doctor, since she talked about it from the time she was seven years old.

wood·work·ing [wŏŏd′wûr′king] *n.* The skill or act of making things out of wood, such as furniture.

work·er [wûr′kər] *n.* **1** A person or animal that does work for another. **2** A female bee, ant, or other insect that cannot have young and that works for her hive, anthill, etc.

writhe [rīth] *v.* To twist the face or body as in pain.

Y

yip [yip] *v.* To cry or bark with short, high sounds as a dog does.

yuc·ca [yuk′ə] *n.* A plant with stiff, pointed leaves and a tall stalk bearing white blossoms. It is the state flower of New Mexico.

Z

zic·zac bird [zik′zak′ bûrd] *n.* An Egyptian bird noted for friendships with crocodiles. It picks out worms that fasten themselves inside a crocodile's mouth. Also called *crocodile bird*.

Index of Titles and Authors

4
E 5
F 6
G 7
H 8
I 9
J 0